STUDY GUIDE
VOLUME II: CHAPTERS 13-26

ACCOUNTING PRINCIPLES

9TH Edition

Douglas W. Kieso, Ph.D., C.P.A.
Aurora University
Aurora, Illinois

Jerry J. Weygandt, Ph.D., C.P.A.
Arthur Andersen Alumni Professor of Accounting
University of Wisconsin - Madison
Madison, Wisconsin

Donald E. Kieso, Ph.D., C.P.A.
KPMG Peat Marwick Emeritus Professor of Accountancy
Northern Illinois University
DeKalb, Illinois

Paul D. Kimmel, Ph.D., C.P.A.
Associate Professor of Accounting
University of Wisconsin - Milwaukee
Milwaukee, Wisconsin

WILEY

John Wiley & Sons, Inc.

Cover Photo Credit: OJO Images/SuperStock

To order books or for customer service call 1-800-CALL-WILEY (225-5945).

ISBN-13 978-0-470-38659-0

Printed in the United States of America

10 9 8 7 6 5 4 3 2 1

Printed and bound by Bind-Rite

CONTENTS

Preface

Chapter 13   Corporations: Organization and Capital Stock Transactions

Chapter 14   Corporations: Dividends, Retained Earnings, and Income Reporting

Chapter 15   Long-Term Liabilities

Chapter 16   Investments

Chapter 17   Statement of Cash Flows

Chapter 18   Financial Statement Analysis

Chapter 19   Managerial Accounting

Chapter 20   Job Order Costing

Chapter 21   Process Costing

Chapter 22   Cost-Volume-Profit

Chapter 23   Budgetary Planning

Chapter 24   Budgetary Control and Responsibility Accounting

Chapter 25   Standard Costs and Balanced Scorecard

Chapter 26   Incremental Analysis and Capital Budgeting

Appendix C   Present Value Concepts

PREFACE

To The Student

This study guide is provided as a significant aid in your study of *Accounting Principles, 9th Edition* by Jerry J. Weygandt and Donald E. Kieso and Paul D. Kimmel. The material in the study guide is designed to reinforce your understanding of the principles and procedures presented in the textbook. **It is important to recognize that the study guide is a supplement to and not a substitute for the textbook.**

This study guide contains the following materials for each chapter in the textbook: (a) study objectives, (b) a preview of the chapter, (c) a chapter review consisting of 20-30 key points, (d) a demonstration problem, (e) 20 true—false statements, (f) 20 multiple choice questions, (g) a matching question pertaining to key terms, and (h) 2-3 exercises. At the end of each chapter, answers to questions and exercises are provided in order to enable you to assess your comprehension of the material. Included are solutions explaining why the answer is what it is, so you get immediate feedback as to what, how, or why.

You will realize the maximum benefit from this study guide by following the approach suggested below.
1. Carefully read and study the chapter material in the textbook.
2. Read the chapter preview and review material in the study guide.
3. Answer the questions and exercises for the chapter in the study guide and compare your answers with those provided in the study guide. For any incorrect answers, refer back to the textbook for a discussion of the point you have missed.
4. Solve the end-of-chapter materials in the textbook assigned by your instructor.

The study guide should be helpful in preparing for examinations. The chapter review points, class notes, and other materials may be used to determine your recall of the information presented in specific chapters. When you have identified topics in need of further study, you can return to the textbook for a complete discussion of the subject matter.

I wish to acknowledge the valuable assistance of the accuracy checker of this study guide, James Emig, Villanova University, and our compositor, Pine Tree Composition.

Douglas W. Kieso

```
┌─────────────────────────────────────────────────────────────┐
│                                                             │
│              MAKING YOUR STUDIES PAY                        │
│                                                             │
│            Suggestions for Effective Studying               │
│                                                             │
└─────────────────────────────────────────────────────────────┘
```

WANT TO GET BETTER GRADES? READ ON!

Good students have a system to their studying. In the next few pages, we'll give you some guidelines that we think can help improve the way you study—not only for this course, but for any course.

> How to Use a Textbook
> How to Read a Chapter
> How to Take Notes
> How to Use a Study Guide (In General)
> How to Take Tests

If you need more specific help, we suggest that you go to your teacher or your school's career counseling center.

And Good Luck in your College Career!

HOW TO USE A TEXTBOOK

Textbooks often include material designed to help you study. It's worth your while to flip through a textbook to look for:

- **The Preface.** If an author has a point of view, you can find it here, along with notes on how the book is meant to be used.

- **The Table of Contents.** Reading the table of contents will tell you how the book will be developed.

- **Glossary.** The most important terms and ideas for you to know will be in a glossary, either at the end of each chapter or at the end of the book.

- **Appendixes.** Found either after certain chapters or at the end of the book, appendixes contain such things as:
    - *   More difficult material.
    - *   Statistics or data, such as the present value of money. You may be able to use such data for most of the book.
    - *   Answers to selected problems.

HOW TO READ A CHAPTER

Before Class: Skim

Unless you're told to know a chapter completely by class time, it's a good idea just to skim an assigned chapter before class.

- Become familiar with the main ideas so that the lecture will make more sense to you.

- As you skim, ask yourself if you know something about the material.

- Keep any questions you have in mind for the lecture, so that you can listen for the answers.

In particular, look for:

- **Study Objectives.** These are what your teacher will expect you to know—and be able to do or explain—by the end of the chapter.

- **Chapter-Opening Vignettes.** This section is linked to the chapter topic, and gives a general idea of how accounting relates to your day-to-day life.

- **Boldface or *Italic* Terms.** These usually indicate important terms, people, or concepts.

- **Headings.** Read the major headings to see how the material fits together. How are the ideas related to each other? Do they make sense to you?

- **Summary.** A good summary will repeat the general ideas and conclusions of the chapter, but it won't explain them. It usually matches up well with the study objectives and chapter introduction.

After Class: Read

After skimming the chapter and attending class, you are ready to read a chapter in detail.

- **Check for Meaning.** Ask yourself as you read if you understand what the material means.

- **Don't Skip the Tables, Figures, and Illustrations.** These items usually contain important material and may all be on the test.

- **Read the "Sidebars."** These are features that are set off, usually in boxes or by color backgrounds. They can include real-world examples, amusing anecdotes, or additional material. The amusing anecdotes may not come up on the test, but the other kinds of sidebars probably will!

- **Review.** Read the chapter again, especially the parts you had trouble with. Review the study objectives, chapter introduction, summary, and key terms to make sure you understand them.
- **End-of-Chapter Questions.** Do all the end-of-chapter questions, exercises, or problems. For the exercises and problems, make sure you have memorized what equations or rules apply, and why. (Do any practice problems that your teacher gives you, too. These will not

only help you but show you what kind of questions might be on the test.) If you have trouble with any:

  *   Review the part of the chapter that applies.
  *   Look for similar questions.
  *   Ask yourself what concept or equation should be applied.

- **Use the Study Guide.** After you've read and studied the chapter, use the study guide to find out what areas you need to review in the text.

HOW TO TAKE NOTES

The ability to take notes is a skill, and one you can learn. First, a few practical tips:

- Arrive in class on time, and don't leave early. You might miss important notes or assignments.

- If you don't have assigned seating, sit close enough to your teachers so that you can hear them and read any overhead transparencies.

- If you don't understand, ask questions.

- Do not read the text during the class—you'll just miss what your teacher is saying. Listen, take notes, and ask questions.

Now, for the note-taking itself:

- **Listen for Ideas.** Don't try to write everything the instructor says. Instead, listen and take notes on the main ideas and any supporting ideas and examples. Make sure you include names, dates, and any new terms. In accounting classes, take down all rules, equations, and theories, as well as every step in a demonstration problem.

- **Use Outlines.** Organize these ideas into outlines. You don't have to use a numbered outline if you don't want to—just indent supporting ideas under the main ones.

- **Abbreviate.** Use any abbreviations you can, whether they're standard or ones you make up. (Leaving out vowels can sometimes help: Lvg out vwls can ...).

- **Leave Space.** Leave enough space in your notes so that you can add material if the instructor goes back to the topic or expands a problem later.

HOW TO USE A STUDY GUIDE (IN GENERAL)

A study guide is devoted to the particular text you're using. It can't replace the text; it can only point out places where you need more work. To make a study guide most effective:

- Use it only after you've read the chapter and reviewed your class notes.

- Ask yourself whether you really understand the chapter's main points and how they relate to one another.

- Go back and reread the sections of your text that deal with any questions you missed. Chances are that a text will not ask the same questions the study guide does, but the text can help you understand the material better. If that doesn't work, ask your instructor for help.

- Remember that a study guide can't cover any extra material that your teacher may have lectured on.

HOW TO TAKE TESTS

Studying for a Test

Studying for tests is a process that starts with the first class and ends only with the last test. All through the semester, it helps to:

- Follow the advice we gave about reading a chapter and taking notes.

- Review your notes:
    * immediately after class. Clear up anything you can't read and circle important items while the lecture is still fresh in your mind.
    * periodically during the semester.
    * before the test.

- Use any videotapes that may be made of lectures.

Now you're ready to do your final studying for this test. Leave as much time as you need, and study under the conditions that are right for you—alone or with a study group, in the library or another quiet place. It helps to schedule several short study sessions rather than to study all at one time.

- **Reread the chapter(s).** Follow this system:
    * Most importantly, look for things you don't remember or don't understand.
    * Reinforce your understanding of the main ideas by rereading the introduction, study objectives, and summary.
    * Read the chapter from beginning to end.

- **Redo the Problems.** Make sure you know what equation to apply or procedure to follow in different situations, and why.

- **Test Yourself.** Cover up something you've just read and try to explain it to yourself—or to a friend—out loud.

- **Use Memory Tricks.** If you're having trouble remembering something—such as a formula or items in a list—try associating it with something you know or by making a sentence up out of the first letters.

- **Study with a Group.** Group study is helpful after you've done all your own studying. You can help each other with problems and by quizzing each other, but you'll probably just distract each other if you try to review a chapter together.

(A Note About Cramming), DON'T! If you cram, you will probably only remember what you've read for a short time, and you'll have trouble knowing how to generalize from it. If you must cram, however, concentrate on the main ideas, the supporting ideas, main headings, boldface or italicized terms, and study objectives.)

Taking a Test

After the following general tips, we'll give you specifics on objective, problem, and essay tests.

- **Before the Test**
  - Make sure you eat well and get enough sleep before the exam.
  - If the instructor doesn't say in class what material will be covered or what kind of test—objective or essay—will be used, ask.
  - Arrive early enough to get settled.
  - Bring everything you need—bluebook, pens, pencils, eraser, calculator—even the book if it's an open-book test.

- **As You Begin the Test**
  - Read the instructions completely. Do you have to answer all of the questions? Do certain questions apply to others? Do some questions count more than others? Will incorrect answers be counted against you?
  - Schedule your time. How many questions are there? Try to estimate how much time to leave for each section. If sections are timed, so that you won't be able to go back to them, make sure you leave enough time to decide which questions to answer.

- **Taking the Test**
  - Read each question completely as you come to it.
  - Answer the easier questions first and go back to the harder ones.
  - Concentrate on questions that count more.
  - Jot notes or equations in the margin if you think it will help.
  - Review your answers, and don't change an answer unless you're sure you were wrong.

- **Dealing with Panic**
  - Relax. Do this by tightening and relaxing one muscle at a time.
  - Breathe deeply.
  - If you don't know an answer, go on to the next question.

Now for some notes on objective, problem, and essay tests.

- **Objective Tests.** (Multiple choice, true/false, matching, and completion or fill-in-the blank.)
  - * Watch out for words like always/all/every/none/never. Very few things are always or never so. If a question or answer includes words like these, be careful.
  - * If you are uncertain about a multiple choice answer, try to narrow the choices down to two and make an educated guess.
  - * Match up the easy ones first on a matching test. This will leave less possibilities for the harder ones.
  - * Make educated guesses for other objective questions. (If you really have no idea and wrong answers count against you, leave it blank.)

- **Problem Test**
  - * If a formula or equation is quite long, jot it down before you work on the problem.
  - * Remember that math builds one equation on another. If you can't remember a particular equation, try to remember how it was derived.
  - * Don't despair if you can't figure out what a question is calling for. Try to figure out part of it first. If that doesn't work, go on; sometimes a later question will jog your memory.
  - * If your teacher grants some credit for partially correct problems, make sure you include the way you worked out a problem.
  - * Make sure you know how your calculator works before the test. And make sure you know how to do the problems without it. Sometimes you can hit the wrong button, so it helps to have a rough idea of what your calculator should be giving you.

- **Essay Test**
  - * Write a rough outline before you begin. If that takes too much time, just jot down all the things you want to say and then number them. Organize what you're going to say into groups of related ideas.
  - * Make a point in each paragraph. The easiest way is to make the point in the paragraph's first sentence and then to back it up.
  - * Use examples, facts, and dates to back up what you are saying.
  - * Do what the question asks for. If it asks you to compare two things, for example, go back and forth between them; don't spend all your time on one of them.
  - * If you have no idea what to write, try to remember ideas that the teacher stressed in class and see if you can relate the question to those ideas.
  - * Check your time. If you're running out, write your last points down without explaining them; your teacher will at least know what you are going to explain.

Chapter 13

CORPORATIONS: ORGANIZATION AND CAPITAL STOCK TRANSACTIONS

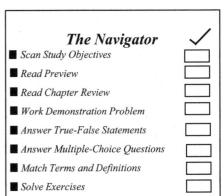

The Navigator ✓
- Scan Study Objectives ☐
- Read Preview ☐
- Read Chapter Review ☐
- Work Demonstration Problem ☐
- Answer True-False Statements ☐
- Answer Multiple-Choice Questions ☐
- Match Terms and Definitions ☐
- Solve Exercises ☐

CHAPTER STUDY OBJECTIVES

After studying this chapter, you should be able to:
1. Identify the major characteristics of a corporation.
2. Differentiate between paid-in capital and retained earnings.
3. Record the issuance of common stock.
4. Explain the accounting for treasury stock.
5. Differentiate preferred stock from common stock.
6. Prepare a stockholders' equity section.

The Navigator

PREVIEW OF CHAPTER 13

The corporation is the dominant form of business organization in the United States in terms of dollar volume of sales, earnings, and employees. All of the 500 largest companies in the United States are corporations. In this chapter we will explain the essential features of a corporation and the accounting for a corporation's capital stock transactions. (In Chapter 14 we will look at other issues related to accounting for corporations.) The content and organization of this chapter is as follows:

Corporations: Organization and Capital Stock Transactions

The Corporate Form of Organization	Accounting for Issues of Common Stock	Accounting for Treasury Stock	Preferred Stock	Statement Presentation
▶Characteristics ▶Formation ▶Stockholder rights ▶Stock issue considerations ▶Corporate capital	▶Issuing par value stock ▶Issuing no-par stock ▶Issue stock for services or noncash assets	▶Purchase of treasury stock ▶Disposal of treasury stock	▶Dividend preferences ▶Liquidation preference	

CHAPTER REVIEW

The Corporate Form of Organization

1. (S.O. 1) A **corporation** is an entity created by law that is separate and distinct from its owners and its continued existence is dependent upon the corporate statutes of the state in which it is incorporated.

2. The characteristics that distinguish a corporation from proprietorships and partnerships are:
   a. The corporation has separate legal existence from its owners.
   b. The stockholders have limited liability.
   c. Ownership is shown in shares of capital stock, which are transferable units.
   d. It is relatively easy for a corporation to obtain capital through the issuance of stock.
   e. The corporation can have a continuous life.
   f. The management in the corporation's organizational structure is at the discretion of the board of directors who are elected by the stockholders.
   g. The corporation is subject to numerous government regulations.
   h. The corporation must pay an income tax on its earnings, and the stockholders are required to pay taxes on the dividends they receive: the result is double taxation of distributed earnings.

Forming a Corporation

3. The formation of a corporation involves (a) filing an application with the Secretary of State, (b) paying an incorporation fee, (c) receiving a charter (articles of incorporation), and (d) developing by-laws.
   a. Costs incurred in forming a corporation are called **organization costs.**
   b. These costs include fees to underwriters, legal fees, state incorporation fees, and promotional expenditures.
   c. Organization costs are expensed as incurred.

Ownership Rights of Stockholders

4. When chartered, the corporation may begin selling ownership rights in the form of shares of stock. Each share of common stock gives the stockholder the following **ownership rights:**
   a. To **vote** for the board of directors and in corporate actions that require stockholder approval.
   b. To **share in corporate earnings** through the receipt of dividends.
   c. To maintain the same percentage ownership when additional shares of common stock are issued **(preemptive right).**
   d. To share in assets upon liquidation **(residual claim).**

Stock Issue Considerations

5. **Authorized stock** is the amount of stock a corporation is allowed to sell as indicated by its charter.
   a. The authorization of capital stock does not result in a formal accounting entry.
   b. The difference between the shares of stock authorized and the shares issued is the number of unissued shares that can be issued without amending the charter.

6. A corporation has the choice of issuing common stock directly to investors or indirectly through an investment banking firm (brokerage house). Direct issue is typical in closely held companies, whereas indirect issue is customary for a publicly held corporation.

7. **Par value stock** is capital stock that has been assigned a value per share in the corporate charter. It represents the **legal capital** per share that must be retained in the business for the protection of corporate creditors.

8. **No-par stock** is capital stock that has not been assigned a value in the corporate charter. In many states the board of directors can assign a **stated value** to the shares which becomes the legal capital per share. When there is no assigned stated value, the entire proceeds are considered to be legal capital.

Corporate Capital

9. (S.O. 2) Owner's equity in a corporation is identified as **stockholders' equity, shareholders' equity, or corporate capital.** The stockholders' equity section of a corporation's balance sheet consists of: (a) paid-in (contributed) capital, and (b) retained earnings (earned capital).

10. **Paid-in capital** is the investment of cash and other assets in the corporation by stockholders in exchange for capital stock.

11. **Retained earnings** is net income retained in a corporation.
    a. Net income is recorded in Retained Earnings by a closing entry with a debit to Income Summary and a credit to Retained Earnings.
    b. Retained earnings (earned capital) is part of the stockholders' equity section of a corporation.

12. (S.O. 3) The **primary objectives** in accounting for the issuance of common stock are to (a) identify the specific sources of paid-in capital and (b) maintain the distinction between paid-in capital and retained earnings.

13. When par value common stock is issued for cash, the par value of the shares is credited to Common Stock and the portion of the proceeds that is above par value is recorded in a separate paid-in capital account.

14. When no-par common stock has a stated value, the stated value is credited to Common Stock. When the selling price exceeds the stated value, the excess is credited to Paid-in Capital in Excess of Stated Value. When no-par stock does not have a stated value, the entire proceeds are credited to Common Stock.

Common Stock for Services or Non-Cash Assets

15. When common stock is issued for **services or non-cash assets,** cost is either the fair market value of the consideration given up or the consideration received, whichever is more clearly determinable.

Treasury Stock

16. (S.O. 4) **Treasury stock** is a corporation's own stock that has been issued, fully paid for, and reacquired but not retired.
    a. Under the cost method, Treasury Stock is debited at the price paid for the shares and the same amount is credited to Treasury Stock when the shares are reissued.
    b. When the Treasury Stock is resold and the selling price of the shares is greater than cost, the difference is credited to Paid-in Capital from Treasury Stock.
    c. When the selling price is less than cost, the excess of cost over selling price is usually debited to Paid-in Capital From Treasury Stock. When there is no remaining balance in Paid-in Capital From Treasury Stock, the remainder is debited to Retained Earnings.

Preferred Stock

17. (S.O. 5) **Preferred stock** has contractual claims that give it priority over common stock. Preferred stockholders usually have a preference to dividends and assets in the event of liquidation. However, they usually do not have voting rights.

18. Preferred stock should be identified separately from other stock (e.g., Preferred Stock, Paid-in Capital in Excess of Par Value—Preferred Stock). Preferred stock is shown first in the stockholders' equity section.

Cumulative Dividend

19. A **cumulative dividend** provides that preferred stockholders must be paid both current and prior year dividends before common stockholders receive any dividends.
    a. Preferred dividends not declared in a given period are called **dividends in arrears.**
    b. Dividends in arrears are not considered a liability, but the amount of the dividends in arrears should be disclosed in the notes to the financial statements.

Stockholders' Equity Presentation

20. (S.O. 6) In the **stockholders' equity section,** paid-in capital and retained earnings are reported and the specific sources of paid-in capital are identified. Within paid-in capital, two classifications are recognized.
    a. **Capital stock,** which consists of preferred and common stock. Preferred stock is shown before common stock because of its preferential rights. Information as to the par value, shares authorized, shares issued, and shares outstanding is reported for each class of stock.
    b. **Additional paid-in capital,** which includes the excess of amounts paid in over par or stated value and paid-in capital from treasury stock.

The Navigator

DEMONSTRATION PROBLEM (S.O. 4)

The Jefferson Corporation and the Franklin Company have the following stockholders' equity accounts on January 1, 2010.

Jefferson Corporation

Common stock, no par stated value $2	$ 600,000
Paid-in capital in excess of stated value	900,000
Retained earnings	300,000
Total	$1,800,000

Franklin Company

Common stock, $3 par	$ 900,000
Paid-in capital in excess of par value	450,000
Retained earnings	750,000
Total	$2,100,000

Both companies use the cost method of accounting for treasury stock. During 2010, the companies had the following treasury stock transactions.

Jefferson Corporation

Feb.   1   Purchased 10,000 shares at $9 per share.
May   2   Sold 2,000 shares at $10 per share.
Aug. 17   Sold 4,000 shares at $13 per share.
Dec. 15   Sold 3,000 shares at $8 per share.

Franklin Company

Mar.   6   Purchased 7,000 shares at $7 per share.
June 19   Sold 1,500 shares at $9 per share.
Sept. 2   Sold 3,000 shares at $6 per share.
Dec. 23   Sold 2,000 shares at $6 per share.

Instructions
(a)   Journalize the treasury stock transactions for both companies (omit explanations).
(b)   Prepare a stockholders' equity section for Franklin Company at December 31, 2010, assuming the company earned $75,000 of net income in 2010.

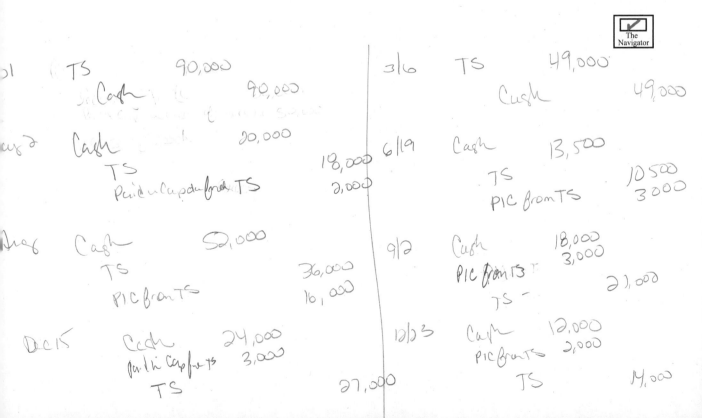

SOLUTION TO DEMONSTRATION PROBLEM

(a)

JEFFERSON CORPORATION—General Journal			J1
Date	**Account Title**	**Debit**	**Credit**
2010			
Feb. 1	Treasury Stock	90,000	
	Cash		90,000
May 2	Cash	20,000	
	Treasury Stock		18,000
	Paid-in Capital from Treasury Stock		2,000
Aug. 17	Cash	52,000	
	Treasury Stock		36,000
	Paid-in Capital from Treasury Stock		16,000
Dec. 15	Cash	24,000	
	Paid-in Capital from Treasury Stock	3,000	
	Treasury Stock		27,000

FRANKLIN CORPORATION—General Journal			J1
Date	**Account Title**	**Debit**	**Credit**
2010			
Mar. 6	Treasury Stock	49,000	
	Cash		49,000
June 19	Cash	13,500	
	Treasury Stock		10,500
	Paid-in Capital from Treasury Stock		3,000
Sept. 2	Cash (3,000 X 6)	18,000	
	Paid-in Capital from Treasury Stock	3,000	
	Treasury Stock		21,000
Dec. 23	Cash	12,000	
	Retained Earnings	2,000	
	Treasury Stock		14,000

(b)

FRANKLIN COMPANY—Stockholders' Equity
December 31, 2010

Stockholders' equity	
Paid-in capital	
Common stock, $3 par value	$ 900,000
Paid-in capital in excess of par value	450,000
Total paid-in capital	1,350,000
Retained earnings..	823,000
Total paid-in capital and retained earnings	2,173,000
Less: Treasury stock (500 shares)...	3,500
Total stockholders' equity	$2,169,500

REVIEW QUESTIONS AND EXERCISES

TRUE—FALSE

Indicate whether each of the following is true (T) or false (F) in the space provided.

_____ 1. (S.O. 1)   A corporation is a legal entity separate and distinct from its owners.

_____ 2. (S.O. 1)   A successful corporation can have a continuous and perpetual life.

_____ 3. (S.O. 1)   Stockholders have the right to directly formulate operating policies for the company.

_____ 4. (S.O. 1)   An advantage of a corporation is that it is subject to very few government regulations.

_____ 5. (S.O. 1)   The issuance of the charter, often referred to as the articles of incorporation, creates the corporation.

_____ 6. (S.O. 1)   Organizational costs are capitalized by debiting an intangible asset entitled Organization Costs.

_____ 7. (S.O. 1)   The amount of stock that a corporation is authorized to sell is indicated in its charter.

_____ 8. (S.O. 1)   Upon the authorization of capital stock, a corporation will record a debit for the asset acquired and a credit to common stock.

_____ 9. (S.O. 1)   Par value is indicative of the worth or market value of the stock.

_____ 10. (S.O. 3)   The cash proceeds from issuing par value stock may be equal to or greater than, but not less than par value.

_____ 11. (S.O. 3)   When no-par stock has a stated value, the entire proceeds from the issue are credited to Common Stock.

_____ 12. (S.O. 3)   The cost of a noncash asset acquired in exchange for common stock should be either the fair market value of the consideration given up or the consideration received, whichever is more clearly determinable.

_____ 13. (S.O. 3)   When stock is issued for noncash assets, the par value of the stock is never a factor in determining the cost of the assets received.

_____ 14. (S.O. 4)   Under the cost method, Treasury Stock is debited at the price paid to reacquire the shares, and the same amount is credited to Treasury Stock when the shares are sold.

_____ 15. (S.O. 4)   Treasury stock is a contra stockholders' equity account.

_____ 16. (S.O. 5) Preferred stockholders usually have the right to vote.

_____ 17. (S.O. 5) Preferred stockholders generally have the right to receive dividends before common stockholders.

_____ 18. (S.O. 5) Most common stocks have a preference over preferred stocks on corporate assets if the corporation fails.

_____ 19. (S.O. 5) Dividends in arrears should be recorded in a liability account.

_____ 20. (S.O. 6) In the stockholders' equity section, paid-in capital and retained earnings are reported and the specific sources of paid-in capital are identified.

MULTIPLE CHOICE

Circle the letter that best answers each of the following statements.

1. (S.O. 1) Which of the following is an **incorrect** statement about a corporation?
    a. A corporation is an entity separate and distinct from its owners.
    b. Creditors ordinarily have recourse only to corporate assets in satisfaction of their claims.
    c. A corporation may be formed in writing, orally, or implied.
    d. A corporation is subject to numerous state and federal regulations.

2. (S.O. 1) Which of the following is **not** considered an advantage of a corporation?
    a. Government regulation.
    b. Limited liability of stockholders.
    c. Continuous life.
    d. Transferable ownership rights.

3. (S.O. 1) Each share of common stock gives the stockholder the following ownership rights.

	Vote	Preemptive right	Residual claim
a.	yes	no	no
b.	yes	yes	no
c.	no	no	yes
d.	yes	yes	yes

4. (S.O. 1) Legal capital per share **cannot** be equal to the:
    a. par value per share of par value stock.
    b. total proceeds from the sale of par value stock above par value.
    c. stated value per share of no-par value stock.
    d. total proceeds from the sale of no-par value stock.

5. (S.O. 2) Assuming that net income for Sponge Bob Co. in its first year of operations is $130,000, the closing entry is:

a.	Retained Earnings	130,000	
	Net Income		130,000
b.	Net Income	130,000	
	Retained Earnings		130,000
c.	Retained Earnings	130,000	
	Income Summary		130,000
d.	Income Summary	130,000	
	Retained Earnings		130,000

6. (S.O. 3) Mary Wells, Inc. issues 2,000 shares of $10 par value common stock at $22 per share. The entry for the issue will include a credit of $24,000 to:
    a. Gain from the Sale of Common Stock.
    b. Paid-in Capital from Treasury Stock.
    c. Paid-in Capital in Excess of Stated Value.
    d. Paid-in Capital in Excess of Par Value.

7. (S.O. 3) Aretha Franklin Inc. issues 10,000 shares of $1 stated value no-par value common stock at $8 per share. The entry for the issue will include a debit to Cash for $80,000 and credits to:
    a. Common Stock, $10,000 and Paid-in Capital in Excess of Stated Value, $70,000.
    b. Common Stock, $10,000 and Paid-in Capital in Excess of Par Value, $70,000.
    c. Common Stock, $80,000.
    d. Common Stock, $10,000 and Retained Earnings, $70,000.

8. (S.O. 3) When common stock is issued for services or non-cash assets, cost should be:
    a. only the fair market value of the consideration given up.
    b. only the fair market value of the consideration received.
    c. the book value of the common stock issued.
    d. either the fair market value of the consideration given up or the consideration received, whichever is more clearly evident.

9. (S.O. 4) Treasury stock was acquired for cash at more than its par value and then sub-sequently sold for cash at more than its acquisition price. What is the effect on additional paid-in capital from treasury stock transactions?

	Purchase of Treasury Stock	Sale of Treasury Stock
a.	No effect	No effect
b.	No effect	Increase
c.	Decrease	Increase
d.	Decrease	No effect

10. (S.O. 4) Elton John Corporation was organized on January 1, 2010, with authorized capital of 500,000 shares of $10 par value common stock. During 2010, Elton John issued 10,000 shares at $12 per share, purchased 1,000 shares of treasury stock at $13 per share, and sold 1,000 shares of treasury stock at $14 per share. What is the amount of additional paid-in capital at December 31, 2010?
    a. $0.
    b. $1,000.
    c. $20,000.
    d. $21,000.

11. (S.O. 4) Big Head Todd sells 2,000 shares of treasury stock purchased for $32,000 at $20 per share. The entry to record this sale should include a credit to:
    a. Gain from Sale of Treasury Stock $8,000.
    b. Paid-in Capital from Treasury Stock $8,000.
    c. Retained Earnings $8,000.
    d. Paid-in Capital from Treasury Stock $12,000.

12. (S.O. 4) The purchase of treasury stock:
    a. decreases common stock authorized.
    b. decreases common stock issued.
    c. decreases common stock outstanding.
    d. has no effect on common stock outstanding.

13. (S.O. 4) What is the effect of the purchase of treasury stock on the amount reported in the balance sheet for each of the following?

	Additional Paid-in Capital	Retained Earnings
a.	No effect	No effect
b.	No effect	Decrease
c.	Decrease	No effect
d.	Decrease	Decrease

14. (S.O. 4) Treasury stock is reported in the balance sheet as:
a. an asset.
b. a deduction in paid-in capital section.
c. a deduction in the retained earnings section.
d. a deduction from total paid-in capital and retained earnings.

15. (S.O. 4) Bob Marley Corporation was organized on January 2, 2010. During 2010, Bob Marley issued 20,000 shares at $12 per share, purchased 3,000 shares of treasury stock at $13 per share, and had net income of $150,000. What is the total amount of stockholders' equity at December 31, 2010?
a. $320,000.
b. $351,000.
c. $354,000.
d. $360,000.

16. (S.O. 5) On January 2, 2008, Poi Dog Corporation issued 5,000 shares of 6% cumulative preferred stock at $100 par value. On December 31, 2011, Poi Dog Corporation declared and paid its first dividend. What dividends are the preferred stockholders entitled to receive in the current year before any distribution is made to common stockholders?
a. $0.
b. $30,000.
c. $90,000.
d. $120,000.

17. (S.O. 5) Dividends in arrears should:
a. be disclosed in the notes to the financial statements.
b. be reported as a liability.
c. be reported as a deduction from retained earnings.
d. not be reported or disclosed.

18. (S.O. 6) In the stockholders' equity section of the balance sheet, the classification of capital stock consists of:
a. additional paid-in capital and common stock.
b. common stock and treasury stock.
c. common stock, preferred stock and treasury stock.
d. common stock and preferred stock.

The Navigator

MATCHING

Match each term with its definition by writing the appropriate letter in the space provided.

Terms	Definitions

Terms

_____ 1.   Authorized stock.

_____ 2.   Paid-in capital.

_____ 3.   Par value stock.

_____ 4.   No-par value stock.

_____ 5.   Treasury stock.

_____ 6.   Cumulative dividend.

_____ 7.   Preferred stock.

_____ 8.   Legal capital.

_____ 9.   By-laws.

Definitions

a.   The amount per share of capital stock that must be retained in the business for the protection of corporate creditors.

b.   Capital stock that has not been assigned a value in the corporate charter.

c.   A feature of preferred stock entitling the stockholder to receive current and unpaid prior-year dividends before common stock-holders receive any dividends.

d.   Capital stock that has been assigned a value per share in the corporate charter.

e.   Total amount paid in on capital stock.

f.   The amount of stock a corporation is allowed to sell as indicated in its charter.

g.   The internal rules and procedures for conducting the affairs of a corporation.

h.   A corporation's own stock that has been issued, fully paid for, and reacquired but not retired.

i.   Capital stock which has contractual prefer-ences over common stock in certain areas.

EXERCISES

EX. 13-1 (S.O. 3, 4) On January 2, The Soup Dragons receive a corporate charter authorizing the sale of 200,000 shares of $10 par value common stock. During the year, The Soup Dragons had the following transactions:

Jan.   5   Issued 20,000 shares of common stock for cash at $10 per share.

       10   Issued 30,000 shares of common stock for cash at $30 per share.

       23   Issued 10,000 shares of common stock for land that had a fair market price of $320,000.

Mar. 15   Issued 1,000 shares of common stock for attorney services used in organizing the corporation valued at $32,000.

Apr. 28   Acquired 5,000 shares of its common stock at $32 per share for the treasury.

June 18   Issued 15,000 shares of common stock for cash at $33 per share.

Sept. 23   Sold 2,000 shares of the treasury stock at $35 per share.

Instructions
Journalize the transactions. (Omit explanations)

General Journal			J1
Date	**Account Title**	**Debit**	**Credit**
1/5	Cash	200,000	
	C/S		200,000
1/10	Cash	900,000	
	PIC - CS		600,000
	C/S		300,000
1/23	Land	320,000	
	PICS		220,000
	C/S		100,000
3/15	Operating Expenses	32,000	
	PIC - C/S		22,000
	C/S		10,000
4/26	T/S	160,000	
	Cash		160,000
6/14	Cash	445,000	
	C/S		100,000
	PIC C/S		345,000
9/23	Cash	70,000	
	T/S		64,000
	PIC-T/S		6,000

EX. 13-2 (S.O. 6)   Charlatans Corporation had the following stockholders' equity accounts at December 31.

Common stock ($1 par value)	$ 150,000
Preferred stock ($50 par value, 6%)	500,000
Paid-in Capital in Excess of Par Value—Common	1,560,000
Paid-in Capital from Treasury Stock—Common	250,000
Retained Earnings	340,000
Treasury stock—common at cost	190,000

At December 31, the number of common and preferred shares were:

	Common	**Preferred**
Authorized	500,000	50,000
Issued	150,000	10,000
Outstanding	140,000	10,000

Instructions
Prepare the stockholders' equity section at December 31.

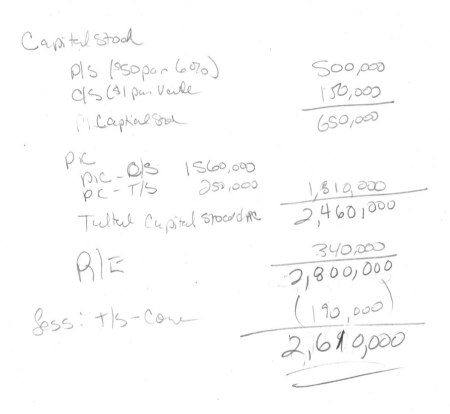

CHARLATANS CORPORATION

Stockholders' equity

SOLUTIONS TO REVIEW QUESTIONS AND EXERCISES

TRUE-FALSE

1. (T)
2. (T)
3. (F)   The operating policies for the company are at the discretion of the board of directors, who are elected by the stockholders.
4. (F)   A corporation is subject to numerous state and federal regulations that add considerably to the cost of doing business.
5. (T)
6. (F)   Organizational costs are expensed as incurred.
7. (T)
8. (F)   The authorization of capital stock does not result in a formal accounting entry, or the acquisition of an asset.
9. (F)   Par value is not indicative of the worth or market value of the stock. The significance of par value is a legal matter.
10. (F)   The sale of common stock may be below par value unless it is legally prohibited.
11. (F)   When the selling price exceeds stated value, the excess is credited to Paid-in Capital in Excess of Stated Value and only the stated value is credited to Common Stock.
12. (T)
13. (T)
14. (T)
15. (T)
16. (F)   Preferred stockholders usually do not have the right to vote.
17. (T)
18. (F)   Most preferred stocks also have a preference on corporate assets if the corporation fails.
19. (F)   Dividends in arrears are not considered a liability because no obligation exists until the dividend is declared by the board of directors. They are disclosed in the footnotes to the financial statements.
20. (T)

MULTIPLE CHOICE

1. (c)   Answers (a), (b), and (d) are all correct statements. Answer (c) is incorrect because a corporation must file an application with the Secretary of State in the state in which incorporation is desired.

2. (a)   Advantages of corporate existence are separate legal existence, limited liability of stockholders, transferable ownership rights, ability to acquire capital, continuous life, corporation management--professional managers. Disadvantages of corporate existence are government regulations, additional taxes and corporation management--separation of ownership and management.

3. (d)   Each share of common stock entitles the owner to vote in the election of the board of directors and other matters of concern. The stockholder has a preemptive right to maintain the same percentage ownership when additional shares of common stock are issued. And, upon liquidation, shareholders share in the distribution of assets according to their residual claim.

4. (b) Legal capital per share for par value stock is par value (a). Answers (c) and (d) are both equal to legal capital.

5. (d) The entry is:

Income Summary	130,000	
Retained Earnings...		130,000

6. (d) The entry is:

Cash..	44,000	
Common Stock...		20,000
Paid-in Capital in Excess of Par value..............		24,000

7. (a) The entry is:

Cash..	80,000	
Common Stock...		10,000
Paid-in Capital in Excess of Stated Value		70,000

8. (d) When common stock is issued for services or non-cash assets, cost should be either the fair market value of the consideration given up or the consideration received, whichever is more clearly evident.

9. (b) The purchase of treasury stock affects only the treasury stock account and the cash account. The sale above cost affects these accounts and also increases paid-in capital from treasury stock.

10. (d) The additional paid-in capital will include both the excess of cash received over par value on the issuance of the stock, $20,000 (10,000 X $2) and Paid-in Capital from Treasury Stock when the treasury stock is sold, $1,000 ($14,000 - $13,000).

11. (b) Because the treasury stock was purchased at a cost of $32,000, the following entry should be made for the sale:

Cash..	40,000	
Treasury Stock		32,000
Paid-in Capital from Treasury Stock..................		8,000

12. (c) Common stock outstanding includes any common stock issued less treasury stock. Treasury stock, however, is still issued stock.

13. (a) The purchase of the treasury stock decreases total stockholders' equity but has no effect on either additional paid-in capital or retained earnings.

14. (d) Treasury stock is not an asset (a). It is a contra stockholders' equity account that is deducted from total paid-in capital and retained earnings.

15. (b) The issuance of 20,000 shares at $12 per share results in $240,000 of stockholders' equity. The purchase of 3,000 shares of treasury stock decreases stockholders' equity by $39,000, and the net income causes stockholders' equity to increase by $150,000.

16. (d) The preferred stockholders are entitled to four years of cumulative dividends of $30,000 per year (5,000 X $100 X .06) for each year between January 2, 2008 and December 31, 2011.

17. (a) Dividends in arrears are not considered to be a liability (b) because the dividends have not been declared. However, they should be disclosed in the notes to the financial statements.

18. (d) In the stockholders' equity section of the balance sheet, the classification of capital stock consists of common stock and preferred stock.

MATCHING

1.	f.	5.	h.	9.	g.
2.	e.	6.	c.		
3.	d.	7.	i.		
4.	b.	8.	a.		

EXERCISES

EX. 13-1

General Journal			J1
Date	**Account Title**	**Debit**	**Credit**
Jan. 5	Cash	200,000	
	Common Stock		200,000
10	Cash	900,000	
	Common Stock		300,000
	Paid-in Capital in Excess of Par Value		600,000
23	Land	320,000	
	Common Stock		100,000
	Paid-in Capital in Excess of Par Value		220,000
Mar. 15	Organization Costs	32,000	
	Common Stock		10,000
	Paid-in Capital in Excess of Par Value		22,000
Apr. 28	Treasury Stock	160,000	
	Cash		160,000
June 18	Cash	495,000	
	Common Stock		150,000
	Paid-in Capital in Excess of Par Value		345,000
Sept. 23	Cash	70,000	
	Treasury Stock (2,000 X $32)		64,000
	Paid-in Capital from Treasury Stock		6,000

EX. 13-2

CHARLATANS CORPORATION

Stockholders' equity
    Paid-in capital
        Capital stock

Preferred stock, $50 par value, 6%, 50,000 shares authorized, 10,000 shares issued and outstanding..		$ 500,000
Common stock, $1 par value, 500,000 shares authorized, 150,000 shares issued and 140,000 shares outstanding............................		150,000
Total capital stock		650,000
Additional paid-in capital		
Excess over par value—common stock	$1,560,000	
From treasury stock—common	250,000	
Total additional paid-in capital.........................		1,810,000
Total paid-in capital...		2,460,000
Retained earnings..		340,000
Total paid-in capital and retained earnings		2,800,000
Less: Treasury stock (10,000 common shares at cost)		(190,000)
Total stockholders' equity................................		$2,610,000

Chapter 14

CORPORATIONS: DIVIDENDS, RETAINED EARNINGS, AND INCOME REPORTING

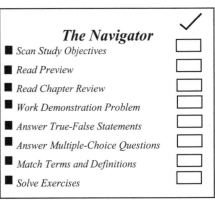

The Navigator
- ☑ Scan Study Objectives
- ☑ Read Preview
- ☑ Read Chapter Review
- ☑ Work Demonstration Problem
- ☑ Answer True-False Statements
- ☑ Answer Multiple-Choice Questions
- ☑ Match Terms and Definitions
- ☑ Solve Exercises

CHAPTER STUDY OBJECTIVES

After studying this chapter, you should be able to:
1. Prepare the entries for cash dividends and stock dividends.
2. Identify the items reported in a retained earnings statement.
3. Prepare and analyze a comprehensive stockholders' equity section.
4. Describe the form and content of corporation income statements.
5. Compute earnings per share.

PREVIEW OF CHAPTER 14

A corporation that is profitable distributes substantial dividends. In addition, it often reinvests a portion of its earnings in the business. This chapter discusses dividends, retained earnings, corporation income statements, and earnings per share. The content and organization of the chapter are as follows:

Corporations: Dividends, Retained Earnings, and Income Reporting

Dividends	Retained Earnings	Statement Presentation and Analysis
▶ Cash dividends	▶ Retained earnings restrictions	▶ Stockholders' equity presentation
▶ Stock dividends	▶ Prior period adjustments	▶ Stockholders' equity analysis
▶ Stock splits	▶ Retained earnings statement	▶ Income statement presentation
		▶ Income statement analysis

CHAPTER REVIEW

Dividends

1. (S.O. 1) A dividend is a distribution by a corporation to its stockholders on a pro rata (proportional) basis. Dividends may be in the form of cash, property, scrip, or stock.

2. A cash dividend is a pro rata distribution of cash to stockholders. For a corporation to pay a cash dividend, it must have (a) retained earnings, (b) adequate cash, and (c) declared dividends.

3. Three dates are important in connection with dividends:
    a. **Declaration date**—the date on which the board of directors formally declares a cash dividend and the liability is recorded.
    b. **Record date**—the date that marks the time when ownership of outstanding shares is determined from the stockholders' records maintained by the corporation.
    c. **Payment date**—the date dividend checks are mailed to the stockholders and the payment of the dividend is recorded.

4. **Preferred stockholders** must be paid dividends before common stockholders receive dividends.
    a. When preferred stock is **cumulative,** any dividends in arrears must be paid to preferred stockholders before allocating any dividends to common stockholders.
    b. When preferred stock is **not** cumulative, only the current dividend must be paid to preferred stockholders before paying any dividends to common stockholders.

Stock Dividend

5. A **stock dividend** is a pro rata distribution to stockholders of the corporation's own stock. A stock dividend results in a decrease in retained earnings and an increase in paid-in capital. At a minimum, the par or stated value must be assigned to the dividend shares; in most cases, however, fair market value is used.

6. When the fair market value of the stock is used, the following entry is made at the declaration date:

Retained Earnings	XXX	
Common Stock Dividends Distributable...............................		XXX
Paid-in Capital in Excess of Par Value...................................		XXX

    a. Common Stock Dividends Distributable is reported in paid-in capital as an addition to common stock issued.
    b. Common Stock Dividends Distributable is debited and Common Stock is credited when the dividend shares are issued.

7. Stock dividends change the composition of stockholders' equity because a portion of retained earnings is transferred to paid-in capital. However, total stockholders' equity and the par or stated value per share remain the same.

Stock Split

8.   A **stock split** involves the issuance of additional shares of stock to stockholders according to their percentage ownership.
  a.   In a stock split, the number of shares is increased in the same proportion that par or stated value per share is decreased.
  b.   A stock split has no effect on total paid-in capital, retained earnings, or total stockholders' equity.
  c.   It is not necessary to formally journalize a stock split.

Retained Earnings

9.   (S.O. 2) **Retained earnings** is net income that is retained in the business. The balance in retained earnings is part of the stockholders' claim on the total assets of the corporation.
  a.   A **net loss** is recorded in Retained Earnings by a closing entry in which Retained Earnings is debited and Income Summary is credited.
  b.   A debit balance in Retained Earnings is identified as a **deficit** and is reported as a deduction in the stockholders' equity section.

10.   In some cases there may be **retained earnings restrictions** that make a portion of the balance currently unavailable for dividends.   Restrictions result from one or more of the following causes: legal, contractual or voluntary. Retained earnings restrictions are generally disclosed in the notes to the financial statements.

11.   A **prior period adjustment** is the correction of a material error in reporting net income in previously issued financial statements. The correction is:
  a.   made directly to Retained Earnings.
  b.   reported in the current year's retained earnings statement as an adjustment of the beginning balance of Retained Earnings.

12.   Many corporations prepare a **retained earnings statement** to explain the changes in **retained earnings** during the year.

Stockholders' Equity Statement

13.   (S.O. 3) Instead of presenting a detailed stockholders' equity section in the balance sheet and a retained earnings statement, many companies prepare a **stockholders' equity statement.**

Form of Income Statement

14.   (S.O. 4) The **income statement** for a corporation includes essentially the same sections as in a proprietorship or a partnership. The major difference is a section for income taxes.

Earnings Per Share

15. (S.O. 5)   Earnings per share (EPS) indicates the net income earned by each share of outstanding common stock.
    a.   The formula for computing earnings per share is:

$$\text{Net income} \div \begin{array}{c}\text{Weighted Average}\\\text{Common Shares}\\\text{Outstanding}\end{array} = \begin{array}{c}\text{Earnings}\\\text{per Share}\end{array}$$

16. When a corporation has both preferred and common stock outstanding, dividends declared on preferred stock are subtracted from net income in determining earnings per share. If the preferred stock is cumulative, the dividend for the current year is deducted whether or not it is declared.

The
Navigator

DEMONSTRATION PROBLEM (S.O. 3)

The following accounts appear in the ledger of Geis Inc. after the books are closed at December 31.

Common Stock, no par, $1 stated value, 700,000 shares authorized, 600,000 shares issued	$ 600,000
Common Stock Dividends Distributable	50,000
Paid-in Capital in Excess of Stated Value-Common Stock	2,400,000
Preferrd Stock, $5 par value, 8%, 400,000 shares authorized; 100,000 shares issued	500,000
Retained Earnings	900,000
Treasury Stock (5,000 common shares)	35,000
Paid-in Capital in Excess of Par Value—Preferred Stock	1,500,000

Instructions
Prepare the stockholders' equity section at December 31, assuming retained earnings is restricted for a new plant in the amount of $400,000.

SOLUTION TO DEMONSTRATION PROBLEM
GEIS INC.
Balance Sheet (partial)

Stockholders' equity		
Paid-in capital		
Capital stock		
8% Preferred stock, $5 par value,		
400,000 shares authorized, 100,000 shares issued and outstanding		$ 500,000
Common stock, no par, $1 stated value,		
700,000 shares authorized, 600,000 shares issued and 595,000 outstanding	$ 600,000	
Common stock dividends distributable	50,000	650,000
Total capital stock		1,150,000
Additional paid-in capital		
In excess of par value—preferred stock	1,500,000	
In excess of stated value—common stock	2,400,000	
Total additional paid-in capital		3,900,000
Total paid-in capital		5,050,000
Retained earnings (see Note A)		900,000
Total paid-in capital and retained earnings		5,950,000
Less: Treasury stock—common (5,000 shares)		(35,000)
Total stockholders' equity		$5,915,000

Note A: Retained earnings is restricted for a new plant, $400,000.

REVIEW QUESTIONS AND EXERCISES

TRUE—FALSE

Indicate whether each of the following is true (T) or false (F) in the space provided.

_____   1. (S.O. 1)   A cash dividend is a pro rata distribution of cash to stockholders.

_____   2. (S.O. 1)   A dividend based on paid-in capital is termed a liquidating dividend.

_____   3. (S.O. 1)   The date that the board of directors formally declares a cash dividend is the date of record.

_____   4. (S.O. 1)   Dividends Payable is a current liability because it will normally be paid within the next several months.

_____   5. (S.O. 1)   A stock dividend results in a decrease in retained earnings and an increase in paid-in capital.

_____   6. (S.O. 1)   Common Stock Dividends Distributable is reported as additional paid-in capital in the stockholders' equity section.

_____   7. (S.O. 1)   A stock split must be formally journalized.

_____   8. (S.O. 2)   A net loss is credited to Retained Earnings in preparing closing entries.

_____   9. (S.O. 2)   Retained earnings restrictions are generally disclosed in the notes to the financial statements.

_____   10. (S.O. 2)   A prior period adjustment is reported as an adjustment of the beginning balance of Retained Earnings.

_____   11. (S.O. 3)   The return on common stockholders' equity ratio shows how many dollars of net income were earned for each dollar invested by the owners.

_____   12. (S.O. 4)   Income tax expense and the related liability for income taxes payable are recorded when taxes are paid.

_____   13. (S.O. 5)   Earnings per share is reported only for common stock.

_____   14. (S.O. 5)   If a company has declared any preferred dividends, they should be added to net income in the calculation of earnings per share.

The
Navigator

MULTIPLE CHOICE

Circle the letter that best answers each of the following statements.

1. (S.O. 1) Which of the following statements about a cash dividend is **incorrect?**
    a. The legality of a cash dividend depends on state corporation laws.
    b. The legality of a dividend does not indicate a company's ability to pay a dividend.
    c. Dividends are not a liability until declared.
    d. Shareholders usually vote to determine the amount of income to be distributed in the form of a dividend.

2. (S.O. 1) On December 31, 2010, Little Richard, Inc. has 2,000 shares of 6% $100 par value cumulative preferred stock and 30,000 shares of $10 par value common stock outstanding. On December 31, 2010, the directors declare an $8,000 cash dividend. The entry to record the declaration of the dividend would include:
    a. a credit of $4,000 to Retained Earnings.
    b. a note in the financial statements that dividends of $8 per share are in arrears on preferred stock for 2010.
    c. a debit of $8,000 to Common Stock.
    d. a credit of $8,000 to Dividends Payable.

3. (S.O. 1) Which of the following statements about a stock dividend is **incorrect?**
    a. A stock dividend is a pro rata distribution of the corporation's own stock to stockholders.
    b. A stock dividend has no effect on total stockholders' equity and book value per share.
    c. Common Stock Dividends Distributable is reported in the stockholders' equity section.
    d. A stock dividend decreases retained earnings and increases paid-in capital.

4. (S.O. 1) Remmers, Inc. declares a 10% common stock dividend when it has 20,000 shares of $10 par value common stock outstanding. If the market value of $24 per share is used, the amounts debited to Retained Earnings and credited to Paid-in Capital in Excess of Par Value are:

	Retained Earnings	Paid-in Capital in Excess of Par Value
a.	$20,000	$0
b.	$48,000	$28,000
c.	$48,000	$20,000
d.	$20,000	$28,000

5. (S.O. 1) Bussan Corporation splits its common stock 4 for 1, when the market value is $80 per share. Prior to the split, Bussan had 50,000 shares of $12 par value common stock issued and outstanding. After the split, the par value of the stock:
    a. remains the same.
    b. is reduced to $2 per share.
    c. is reduced to $3 per share.
    d. is reduced to $4 per share.

6. (S.O. 2)   Which of the following statements about retained earnings restrictions is **incorrect?**
    a.   Many states require a corporation to restrict retained earnings for the cost of treasury stock purchased.
    b.   Long-term debt contracts may impose a restriction on retained earnings as a condition for the loan.
    c.   The board of directors of a corporation may voluntarily create retained earnings restrictions for specific purposes.
    d.   Retained earnings restrictions are generally disclosed through a journal entry on the books of a company.

7. (S.O. 2) A prior period adjustment should be reported in the:
    a.   income statement after income from continuing operations and before extraordinary items.
    b.   income statement after income from continuing operations and after extraordinary items.
    c.   retained earnings statement after net income but before dividends.
    d.   retained earnings statement as an adjustment of the beginning balance.

8. (S.O. 4) Jennifer Company reports the following amounts for 2010:

Net income	$ 100,000
Average stockholders' equity	1,000,000
Preferred dividends	28,000
Par value preferred stock	200,000

    The 2010 rate of return on common stockholders' equity is:
    a.   7.2%.
    b.   9.0%.
    c.   10.0%.
    d.   12.5%.

9. (S.O. 5) In determining earnings per share, dividends for the current year on noncumulative preferred stock should be:
    a.   disregarded.
    b.   added back to net income whether declared or not.
    c.   deducted from net income only if declared.
    d.   deducted from net income whether declared or not.

10. (S.O. 5) Kepler Corporation had 300,000 shares of common stock outstanding during the year. Kepler declared and paid cash dividends of $150,000 on the common stock and $120,000 on the preferred stock. Net income for the year was $660,000. What is Kepler's earnings per share?
    a. $1.30.
    b. $1.70.
    c. $1.80.
    d. $2.20.

11. (S.O. 5) On January 1, Lindsey Company had 44,000 shares of common stock outstanding. On May 1, they sold an additional 3,000 shares of common stock. The number of shares on which earnings per share for the year should be based is:
  a.   44,000.
  b.   45,000.
  c.   46,000.
  d.   47,000.
  (Note: The calculation of weighted average of common shares outstanding is typically covered in an advanced accounting course, not an introductory accounting course.)

12. (S.O. 5)   The income statement for Monkey, Co. shows income before income taxes $400,000, income tax expense $120,000, and net income $280,000. If Monkey has 100,000 shares of common stock outstanding throughout the year, earnings per share is:
  a. $4.00.
  b. $2.80.
  c. $1.20.
  d. $1.00.

$$\frac{280,000}{100,000}$$

The
Navigator

MATCHING

Match each term with its definition by writing the appropriate letter in the space provided.

Terms	Definitions

Terms

_c_   1.   Liquidating dividend.

_f_   2.   Cash dividend.

_e_   3.   Retained earnings restrictions.

_j_   4.   Stock dividend.

_g_   5.   Retained earnings.

_b_   6.   Record date.

_d_   7.   Earnings per share.

_h_   8.   Prior period adjustment.

_i_   9.   Stock split.

_a_   10.   Declaration date.

Definitions

a. The date the board of directors formally declares the dividend and announces it to stockholders.

b. The date when ownership of outstanding shares is determined for dividend purposes.

c. A dividend declared out of paid-in capital.

d. The net income earned by each share of outstanding common stock.

e. Circumstances that make a portion of retained earnings currently unavailable for dividends.

f. A pro rata distribution of cash to stock-holders.

g. Net income that is retained in the business.

h. The correction of an error in previously issued financial statements.

i. The issuance of additional shares of stock to stockholders accompanied by a reduction in the par or stated value per share of the stock.

j. A pro rata distribution of the corporation's own stock to stockholders with no change in par or stated value per share.

EXERCISES

EX. 14-1   (S.O. 1 and 2) Tycho Corporation started business operations on January 1, 2010. On January 1, 2011, Tycho has 400,000 shares of $10 par value common stock outstanding and $300,000 of retained earnings. During 2011, Tycho had the following transactions:

Apr. 1   Declared a 10 cent per share cash dividend on common stock outstanding.

Apr. 15   Discovered an error made in 2006 that understated depreciation by $800. (Ignore tax effects).

May 15   Paid the cash dividend declared on April 1.

July 1   Declared a 2% stock dividend when the fair market value of the stock was $15.

Aug. 1   Issued the shares for the stock dividend.

Nov. 1   Effected a 2 for 1 stock split.

Dec. 1   Declared a 10 cent per share cash dividend on common stock outstanding.

Instructions
Record the transactions above in the general journal. (Omit explanations).

General Journal			J1
Date	Account Title	Debit	Credit

EX. 14-2   (S.O. 3) The following accounts appear in the ledger of Jewel Corp. after the books are closed at December 31.

Common Stock, $2 par value, 900,000 shares authorized, 200,000 shares issued	$ 400,000
Common Stock Dividends Distributable	20,000
Paid-in Capital in Excess of Par Value—Common Stock	1,600,000
Preferred Stock, $10 par value, 9%, 800,000 shares authorized, 50,000 shares issued	500,000
Retained Earnings	700,000
Treasury Stock (10,000 common shares)	110,000
Paid-in Capital in Excess of Par Value—Preferred Stock	800,000

Instructions
Prepare the stockholders' equity section at December 31.

SOLUTIONS TO REVIEW QUESTIONS AND EXERCISES

TRUE-FALSE

1.   (T)
2.   (T)
3.   (F)   The date that the board of directors formally declares a cash dividend is the date of the declaration.
4.   (T)
5.   (T)
6.   (F)   Common Stock Dividends Distributable is reported in paid-in capital as an addition to common stock issued.
7.   (F)   Because a stock split does not affect the balances in any stockholders' equity accounts, it is not necessary to journalize a stock split.
8.   (F)   A net loss is debited to Retained Earnings in preparing closing entries.
9.   (T)
10.   (T)
11.   (T)
12.   (F)   Income tax expense and the related liability for income taxes payable are recorded as part of the adjusting process preceding financial statement preparation.
13.   (T)
14.   (F)   Preferred dividends should be subtracted from net income in the calculation of earnings per share.

MULTIPLE CHOICE

1.   (d)   The board of directors has full authority to determine the amount of income to be distributed in the form of a dividend.   The other answer choices are correct statements.

2.   (d)   The entry on December 31, 2010 to record the declaration of the dividend would be as follows:

Retained Earnings...	8,000	
Dividends Payable		8,000

In addition, because of the cumulative feature, dividends in arrears of $4,000 should be disclosed in the financial statements.

3.   (b)   Because of the additional shares that are issued, book value per share decreases as a result of the stock dividend. The other answer choices are correct statements.

4.   (b)   The stock dividend results in the following entry:

Retained Earnings...	48,000	
Common Stock Dividends Distributable............		20,000
Paid-in Capital in Excess of Par Value		28,000

5. (c)   The stock split results in an inversely proportional decrease in the par value of the stock ($3 = $12/4).

6. (d)   Retained earnings restrictions are generally disclosed in the notes to the financial statements. The other answers are correct.

7. (d)   A prior period adjustment is reported in the retained earnings statement as an adjustment of the beginning balance.

8. (b)   The basic computation for the rate of return on common stockholders' equity is net income divided by average common stockholders' equity. When preferred stock is present, preferred dividends must be subtracted from the numerator and the par value of preferred stock must be subtracted from the denominator.

The result is: $\dfrac{\$100,000 - \$28,000}{\$1,000,000 - \$200,000} = 9\%$

9. (c)   In determining earnings per share, dividends on noncumulative preferred stock should be deducted from net income only if declared.

10. (c)   The earnings per share is calculated as follows: $\dfrac{\$660,000 - \$120,000}{300,000} = \$1.80.$

11. (c)   The weighted average shares are computed by determining the time a given number of shares is outstanding during the period as follows:

44,000 shares X 4/12 of a year...	14,666.67
47,000 shares X 8/12 of a year...	31,333.33
Weighted average shares outstanding......................................	46,000.00

12. (b)   The earnings per share is calculated as $2.80 ($280,000 ÷ 100,000).

MATCHING

1.	c	6.	b
2.	f	7.	d
3.	e	8.	h
4.	j	9.	i
5.	g	10.	a

EXERCISES

EX. 14-1

General Journal			J1
Date	**Account Title**	**Debit**	**Credit**
2011			
Apr. 1	Retained Earnings (400,000 X $.10)	40,000	
	Dividends Payable		40,000
Apr. 15	Retained Earnings	800	
	Accumulated Depreciation		800
May 15	Dividends Payable	40,000	
	Cash		40,000
July 1	Retained Earnings (400,000 X 2% X $15)	120,000	
	Common Stock Dividends Distributable		80,000
	(400,000 X 2% X $10)		
	Paid-in Capital In Excess of Par Value		40,000
Aug. 1	Common Stock Dividends Distributable	80,000	
	Common Stock		80,000
Nov. 1	No entry needed; total shares are 816,000		
	(408,000 X 2)		
Dec. 1	Retained Earnings (816,000 X $.10)	81,600	
	Dividends Payable		81,600

EX. 14-2

JEWEL CORP.
Balance Sheet (partial)

Stockholders' equity		
Paid-in capital		
Capital stock		
9% Preferred stock, $10 par value,		
800,000 shares authorized, 50,000 shares		
issued and outstanding		$ 500,000
Common stock, $2 par value, 900,000 shares		
authorized, 200,000 shares issued and		
190,000 outstanding	$ 400,000	
Common stock dividends distributable	20,000	420,000
Total Capital stock		920,000
Additional paid-in capital		
In excess of par value—preferred stock	800,000	
In excess of par value—common stock	1,600,000	
Total additional paid-in capital		2,400,000
Total paid-in capital		3,320,000
Retained earnings		700,000
Total paid-in capital and retained earnings		4,020,000
Less: Treasury stock—common (10,000 shares)		(110,000)
Total stockholders' equity		$3,910,000

Chapter 15

LONG-TERM LIABILITIES

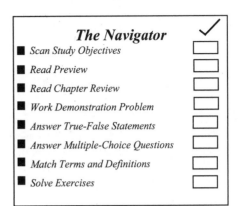

The Navigator
- ☐ Scan Study Objectives
- ☐ Read Preview
- ☐ Read Chapter Review
- ☐ Work Demonstration Problem
- ☐ Answer True-False Statements
- ☐ Answer Multiple-Choice Questions
- ☐ Match Terms and Definitions
- ☐ Solve Exercises

CHAPTER STUDY OBJECTIVES

After studying this chapter, you should be able to:
1. Explain why bonds are issued.
2. Prepare the entries for the issuance of bonds and interest expense.
3. Describe the entries when bonds are redeemed or converted.
4. Describe the accounting for long-term notes payable.
5. Contrast the accounting for operating and capital leases.
6. Identify the methods for the presentation and analysis of long-term liabilities.
*7. Compute the market price of a bond.
*8. Apply the effective-interest method of amortizing bond discount and bond premium.
*9. Apply the straight-line method of amortizing bond discount and bond premium.

*Note: All **asterisked** (*) items relate to material contained in the Appendix to the chapter.

The Navigator

PREVIEW OF CHAPTER 15

In this chapter we will explain the accounting for the major types of long-term liabilities reported on the balance sheet. These liabilities may be bonds, long-term notes, or lease obligations.   The content and organization of the chapter are as follows:

Long-Term Liabilities

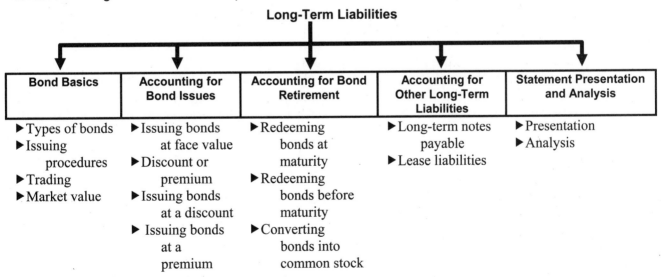

Bond Basics	Accounting for Bond Issues	Accounting for Bond Retirement	Accounting for Other Long-Term Liabilities	Statement Presentation and Analysis
▶Types of bonds ▶Issuing procedures ▶Trading ▶Market value	▶Issuing bonds at face value ▶Discount or premium ▶Issuing bonds at a discount ▶Issuing bonds at a premium	▶Redeeming bonds at maturity ▶Redeeming bonds before maturity ▶Converting bonds into common stock	▶Long-term notes payable ▶Lease liabilities	▶Presentation ▶Analysis

CHAPTER REVIEW

Bonds

1. (S.O. 1) **Long-term liabilities** are obligations that are expected to be paid after one year. Long-term liabilities include bonds, long-term notes, and lease obligations.

2. Bonds offer the following **advantages** over common stock:
    a. Stockholder control is not affected.
    b. Tax savings result.
    c. Earnings per share of common stock may be higher.

3. The **major disadvantages** resulting from the use of bonds are that interest must be paid on a periodic basis, and the principal (face value) of the bonds must be paid at maturity.

Types of Bonds

4. **Secured bonds** have specific assets of the issuer pledged as collateral for the bonds. A **mortgage bond** is secured by real estate. **Unsecured bonds** are issued against the general credit of the borrower; they are also called **debenture bonds.**

5. Bonds that mature at a single specified future date are called **term bonds.** In contrast, bonds that mature in installments are called **serial bonds.**

6. **Registered bonds** are issued in the name of the owner and have interest payments made by check to bondholders of record. **Bearer or coupon bonds** are not registered; thus bondholders must send in coupons to receive interest payments.

7. **Convertible bonds** permit bondholders to convert the bonds into common stock at their option. **Callable bonds** are subject to call and retirement at a stated dollar amount prior to maturity at the option of the issuer.

8. State laws grant corporations the power to issue bonds.
    a. Within the corporation, formal approval by both the board of directors and stockholders is usually required before bonds can be issued.
    b. In authorizing a bond issue, the board of directors must stipulate the total number of bonds to be authorized, total face value, and the contractual interest rate.
    c. The terms of the bond issue are set forth in a formal legal document called a **bond indenture.**

Market Value of Bonds

9. The **market value** (present value) of a bond is a function of three factors: (a) the dollar amounts to be received, (b) the length of time until the amounts are received, and (c) the market rate of interest.

Bond Issues

10. (S.O. 2) The issuance of bonds at **face value** results in a debit to Cash and a credit to Bonds Payable.
    a. Over the term of the bonds, entries are required for bond interest.
    b. At the maturity date, it is necessary to record the final payment of interest and payment of the face value of the bonds.

11. Bonds may be issued below or above face value.
    a. If the market (effective) rate of interest is higher than the contractual (stated) rate, the bonds will sell at less than face value, or at a discount.
    b. If the market rate of interest is less than the contractual rate on the bonds, the bonds will sell above face value, or at a premium.

Bond Issues at Discount

12. When bonds are issued at a **discount,**
    a. The discount is debited to a contra account, Discount on Bonds Payable, and it is deducted from Bonds Payable in the balance sheet to show the carrying (or book) value of the bonds.
    b. Bond discount is an additional cost of borrowing that should be recorded as bond interest expense over the life of the bonds.

Bond Issues at Premium

13. When bonds are issued at a **premium,**
    a. The premium is credited to the account, Premium on Bonds Payable, and it is added to Bonds Payable in the balance sheet.
    b. Bond premium is a reduction in the cost of borrowing that should be credited to Bond Interest Expense over the life of the bonds.

Bond Retirements

14. (S.O. 3) When bonds are **retired before maturity** it is necessary to (a) eliminate the carrying value of the bonds at the redemption date, (b) record the cash paid, and (c) recognize the gain or loss on redemption.

15. In recording the **conversion of bonds** into common stock the current market prices of the bonds and the stock are ignored. Instead, the carrying value of the bonds is transferred to paid-in capital accounts and no gain or loss is recognized.

Long-term Notes Payable

16. (S.O. 4) A **long-term note payable** may be secured by a document called a mortgage that pledges title to specific assets as security for a loan.
    a. Typically, the terms require the borrower to make installment payments consisting of (1) interest on the unpaid balance of the loan and (2) a reduction of loan principal.
    b. Mortgage notes payable are recorded initially at face value; each installment payment results in a debit to Interest Expense, a debit to Mortgage Notes Payable, and a credit to Cash.

Leases

17. (S.O. 5) A **lease** is a contractual agreement between a lessor (owner) and a lessee (renter) that grants the right to use specific property for a period of time in return for cash payments.

Operating Leases

18. In an **operating lease** the intent is temporary use of the property by the lessee with continued ownership of the property by the lessor. The lease (or rental) payments are recorded as an expense by the lessee and as revenue by the lessor.

Capital Leases

19. A **capital lease** transfers substantially all the benefits and risks of ownership from the lessor to the lessee.
    a. The lessee is required to record an asset and the related obligation at the present value of the future lease payments.
    b. The leased asset is reported on the balance sheet under plant assets.
    c. The portion of the lease liability to be paid in the next year is a current liability, and the remainder is classified as a long-term liability.

Presentation and Analysis

20. (S.O. 6) Long-term liabilities are reported in a separate section of the balance sheet immediately following current liabilities.

21. The **debt to total assets ratio** measures the percentage of the total assets provided by creditors. It is computed by dividing total debt by total assets.

22. The **times interest earned ratio** provides an indication of the company's ability to meet interest payments as they become due. It is computed by dividing income before interest expense and income taxes by interest expense.

Effective-Interest Method

*23. (S.O. 8) The **effective interest method** of amortization is an alternative to the straight-line method. Under this method,
    a. Bond Interest Expense is computed first by multiplying the carrying value of the bonds at the beginning of the period by the effective interest rate.
    b. The credit to Cash (or Bond Interest Payable) is computed by multiplying the face value of the bonds by the contractual interest rate.
    c. The bond discount or premium amortization amount is then determined by comparing bond interest expense with the interest paid or accrued.

*24. The effective interest method produces a periodic interest expense equal to a constant percentage of the carrying value of the bonds. When the amounts of bond interest expense are materially different under the two methods, the effective interest method is required under generally accepted accounting principles.

Straight-Line Method

*25. (S.O. 9) The **straight-line method** of amortization allocates the same amount of bond discount (premium) each interest period. The formula is:

Bond Discount (Premium) ÷ Number of Interest Periods = Bond Discount (Premium) Amortization

Bond discount amortization is recorded by debiting Bond Interest Expense and crediting Discount on Bonds Payable. Bond premium amortization is recorded by crediting Bond Interest Expense and debiting Premium on Bonds Payable.

DEMONSTRATION PROBLEM (S.O. 2 and 3)

The following is taken from the Brent Company balance sheet at December 31, 2010:

Current liabilities		
Bond interest payable		$ 225,000
Long-term liabilities		
Bonds payable, 10%, due December 31, 2020.........................	$4,500,000	
Add: Premium on Bonds Payable	300,000	4,800,000

The bonds originally sold for $5,100,000 when they were issued on January 1, 2001. Bond interest is payable semiannually on January 1 and July 1. The bonds are callable on any semiannual interest date. Brent uses straight-line amortization for any bond premium or discount.

Instructions
(a) Prepare the necessary journal entries to record the semiannual interest payments, the premium amortization, and accrued interest in 2011. (Note that as of December 31, 2010, the bonds will be outstanding for 10 additional years.)
(b) Prepare the journal entry to record the redemption of $2,000,000 face value of bonds on January 1, 2012 after accrued interest was paid. The bonds were called at 103.
(c) Prepare the journal entry to record the payment of bond interest on July 1, 2012 on the remaining bonds. Include the amortization of the remaining bond premium.

SOLUTION TO DEMONSTRATION PROBLEM

(a) Jan. 1 Bond Interest Payable.. 225,000
          Cash.. 225,000

    July 1 Bond Interest Expense.. 210,000
           Premium on Bonds Payable ($300,000 X 6/120).... 15,000
              Cash.. 225,000

    Dec. 31 Bond Interest Expense....................................... 210,000
            Premium on Bonds Payable................................ 15,000
               Bond Interest Payable................................... 225,000

(b) Jan. 1 Bonds Payable 2,000,000
           Premium on Bonds Payable............................... 120,000
              Gain on Bond Redemption............................. 60,000
              Cash ($2,000,000 X 1.03)............................. 2,060,000
                 Premium on Bonds Payable:

Balance, Dec. 31, 2011	$300,000
July 1, 2011 amortization	(15,000)
Dec. 31, 2011	(15,000)
Balance, January 1	270,000
Pro rata	X 20/45
Amount redeemed	$120,000

(c) July 1 Bond Interest Expense.. 116,667
           Premium on Bonds Payable ($15,000 X 25/45)...... 8,333
              Cash ($2,500,000 X 5%)................................. 125,000
                 Alternatively:
                 Premium on Bonds Payable:

Amount before redemption	$270,000
Amount redeemed	120,000
Total	150,000
Months outstanding at Jan. 1	÷ 108
Amortized per month	1,389
Six months of 2012	X 6
Total amortization	$ 8,334

REVIEW QUESTIONS AND EXERCISES

TRUE—FALSE

Indicate whether each of the following is true (T) or false (F) in the space provided.

_____ 1. (S.O. 1)   An advantage of issuing bonds over common stock is that a tax savings may result.

_____ 2. (S.O. 1)   A disadvantage of issuing bonds over common stock is that bondholders do **not** have voter rights.

_____ 3. (S.O. 1)   Unsecured bonds, also known as debenture bonds, are issued against the general credit of the borrower.

_____ 4. (S.O. 1)   Bonds that mature at a single specified future date are called term bonds.

_____ 5. (S.O. 1)   Bonds that permit bondholders to convert them into common stock at their option are known as callable bonds.

_____ 6. (S.O. 1)   The terms of the bond issue are set forth in a formal legal document called a bond indenture.

_____ 7. (S.O. 1)   The market price of a bond is equal to the future value of the principal and interest payments.

_____ 8. (S.O. 2)   Bond Interest Payable on long-term bonds is classified as a long-term liability.

_____ 9. (S.O. 2)   If the market (effective) interest rate is higher than the contractual (stated) rate, the bonds will sell at less than face value, or at a discount.

_____ 10. (S.O. 2)   The carrying value of bonds at maturity should be equal to the face value of the bonds.

_____ 11. (S.O. 2)   Premium on Bonds Payable is a contra account to Bonds Payable.

_____ 12. (S.O. 2)   The sale of bonds above face value causes the total cost at borrowing to be less than the bond interest cost.

_____ 13. (S.O. 3)   A gain or loss on the redemption of bonds is reported as an extraordinary item in the income statement.

_____ 14. (S.O. 3)   When bonds are converted into common stock, the carrying value of the bonds is transferred to paid-in capital accounts.

_____ 15. (S.O. 5)   Operating leases are leases that the lessee must capitalize on its balance sheet as an asset.

_____ 16. (S.O. 5)   A capital lease occurs when the lease transfers substantially all the benefits and risks of ownership from the lessor to the lessee.

_____ 17. (S.O. 5)   Under a capital lease the lease/asset is reported on the balance sheet under plant assets.

_____ 18. (S.O. 6)   Long-term liabilities are reported in a separate section of the balance sheet immediately following current liabilities.

_____ *19. (S.O. 8) Generally accepted accounting principles require that the straight-line method be used when the annual amounts of bond interest expense for the straight-line method and the effective-interest method are materially different.

_____ *20. (S.O. 8) The effective-interest method results in a varying amount of interest expense but a constant rate of interest each interest period.

MULTIPLE CHOICE

Circle the letter that best answers each of the following statements.

1. (S.O. 1) The market price of a bond is the:
   a. Present value of its principal amount at maturity plus the present value of all future interest payments.
   b. Principal amount plus the present value of all future interest payments.
   c. Principal amount plus all future interest payments.
   d. Present value of its principal amount only.

2. (S.O. 2) When bonds are sold at face value on the issue date, Bonds Payable is credited for:
   a. maturity value plus interest payable.
   b. face value.
   c. call price.
   d. conversion price.

3. (S.O. 3) On the maturity date, January 1, Livingston Corporation pays the accrued interest recorded on December 31 and the face value of the bonds. The entry to record the payment will result in a credit to Cash and a debit to:
   a. Bonds Payable for the total payment.
   b. Bonds Payable for the face amount and a debit to Bond Interest Expense for the interest due.
   c. Bonds Payable for the face amount and a debit to Bond Interest Payable for the interest due.
   d. none of the above.

4. (S.O. 2) On the date of issue, Jagielo Corporation sells $2 million of 5-year bonds at 97. The entry to record the sale will include the following debits and credits:

	Bonds Payable	Discount on Bonds Payable
a.	$1,940,000 Cr.	$0 Dr.
b.	$2,000,000 Cr.	$60,000 Dr.
c.	$2,000,000 Cr.	$500,000 Dr.
d.	$2,000,000 Cr.	$6,000 Dr.

5. (S.O. 2) On the issue date, Wellington Corporation sells $1,000,000 bonds at 103. The entry to record the sale will include a credit to Premium on Bonds Payable of:
    a. $0.
    b. $3,000.
    c. $30,000.
    d. $300,000.

6. (S.O. 2) How does the amortization of discount on bonds payable affect each of the following?

	Carrying Value of Bond	**Net Income**
a.	Increase	Decrease
b.	Increase	Increase
c.	Decrease	Decrease
d.	Decrease	Increase

7. (S.O. 2) The market rate of interest for a bond issue which sells for more than its par value is:
    a. Independent of the interest rate stated on the bond.
    b. Higher than the interest rate stated on the bond.
    c. Equal to the interest rate stated on the bond.
    d. Less than the interest rate stated on the bond.

8. (S.O. 2) How does the amortization of premium on bonds payable affect each of the following?

	Carrying Value of Bond	**Net Income**
a.	Increase	Decrease
b.	Increase	Increase
c.	Decrease	Decrease
d.	Decrease	Increase

9. (S.O. 3) Hoffman Corporation retires its bonds at 106 on January 1, following the payment of semiannual interest. The face value of the bonds is $100,000. The carrying value of the bonds at the redemption date is $104,950. The entry to record the redemption will include a:
    a. credit of $4,950 to Loss on Bond Redemption.
    b. debit of $6,000 to Premium on Bonds Payable.
    c. credit of $1,050 to Gain on Bond Redemption.
    d. debit of $4,950 to Premium on Bonds Payable.

10. (S.O. 3) Ray Corporation's $100,000 convertible bonds are converted into 3,000 shares of $20 par value common stock when the market price of the stock is $40 per share. Using the book value method, the entry to record the conversion will include a:
    a. credit to Paid-in Capital in Excess of Par Value of $40,000.
    b. debit to Loss on Bond Conversion of $20,000.
    c. credit to Paid-in Capital in Excess of Par Value of $20,000.
    d. debit to Loss on Bond Conversion of $60,000.

11.   (S.O. 4) Buffon Electronics Company issues a $300,000, 10%, 20-year mortgage note on January 1. The terms provide for semiannual installment payments, exclusive of real estate taxes and insurance, of $17,483. After the first installment payment, the principal balance is:
      a. $300,000.
      b. $294,910.
      c. $297,517.
      d. $292,172.

12.   (S.O. 4) Portly Cihla, Inc. issues a $1,000,000, 10%, 20-year mortgage note on January 1, 2010. The note will be paid in annual installments of $140,000 each payable at the end of the year. What is the amount of interest expense that should be recognized by Portly Cihla, Inc. in the second year?
      a. $36,000.
      b. $86,000.
      c. $96,000.
      d. $100,000.

13.   (S.O. 5) Which of the following is **not** a condition under which the lessee must record the lease as an asset?
      a.   The lease contains a bargain purchase option.
      b.   The lease transfers ownership of the property to the lessee.
      c.   The lease term is equal to 60% of the economic life of the lease property.
      d.   The present value of the lease payments is 95% of the fair market value of the leased property.

*14. (S.O. 8) Under the effective interest method of amortization, interest expense is computed by multiplying:
      a.   the face value of the bonds by the contractual interest rate.
      b.   the carrying value of the bonds at the beginning of the period by the effective interest rate.
      c.   the carrying value of the bonds at the beginning of the period by the contractual interest rate.
      d.   the carrying value of the bonds at the end of the period by the effective interest rate.

*15. (S.O. 8) On January 1, Arawak, Inc. issued $2,000,000 of 9% bonds for $1,900,000. The bonds were issued to yield 10%. Interest is payable annually on December 31. Arawak uses the effective interest method of amortizing bond discount. At the end of the first year. Arawak should report unamortized bond discount of:
      a. $90,000.
      b. $71,000.
      c. $51,610.
      d. $51,000.

*16. (S.O. 8) On January 1, when the market interest rate was 14%, Santorio Corporation issued bonds in the face amount of $500,000, with interest at 12% payable semiannually. The bonds were issued at a discount of $53,180. How much of the discount should be amortized by the effective interest method for the first interest period?
      a. $1,277.
      b. $2,659.
      c. $3,191.
      d. $3,723.

*17. (S.O. 8) On January 1, Abbie Corporation issued $500,000 of 12%, six-year bonds with interest payable on July 1 and January 1. The bonds sold for $549,300 at an effective interest rate of 10%. On the first interest date, using the effective interest method, the debit entry to Bond Interest Expense is for:
   a. $25,000.
   b. $27,465.
   c. $32,958.
   d. $50,000.

*18. (S.O. 9) The effects of the straight-line method of amortization on the following in each interest period (assuming discount or premium amortization) are:

	Amount of Interest Expense	Carrying Value of Bonds
a.	Same	Increases or decreases
b.	Same	No effect
c.	Different	Increases or decreases
d.	Different	No effect

*19. (S.O. 9) On January 1, the Montesque Corporation sells $300,000 of 5-year, 10% bonds at 98 with interest payable on July 1 and January 1. The entry on July 1 to record payment of bond interest and the amortization of bond discount using the straight-line method will include a:
   a. debit to Interest Expense, $15,000.
   b. debit to Interest Expense, $30,000.
   c. credit to Discount on Bonds Payable, $600.
   d. credit to Discount on Bonds Payable, $1,200.

*20. (S.O. 9) For the bonds issued in question 19, above, what is the carrying value of the bonds at the end of the fourth interest period?
   a. $297,600.
   b. $296,400.
   c. $294,000.
   d. $291,600.

The Navigator

MATCHING

Match each term with its definition by writing the appropriate letter in the space provided.

Terms	**Definitions**
_____ 1. Bond indenture.	a. A method of amortizing bond discount or bond premium that allocates the same amount to interest expense in each interest period.
_____ 2. Long-term liabilities.	b. Obligations that are expected to be paid after one year.
_____ 3. Mortgage bond.	c. Rate used to determine the amount of interest the borrower pays and the investor receives.
_____ 4. Capital lease.	d. Bonds that permit bondholders to convert them into common stock at their option.
_____ 5. Callable bonds.	e. The rate investors demand for loaning funds to the corporation.
_____ 6. Operating lease.	f. A legal document that sets forth the terms of the bond issue.
_____ 7. Convertible bonds.	g. A bond secured by real estate.
_____ *8. Effective interest method of amortization.	h. A contractual arrangement that transfers substantially all the benefits and risks of ownership to the lessee so that the lease is in effect a purchase of the property.
_____ 9. Market interest rate.	i. Bonds subject to retirement at a stated dollar amount prior to maturity at the option of the issuer.
_____ 10. Contractual interest rate.	j. A contractual arrangement giving the lessee temporary use of the property with continued ownership of the property by the lessor.
_____ *11. Straight-line method of amortization.	k. A method of writing off bond discount or bond premium that results in a periodic interest expense equal to a constant percentage of the carrying value of the bonds.

The
Navigator

EXERCISES

EX. 15-1   (S.O. 2 and *8) On January 1, Gutenberg Printers Inc. issues $400,000 of 10-year 12% bonds at 98 with interest payable on July 1 and January 1.

Instructions
(a)   Journalize the issuance of the bonds and the entries on July 1 and December 31 for interest and the amortization of bond discount using the straight-line method. (Omit explanations.)
(b)   Journalize the July 1 and December 31 entries assuming the effective interest rate on the bonds is 12.4% and the effective interest method is used. (Omit explanations.)

	General Journal		J1
Date	Account Title	Debit	Credit
(a)			
(b)			

EX. 15-2 (S.O. 3, 5 and *9) Sonoda Computers Inc. has the following transactions concerning long-term liabilities during the current year.

Apr.　2　Convertible bonds issued by Sonoda at face value are converted into common stock. The $100,000 bond issue has a conversion price of $25 per share of common stock with one $1,000 bond convertible into 40 shares of stock. The common stock has a par value of $10 and a fair market price of $30 at the time of conversion.

June　30　The first installment payment on a $100,000, 10%, 10-year mortgage note is made by Sonoda. The terms of the mortgage contract provided for semi-annual installment payments, exclusive of real estate taxes and insurance of $8,024.

Dec.　31　The second installment payment is made on the mortgage note.

Instructions
Journalize the transactions. (Omit explanations.)

	General Journal		J1
Date	**Account Title**	**Debit**	**Credit**

The
Navigator

SOLUTIONS TO REVIEW QUESTIONS AND EXERCISES

TRUE-FALSE

1. (T)
2. (F)   The fact that bondholders do not have voting rights is an advantage for common stockholders because their control is not affected.
3. (T)
4. (T)
5. (F)   Bonds that permit bondholders to convert the bonds into common stock at their option are known as convertible bonds.
6. (T)
7. (F)   The market price of a bond is equal to the present value of the principal and interest payments.
8. (F)   Because interest on bonds is usually payable annually or semiannually, the interest is expected to be paid within the following year and thus is a current liability.
9. (T)
10. (T)
11. (F)   The premium account is added to Bonds Payable on the balance sheet.
12. (T)
13. (F)   The redemption of bonds results in an ordinary gain or loss in the income statement.
14. (T)
15. (F)   For operating leases the lessee simply records the lease payments as an expense in the income statement. No asset is recorded.
16. (T)
17. (T)
18. (T)
*19. (F)   When the amounts are materially different, the effective-interest method is required under generally accepted accounting principles.
*20. (T)

MULTIPLE CHOICE

1. (a)   The market price of a bond is equal to the present value of its principal amount at maturity plus the present value of all future interest payments.

2. (b)   When bonds are sold at face value on the issue date, Bonds Payable is credited for the face value of the bonds issued. Bonds Payable is always credited for face value.

3. (c)   The interest due was recorded on December 31 through an adjusting entry for accrued interest. Thus, the entry on January 1 will result in debits to Bonds Payable for the face amount and to Bond Interest Payable for the interest due.

4. (b)   The proceeds from the sale are $1,940,000 ($2,000,000 X .97). Thus, Discount on Bonds Payable is debited for $60,000 and Bonds Payable is credited for the face amount, $2,000,000.

5. (c)   The proceeds from the sale are $1,030,000 ($1,000,000 X 1.03). Thus, Premium on Bonds Payable is credited for $30,000 in the entry.

6. (a)   The amortization of discount on bonds payable decreases Discount on Bonds Payable which is a contra account for Bonds Payable. Thus, the carrying value of the bonds increases. The amortized discount increases the amount of interest expense and therefore decreases net income.

7. (d)   When bonds are sold at a premium, the market rate of interest is less than the contractual interest rate on the bonds.

8. (d)   The amortization of a premium on bonds payable decreases Premium on Bonds Payable which is reported as an addition to Bonds Payable. Thus, the carrying value of the bonds decreases. The amortized premium reduces the amount of interest expense and therefore increases net income.

9. (d)   The entry to record the redemption is as follows:

Bonds Payable	100,000	
Premium on Bonds Payable.................................	4,950	
Loss on Bond Redemption	1,050	
Cash..		106,000

10. (a)   The entry to record the conversion of the bonds into common stock is as follows:

Bonds Payable	100,000	
Common Stock...		60,000
Paid-in Capital in Excess of Par Value................		40,000

11. (c)   The installment payment schedule for the first payment is:

Payment Date	Cash Payment	Interest Expense	Reduction of Principal	Principal Balance
1/1				$300,000
7/1	$17,483	$15,000*	$2,483	297,517

*Interest expense is the principal balance times the semiannual interest rate of 5%.

12. (c)   The installment payment schedule for the first two payments is:

Payment Date	Cash Payment	Interest Expense	Reduction of Principal	Principal Balance
1/1/10				$1,000,000
12/31/10	$140,000	$100,000*	$40,000	960,000
12/31/11	$140,000	$ 96,000*		

*Interest expense is the principal balance times the annual interest rate of 10%.

13. (c)   The lease term must be equal to 75% or more of the economic life of the lease.

*14. (b)   The first step in the effective interest method is to determine the bond interest expense by multiplying the carrying value of the bonds at the beginning of the period by the effective interest rate.

*15.   (a)   The amount in Discount on Bonds Payable on January 1 is $100,000 ($2,000,000 - $1,900,000). At December 31, Bond Interest Expense is $190,000 ($1,900,000 X 10%) and the interest payable is $180,000 ($2,000,000 X 9%). The discount amortization is $10,000 and the balance in Discount on Bonds Payable is $90,000 ($100,000 - $10,000).

*16.   (a)   The entry on July 1 for the interest payment is:

Bond Interest Expense ($446,820 X 7%)...................	31,277	
Discount on Bonds Payable.............................		1,277
Cash ($500,000 X 6%)..		30,000

*17.   (b)   The debit to Bond Interest Expense is ($549,300 X 10% X 1/2) = $27,465.

*18.   (a)   Under the straight-line method, the amortization amount is the same each interest period. Thus, the amount of interest expense is the same each period but the carrying value of the bonds increases if a discount and decreases if a premium.

*19.   (c)   Bond discount of $6,000 ($300,000 - $294,000) should be amortized over 10 interest periods. The entry on July 1 is:

Bond Interest Expense...	15,600	
Discount on Bonds Payable ($6,000 ÷ 10)		600
Cash ($300,000 X 10% X 1/2)		15,000

*20.   (b)   Under the straight-line method, the amortization amount is the same each interest period. After four periods, $2,400 will be amortized, and the balance in Discount on Bonds Payable will be $3,600 ($6,000 - $2,400). Thus, the carrying value of the bonds is $296,400 ($300,000 - $3,600).

MATCHING

1.	f	5.	i	9.	e
2.	b	6.	j	10.	c
3.	g	7.	d	11.	a
4.	h	8.	k		

EXERCISES

EX. 15-1

General Journal			J1
Date	**Account Title**	**Debit**	**Credit**
(a)			
Jan. 1	Cash ($400,000 X 98%)	392,000	
	Discount on Bonds Payable	8,000	
	Bonds Payable		400,000
July 1	Bond Interest Expense	24,400	
	Discount on Bonds Payable ($8,000 ÷ 20)		400
	Cash ($400,000 X 6%)		24,000
Dec. 31	Bond Interest Expense	24,400	
	Discount on Bonds Payable		400
	Bond Interest Payable		24,000
(b)			
July 1	Bond Interest Expense ($392,000 X 6.2%)	24,304	
	Discount on Bonds Payable		304
	Cash ($400,000 X 6%)		24,000
Dec. 31	Bond Interest Expense [($392,000 + $304) X 6.2%]	24,323	
	Discount on Bonds Payable		323
	Bond Interest Payable		24,000

EX. 15-2

General Journal			J1
Date	**Account Title**	**Debit**	**Credit**
Apr. 2	Bonds Payable	100,000	
	Common Stock		40,000
	Paid-in Capital in Excess of Par Value		60,000
June 30	Interest Expense ($100,000 X 5%)	5,000	
	Mortgage Note Payable	3,024	
	Cash		8,024
Dec. 31	Interest Expense ($96,976 X 5%)	4,849	
	Mortgage Note Payable	3,175	
	Cash		8,024

Chapter 16

INVESTMENTS

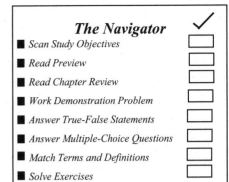

The Navigator ✓
- Scan Study Objectives ☐
- Read Preview ☐
- Read Chapter Review ☐
- Work Demonstration Problem ☐
- Answer True-False Statements ☐
- Answer Multiple-Choice Questions ☐
- Match Terms and Definitions ☐
- Solve Exercises ☐

CHAPTER STUDY OBJECTIVES

After studying this chapter, you should be able to:
1. Discuss why corporations invest in debt and stock securities.
2. Explain the accounting for debt investments.
3. Explain the accounting for stock investments.
4. Describe the use of consolidated financial statements.
5. Indicate how debt and stock investments are reported in financial statements.
6. Distinguish between short-term and long-term investments.

The Navigator ☑

PREVIEW OF CHAPTER 16

Investment clubs represent one of a vast assortment of ways that investments can be purchased. Investments also can be made by individuals, mutual funds, banks, pension funds, and corporations. In addition, investments can be purchased for a short or a long period of time, as a passive investment, or with the intent to control the firm. As you will see in this chapter, the way in which a company accounts for its investments is determined by a number of factors. The content and organization of this chapter is as follows:

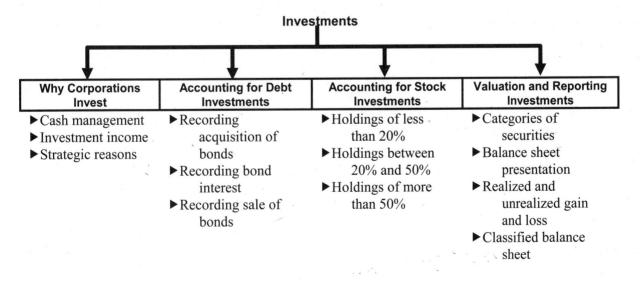

Why Corporations Invest	Accounting for Debt Investments	Accounting for Stock Investments	Valuation and Reporting Investments
▶ Cash management ▶ Investment income ▶ Strategic reasons	▶ Recording acquisition of bonds ▶ Recording bond interest ▶ Recording sale of bonds	▶ Holdings of less than 20% ▶ Holdings between 20% and 50% ▶ Holdings of more than 50%	▶ Categories of securities ▶ Balance sheet presentation ▶ Realized and unrealized gain and loss ▶ Classified balance sheet

Investments

CHAPTER REVIEW

Why Corporations Invest

1. (S.O. 1) Corporations purchase investments because (1) they may have excess cash, (2) they generate earnings from investment income, and (3) for strategic reasons.

Accounting for Short-Term Debt Investments

2. (S.O. 2) **Debt investments** are investments in government and corporation bonds. At acquisition, the cost principle is applied and all expenditures necessary to acquire these investments are included in the cost (e.g., brokerage fees). At acquisition, Debt Investments is debited and Cash is credited for the cost of the investment.

3. Interest revenue must also be recorded on debt investments. Assume Bodhi Company (fiscal year ends December 31) receives $2,000 interest July 1 and January 1 on a debt investment purchased July 1, 2010. The following entries are required:

Dec. 31	Interest Receivable	2,000	
	Interest Revenue		2,000
Jan. 1	Cash...	2,000	
	Interest Receivable...		2,000
Jul. 1	Cash...	2,000	
	Interest Revenue		2,000

4. When bonds are sold, it is necessary to credit the Investment account for the cost of the bonds, debit Cash, and any difference between the sale price and cost of bonds is recorded as a gain or loss. The gain or loss on the sale of debt investments is reported under Other Revenues and Gains or Other Expenses and Losses, respectively, in the income statement.

Accounting for Stock Investments

5. (S.O. 3) **Stock investments** are investments in the capital stock of corporations. The accounting for stock investments differs depending on the degree of influence the investor has over the issuing corporation. The presumed influences based on the investor's ownership interest and the accounting guidelines that are to be used are as follows:

Investor's Ownership Interest in Investee's Common Stock	Presumed Influence on Investee	Accounting Guidelines
Less than 20%	Insignificant	Cost Method
Between 20% and 50%	Significant	Equity Method
More than 50%	Controlling	Consolidated financial statements

Holdings Less than 20%

6. In accounting for stock investments of less than 20%, the **cost method** is used. Under the **cost method,** the investment is recorded at cost and revenue is recognized only when cash dividends are received.
   a. At acquisition, the cost principle applies and Stock Investments is debited and Cash is credited.
   b. When dividends are received, Cash is debited and Dividend Revenue is credited.
   c. When stock is sold, Cash is debited, Stock Investments is credited, and any difference between the two is debited or credited to Loss or Gain on Sale of Stock Investments, respectively. The loss or gain is reported under Other Expenses and Losses or Other Revenues and Gains in the income statement.

Holdings Between 20% and 50%

7. When an investor owns between 20% and 50% of the common stock of a corporation, it is generally presumed that the investor has a significant influence over the financial and operating activities of the investee; and therefore the **equity method** is used. Under the equity method, the investor does not record its share of the investee until the investee has earned income.
   a. At acquisition, the cost principle applies and Stock Investments is debited and Cash is credited.
   b. Each year, the investor records its share of the investee's income (investee's income X % of ownership in investee) with a debit to Stock Investments and a credit to Revenue from Investee Company (if the investee incurred a loss, then the opposite entry is made).
   c. Upon receiving dividends from the investee, the investor makes a debit to Cash and a credit to Stock Investments.

Holdings of More Than 50%

8. (S.O. 4) A company that owns more than 50% of the common stock of another entity is known as the **parent company.** The entity whose stock is owned by the parent company is called the **Subisidiary (affiliated) company.** Because of its stock ownership, the parent company has a **controlling interest** in the subsidiary company.

9. When a company owns more than 50% of the common stock of another company, **consolidated financial statements** are usually prepared. Consolidated financial statements present the assets and liabilities controlled by the parent company and the aggregate profitability of the subsidiary companies.

Valuation and Reporting of Investments

10. (S.O. 5) For purposes of valuation and reporting at a financial statement date, debt and stock investments are classified into the following three categories.
    a. **Trading securities** are securities bought and held primarily for sale in the near term to generate income on short-term price differences.
    b. **Available-for-sale securities** are securities that may be sold in the future.
    c. **Held-to-maturity securities** are debt securities that the investor has the intent and ability to hold to maturity.

11.   The valuation guidelines for the above securities are as follows:

Trading	**Available-for-sale**	**Held-to-maturity**
At fair value with changes reported in net income	At fair value with changes reported in the stock-holders' equity section	At amortized cost

Trading Securities

12.   When the trading securities are not sold, the difference between the total cost of the securities and their total fair value is reported as unrealized gains or losses in the income statement. The adjusting entry to record an unrealized gain would include a debit to Market Adjustment—Trading and a credit to Unrealized Gain—Income. The adjusting entry to record an unrealized loss would include a debit to Unrealized Loss—Income and a credit to Market Adjustment—Trading. The unrealized gains or losses are reported in the income statement under Other Revenues and Gains or Other Expenses and Losses, respectively.

Available-for-Sale

13.   If available-for-sale securities are held with the intent to sell them within the next year or operating cycle, the securities are classified as current assets in the balance sheet. Otherwise, they are classified as long-term assets in the investments section of the balance sheet.

14.   The available-for-sale securities adjusting entry is made in the same way as the trading securities adjusting entry except that the unrealized gain or loss is reported in the stockholders' equity section of the balance sheet. This balance is then adjusted with the market adjustment account to show the difference between the cost and fair value at that time.

Balance Sheet Presentation

15.   (S.O. 6)   **Short-term investments** are securities held by a company that are (a) readily marketable and (b) intended to be converted into cash within the next year or operating cycle, whichever is longer. Investments that do not meet **both** criteria are classified as **long-term investments.**

16.   An investment is **readily marketable** when it can be sold easily whenever the need for cash arises. **Intent to convert** means that management intends to sell the investment within the next year or the operating cycle, whichever is longer.

17.   Short-term investments are listed immediately below cash in the current asset section of the balance sheet. Short-term investments are reported at fair value. Long-term investments are generally reported in a separate section of the balance sheet immediately below current assets; and available-for-sale securities are reported at fair value, and investments in common stock accounted for under the equity method are reported at equity.

Presentation of Realized and Unrealized Gain or Loss

18. In the income statement, the following items are reported in the nonoperating section:

Other Revenue and Gains	**Other Expenses and Losses**
Interest Revenue	Loss on Sale of Investments
Dividend Revenue	Unrealized Loss—Income
Gain on Sale of Investments	
Unrealized Gain—Income	

The unrealized gain or loss on available-for-sale securities is reported as a separate component of stockholders' equity.

DEMONSTRATION PROBLEM (S.O. 3 and S.O. 5)

During 2010, its first year of operation, the Zimmer Company had the following transactions in stock investments which are considered trading securities.

June 18   Purchased 1,000 shares of McClendon Corporation common stock for cash at $30 per share plus broker's fees of $300.

Aug.   3   Purchased 1,500 shares of Berryhill Corporation common stock for cash at $25 per share plus broker's fees of $400.

Dec. 31   Dividends are received from investments; McClendon Corporation $2 per share, and Berryhill Corporation $1.50 per share.

At December 31, the McClendon common stock had a market price of $29 per share and the Berryhill common stock had a $24 market price.

Instructions
(a) Journalize the transactions and the December 31 adjusting entry. (Omit explanations)
(b) Journalize the sale of 500 shares of McClendon common stock on March 1, 2011, assuming the shares were sold for $14,800 less broker's fees of $150.

[Handwritten journal entries:]

6/18 Stock Investment   30800
       Cash   30800

1500
25
7500
30000
37500

8/3 Stock Investment 37900
       Cash   37900

12/31 Cash   2000
       Dividend Revenue 2000

1500
1.50
2250

12/31 Cash   2250
       Div Revenue 2250

SOLUTION TO DEMONSTRATION PROBLEM

(a)

General Journal			J1	
Date	Account Title	Debit	Credit
2010			
June 18	Stock Investments	30,300	
	Cash		30,300
Aug. 3	Stock Investments	37,900	
	Cash		37,900
Dec. 31	Cash	4,250	
	Dividend Revenue [(1,000 X 2) +		
	(1,500 X 1.5)]		4,250
31	Unrealized Loss—Income	3,200	
	Market Adjustment—Trading		3,200

	Cost	Fair Value	Unrealized Gain (Loss)
McClendon	$30,300	$29,000	$(1,300)
Berryhill	37,900	36,000	(1,900)
	$68,200	$65,000	$(3,200)

(b) 2011
Mar. 1   Cash ($14,800 - $150)..   14,650
            Loss on Sale of Stock Investments...................................   500
                Stock Investments ($30,300 X 1/2)   15,150

REVIEW QUESTIONS AND EXERCISES

TRUE—FALSE

Indicate whether each of the following is true (T) or false (F) in the space provided.

_T_   **1.** (S.O. 1) One of the reasons a corporation may purchase investments is that they have excess cash.

_T_   **2.** (S.O. 2) Debt investments are investments in government and corporation bonds.

_F_   **3.** (S.O. 2) When recording bond interest, Interest Receivable is reported as a fixed asset in the balance sheet.

_F_   **4.** (S.O. 2) The gain on sale of debt investments is reported as an extraordinary gain in the income statement.

_F_   **5.** (S.O. 3) If an investor's common stock ownership interest in an investee is less than 20%, the investment should be accounted for using the equity method.

_T_   **6.** (S.O. 3) Under the cost method, the investment is recorded at cost and revenue is recognized only when cash dividends are received.

_T_   **7.** (S.O. 3) Under the equity method, the investment in common stock is initially recorded at cost, and the investment account is adjusted annually to show the investor's equity in the investee.

_F_   **8.** (S.O. 3) Under the equity method, the investor debits revenue and credits the investment account for its share of the investee's net income.

_F_   **9.** (S.O. 4) If an investor has over a 50% ownership interest in the preferred stock of a company, it is generally assumed that the investor can exert significant influence over the affairs of the investee.

_T_   **10.** (S.O. 4) When a company owns more than 50% of the common stock of another company, consolidated financial statements are usually prepared.

_F_   **11.** (S.O. 4) Consolidated financial statements present a condensed version of the financial statements so investors will **not** experience information overload.

_T_   **12.** (S.O. 5) Trading securities are held with the intention of selling them in a short period of time (generally less than a month).

_F_   **13.** (S.O. 5) Available-for-sale securities are securities bought and held primarily for sale in the near term to generate income on short-term price differences.

_T_   **14.** (S.O. 5) The unrealized gain or loss on trading securities is reported in the income statement.

_T_   **15.** (S.O. 5) Available-for-sale securities can be classified as current assets or long-term assets.

___F___ 16. (S.O. 5) The unrealized gain or loss on available-for-sale securities is reported in the income statement.

___T___ 17. (S.O. 5) The adjusting entry to record an unrealized loss for available-for-sale securities would include a credit to Market Adjustment—Available-for-Sale Securities.

___T___ 18. (S.O. 6) To be considered short-term, an investment must be readily marketable and management should intend to convert the investment into cash within the next year or operating cycle, whichever is longer.

___T___ 19. (S.O. 6) "Intent to convert" does **not** include an investment used as a resource that will be used whenever the need for cash arises.

MULTIPLE CHOICE

Circle the letter that best answers each of the following statements.

1. (S.O. 1) Which of the following reasons best explains why a company that experiences seasonal fluctuations in sales may purchase investments in debt or equity securities?
   a. The company may have excess cash.
   b. The company may generate a significant portion of their earnings from investment income.
   c. The company may invest for the strategic reason of establishing a presence in a related industry.
   d. The company may invest for speculative reasons to increase the value in pension funds.

2. (S.O. 2) Debt investments are investments in:

	Government Bonds	Corporate Bonds
a.	Yes	Yes
b.	Yes	No
c.	No	Yes
d.	No	No

The following information is to be used for questions 3, 4, and 5.

Assume that Sutcliff Company acquires 100 Trout Inc. 10%, semi-annual, 20-year, $1,000 bonds on January 1, 2010, for $106,000, plus brokerage fees of $2,000 as a short-term investment.

3. (S.O. 2) The entry to record the investment includes a debit to Debt Investments of:
   a. $100,000.
   b. $106,000.
   c. $108,000.
   d. $110,000.

Debt Investment 108,000
   Cash   108,000

4. (S.O. 2) The entry for the receipt of interest on July 1 includes a credit to Interest Revenue of:
    a. $5,000.   1000 (100)   10,000 (1b) 5000
    b. $5,600.
    c. $5,800.
    d. $10,000.

5. (S.O. 2) Assuming that Sutcliff Company receives net proceeds of $103,000 on the sale of Trout Inc. bonds on January 1, 2011, after receiving the interest due, the entry would include:
    a. a debit to Loss on Sale of Debt Investments of $3,000.
    b. a debit to Loss on Sale of Debt Investments of $5,000.
    c. a credit to Gain on Sale of Debt Investments of $3,000.
    d. a credit to Gain on Sale of Debt Investments of $5,000.

6. (S.O. 3) A company that acquires less than 20% ownership interest in another company should account for the stock investment in that company using:
    a. the cost method.
    b. the equity method.
    c. the significant method.
    d. consolidated financial statements.

7. (S.O. 3) Under the cost method, cash dividends received by the investor from the investee should be recorded as:
    a. dividend revenue.
    b. an addition to the investor's share of the investee's profit.
    c. a deduction from the investor's share of the investee's profit.
    d. a deduction from the investment account.

8. (S.O. 3) On January 1, 2010, Moreland Company bought 15% of Lopes Corporation's common stock for $30,000. Lopes' net income for 2010 and 2011 were $10,000 and $50,000 respectively. During 2011, Lopes paid a cash dividend of $70,000. How much should Moreland show on its 2011 income statement as income from this investment under the cost method?
    a. $1,575.
    b. $7,500.
    c. $9,000.
    d. $10,500.

    2010   2010   2011
    Lopes 30,000   10,000   50,000

9. (S.O. 3) On January 1, 2010, Trillo Corporation paid $150,000 for 10,000 shares of Davis Corporation's common stock, representing a 15% investment in Davis. Davis declared and paid a cash dividend of $1 per share in 2010 when its net income was $130,000. At what amount should Trillo's investment in Davis be reported at December 31, 2010?
    a. $140,000.
    b. $150,000.
    c. $159,500.
    d. $169,500.

10. (S.O. 3) The equity method of accounting for an investment in the common stock of another company should be used by the investor when the investment:
    a. is composed of common stock and it is the investor's intent to vote the common stock.
    b. ensures a source of supply of raw materials for the investor.
    c. enables the investor to exercise significant influence over the investee.
    d. is obtained by an exchange of stock for stock.

11. (S.O. 3) Cash dividends declared out of current earnings are distributed to an investor. How will the investor's investment account be affected by those dividends under each of the following accounting methods?

	Cost Method	**Equity Method**
a.	Decrease	No effect
b.	Decrease	Decrease
c.	No effect	Decrease
d.	No effect	No effect

12. (S.O. 3) When an investor uses the equity method, the investment account will be increased when the investor recognizes a:
    a. proportionate equity in the net income of the investee.
    b. cash dividend received from the investee.
    c. stock dividend received from the investee.
    d. proportionate equity in the net loss of the investee.

13. (S.O. 3) When an investor uses the equity method to account for investments in common stock, cash dividends received by the investor from the investee should be recorded as:
    a. dividend revenue.
    b. a deduction from the investor's share of the investee's profits.
    c. a deduction from the investment account.
    d. a deduction from the stockholders' equity account, dividends to stockholders.

14. (S.O. 3) On January 2, Matthews Corporation acquired 20% of the outstanding common stock of Dernier Company for $700,000. For the year ended December 31, Dernier reported net income of $180,000 and paid cash dividends of $60,000 on its common stock. At December 31, the carrying value of Matthews' investment in Dernier under the equity method is:
    a. $688,000.
    b. $700,000.
    c. $712,000.
    d. $724,000.

15. (S.O. 4) Wilson Company purchases 54% of Pico Company's common stock. Wilson Company should present its interest in Pico Company using:
    a. the cost method.
    b. the equity method.
    c. the significant method.
    d. consolidated financial statements.

16. (S.O. 5) Securities bought and held primarily for sale in the near term to generate income on short-term price differences are:
    a. Trading securities.
    b. Available-for-sale securities.
    c. Never-sell securities.
    d. Held-to-maturity securities.

17. (S.O. 5) On December 31, 2010, Mumphrey Co. has the following costs and fair values for its investments classified as trading securities:

Investments	Cost	Fair Value
Cub Co.	$20,000	$25,000
Wrigley Co.	34,000	32,000

The adjusting entry for Mumphrey Co. will include a debit to:
a. Unrealized Loss—Income of $5,000.
b. Market Adjustment—Trading of $2,000.
c. Market Adjustment—Trading of $3,000.
d. Unrealized Gain—Income of $3,000.

18. (S.O. 5) On December 31, 2010, Dunston Co. has the following investments that are classified as available-for-sale securities:

Investments	Cost	Fair Value
Shawon Co.	$40,000	$35,000
Cihla Co.	38,000	39,000

The amount of the unrealized gain or loss would be reported on the income statement as a:
a. $5,000 unrealized loss.
b. $4,000 unrealized loss.
c. $1,000 unrealized gain.
d. No unrealized loss or gain is reported on the income statement.

19. (S.O. 6) Short-term investments are:
a. (1) readily marketable and (2) intended to be converted into cash after the current year or operating cycle, whichever is shorter.
b. (1) readily marketable and (2) intended to be converted into cash within the current year or operating cycle, whichever is longer.
c. (1) readily marketable and (2) intended to be converted into cash after the current year or operating cycle, whichever is longer.
d. (1) readily marketable and (2) intended to be converted into cash within the current year or operating cycle, whichever is shorter.

The
Navigator

MATCHING

Match each term with its definition by writing the appropriate letter in the space provided.

Terms

_____ 1. Equity method.

_____ 2. Parent company.

_____ 3. Available-for-sale securities.

_____ 4. Consolidated financial statements.

_____ 5. Trading securities.

_____ 6. Held-to-maturity securities.

_____ 7. Debt investments.

_____ 8. Affiliated companies.

_____ 9. Subsidiary company.

_____ 10. Fair value.

_____ 11. Short-term investments.

_____ 12. Cost method.

_____ 13. Stock investments.

Definitions

a. A company that owns more than 50% of the common stock of another entity.

b. Investments in government and corporate bonds.

c. Amount for which a security could be sold in a normal market.

d. Debt securities that the investor has the intent and ability to hold to maturity.

e. A method in which the investment in common stock is initially recorded at cost, and the investment account is adjusted annually to show the investors' equity in the investee.

f. Securities that may be sold in the future.

g. Financial statements that present the assets and liabilities controlled by a parent company and the aggregate profitability of the affiliated companies.

h. Securities bought and held primarily for sale in the near term to generate income on short-term price differences.

i. Companies under common control of a single company.

j. Investments in capital stock of corporations.

k. A method of accounting in which the investment in common stock is recorded at cost and revenue is recognized only when cash dividends are received.

l. A company in which more than 50% of its stock is owned by another company.

m. Investments that are readily marketable and intended to be converted into cash within the next year or operating cycle, whichever is longer.

The Navigator

EXERCISES

EX. 16-1   (S.O. 2 and 3)   The Williams Corporation accumulated the following data for its investments made on January 1, 2010.

1.   Purchased $100,000, 10%, 10-year Kilgus Corporation bonds for $105,000 in cash as a long-term investment. The bonds pay interest semi-annually on January 1 and July 1. Received the interest due on July 1.

2.   Purchased for cash 10% of Walton Inc.'s 400,000 shares of common stock at a cost of $20 per share plus brokers' fees of $5,000. In 2010, Walton reports net income of $100,000, and it declares and pays a $30,000 cash dividend on December 31.

3.   Acquired 40% of the common stock of Wilkerson Company for $500,000 cash. In 2010, Wilkerson Company reports net income of $70,000, and it declares and pays a $60,000 cash dividend on December 31.

Instructions
(a)   Journalize the entries for the bonds on January 1 and July 1.
(b)   Journalize the 2010 entries for the Walton stock, assuming the cost method is used.
(c)   Journalize the 2010 entries for the Wilkerson stock, assuming the equity method is used.

Date	Account Title	Debit	Credit
General Journal			J1
2010			
(a)			
(b)			

	General Journal		J
Date	**Account Title**	**Debit**	**Credit**
(c)			

EX. 16-2   (S.O. 5) Harry Caray Co. has the following data at December 31, 2010:

Securities	Cost	Fair value
Trading	$103,000	$99,000
Available-for-sale	70,000	75,000

The available-for-sale securities are held as a long-term investment.

Instructions
(a)   Prepare the adjusting entries to report each class of securities at fair value.
(b)   Indicate the statement presentation of each class of securities and the related unrealized gain (loss) accounts.

(a)

	General Journal		J
Date	**Account Title**	**Debit**	**Credit**

(b)

_____

_____

_____

_____

_____

_____

The
Navigator

SOLUTIONS TO REVIEW QUESTIONS AND EXERCISES

TRUE-FALSE

1. (T)
2. (T)
3. (F) When recording bond interest, Interest Receivable is reported as a current asset in the balance sheet.
4. (F) The gain on the sale of debt investments is reported under Other Revenues and Gains in the income statement.
5. (F) If an investor's common stock ownership interest in an investee is less than 20%, the investment should be accounted for using the cost method.
6. (T)
7. (T)
8. (F) Under the equity method, the investor debits the investment account and credits revenue for its share of the investee's net income.
9. (F) Regardless of the number of shares held, ownership of preferred stock does not give the investor an opportunity to exert significant influence over the affairs of the investee because preferred stock is usually nonvoting.
10. (T)
11. (F) Consolidated financial statements present the assets and liabilities controlled by the parent company and the aggregate profitability of the subsidiary companies.
12. (T)
13. (F) Trading securities are securities bought and held primarily for sale in the near term to generate income on short-term price differences.
14. (T)
15. (T)
16. (F) The unrealized gain or loss on available-for-sale securities is reported in the balance sheet as a separate component of stockholders' equity.
17. (T)
18. (T)
19. (F) "Intent to convert" is generally satisfied when the investment is considered a resource that will be used whenever the need for cash arises.

MULTIPLE CHOICE

1. (a)   A company that experiences seasonal fluctuations in sales may have excess cash and therefore may be likely to purchase investments in debt or equity securities.

2. (a)   Debt investments are investments in government and corporate bonds.

3. (c)   At acquisition of debt investments, the cost principle applies. Cost includes all expenditures necessary to acquire these investments, such as the price paid plus brokerage fees (commissions), if any. Thus, the total cost of $108,000 is debited to Debt Investments.

4. (a)   The bonds pay interest on July 1 of $5,000 ($100,000 X 10% X 1/2).

5. (b)   Since the securities cost $108,000, a loss of $5,000 ($108,000 - $103,000) is realized.

6. (a)   A company that acquires less than 20% ownership interest in another company should account for the stock investment in that company using the cost method.

7. (a)   Under the cost method, cash dividends received by the investor are recorded as dividend revenue.

8. (d)   Under the cost method, the income statement of the investor is only affected by cash dividends received. During 2011 Lopes Company paid $70,000 of cash dividends of which Moreland received 15% or $10,500.

9. (b)   Under the cost method, the investment in common stock is initially recorded at cost, and the investment account continues to be carried at cost until the shares are sold.

10. (c)   The equity method of accounting for an investment in the common stock of another company should be used when the investment enables the investor to exercise significant influence over the investee.

11. (c)   Under the cost method, cash dividends received by an investor are credited to Dividend Revenue. Under the equity method, the cash dividends received are credited to the Investment account.

12. (a)   Each year, the investor debits the investment account and credits income for its share of the investee's net income.

13. (c)   Each year, the investor credits cash dividends received to the investment account.

14. (d)   Matthews should debit the investment account for $36,000 ($180,000 X 20%) and credit the investment account for $12,000 ($60,000 X 20%). Thus, the investment balance will increase to $724,000 ($700,000 + $36,000 - $12,000).

15. (d)   Because Wilson Company has acquired over 50% of Pico Company's common stock, Wilson should present its interest in Pico Company using consolidated financial statements.

16. (a) Securities bought and held primarily for sale in the near term to generate income on short-term price differences are trading securities. Available-for-sale securities (b) are securities that may be sold in the future. Never-sell securities (c) is not a defined term. Held-to-maturity securities (d) are debt securities that the investor has the intent and ability to hold to maturity.

17. (c) Mumphrey Co. has an unrealized gain of $3,000 because total fair value ($57,000) is $3,000 greater than the total cost ($54,000). The adjusting entry would therefore be as follows:

Market Adjustment—Trading......................................	3,000	
Unrealized Gain—Income		3,000

18. (d) An unrealized gain or loss on available-for-sale securities is not reported in the income statement. Instead, it is reported as a separate component of stockholders' equity. Therefore, Dunston would report a $4,000 ($5,000 - $1,000) unrealized loss as a separate component of stockholders' equity.

19. (b) Short-term investments are (1) readily marketable and (2) intended to be converted into cash within the current year or operating cycle, whichever is longer.

MATCHING

1. e	6. d	11. m	
2. a	7. b	12. k	
3. f	8. i	13. j	
4. g	9. l		
5. h	10. c		

EX. 16-1

General Journal			J1
Date	**Account Title**	**Debit**	**Credit**
2010			
(a)			
Jan. 1	Debt Investment in Kilgus Bonds	105,000	
	Cash		105,000
July 1	Cash ($100,000 X 10% X 6/12)	5,000	
	Interest Revenue		5,000
(b)			
Jan. 1	Equity Investment in Walton Common Stock	805,000	
	Cash		805,000
Dec. 31	Cash ($30,000 X 10%)	3,000	
	Dividend Revenue		3,000
(c)			
Jan. 1	Equity Investment in Wilkerson Common Stock	500,000	
	Cash		500,000
Dec. 31	Equity Investment in Wilkerson Common Stock	28,000	
	Income from Equity Investment in Wilkerson		
	Common Stock ($70,000 X 40%)		28,000
31	Cash ($60,000 X 40%)	24,000	
	Equity Investment in Wilkerson Common Stock		24,000

EX. 16-2

General Journal			J1
Date	**Account Title**	**Debit**	**Credit**
(a)			
Dec. 31	Unrealized Loss--Income	4,000	
	Market Adjustment--Trading		4,000
	Market Adjustment--Available-for-sale	5,000	
	Unrealized Gain--Equity		5,000

(b) The trading securities are considered short-term and because of their high liquidity are listed immediately below cash in the current assets section of the balance sheet. They are reported at their fair value of $99,000. The available-for-sale securities are listed as long-term in this problem and therefore would generally be reported in a separate section of the balance sheet immediately below current assets at their fair value of $75,000.

The unrealized loss—income on the trading securities would be reported on the income statement in the Other Expenses and Losses section for $4,000. The unrealized gain—equity on the available-for-sale securities would be reported on the balance sheet as a separate component of stockholders' equity for $5,000.

Chapter 17

STATEMENT OF CASH FLOWS

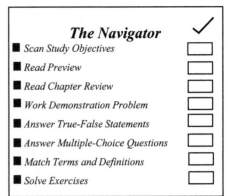

The Navigator
- Scan Study Objectives ☐
- Read Preview ☐
- Read Chapter Review ☐
- Work Demonstration Problem ☐
- Answer True-False Statements ☐
- Answer Multiple-Choice Questions ☐
- Match Terms and Definitions ☐
- Solve Exercises ☐

CHAPTER STUDY OBJECTIVES

After studying this chapter, you should be able to:
1. Indicate the usefulness of the statement of cash flows.
2. Distinguish among operating, investing, and financing activities.
3. Prepare a statement of cash flows using the indirect method.
4. Analyze the statement of cash flows.
*5. Explain how to use a worksheet to prepare the statement of cash flows using the indirect method.
*6. Prepare a statement of cash flows using the direct method.

*Note: All **asterisked** (*) items relate to material contained in the Appendix to the chapter.

PREVIEW OF CHAPTER 17

The balance sheet, income statement, and retained earnings statement do not always show the whole picture of the financial condition of a company or institution. For example, how did Eastman Kodak finance cash dividends of $649 million in a year in which it earned only $17 million? The answer to this and similar questions can be found in this chapter, which presents the **statement of cash flows.** The content and organization of this chapter are as follows:

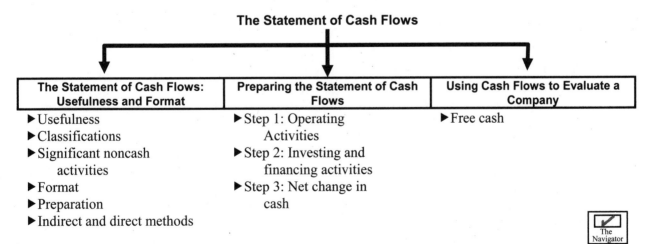

The Statement of Cash Flows

The Statement of Cash Flows: Usefulness and Format	Preparing the Statement of Cash Flows	Using Cash Flows to Evaluate a Company
▶ Usefulness	▶ Step 1: Operating Activities	▶ Free cash
▶ Classifications	▶ Step 2: Investing and financing activities	
▶ Significant noncash activities	▶ Step 3: Net change in cash	
▶ Format		
▶ Preparation		
▶ Indirect and direct methods		

CHAPTER REVIEW

Purpose of the Statement of Cash Flows

1. (S.O. 1) The fourth basic financial statement is the **statement of cash flows.** The primary purpose of the statement is to provide information about an entity's cash receipts and cash payments during a period.

2. The information in the statement of cash flows should help investors to assess the
    a. entity's ability to generate future cash flows.
    b. entity's ability to pay dividends and meet obligations.
    c. reasons for the difference between net income and net cash flow from operating activities.
    d. cash investing and financing transactions during the period.

Classification of Cash Flows

3. (S.O. 2) The statement of cash flows classifies cash receipts and cash payments by:
    a. **Operating activities** which include cash effects of transactions that create revenues and expenses and thus enter into the determination of net income.
    b. **Investing activities** which include (1) acquiring and disposing of property, plant, and equipment, (2) acquiring and disposing of investments, and (3) lending money and collecting the loans.
    c. **Financing activities** which involve liability and stockholders' equity items and include (1) obtaining cash from issuing debt and repaying the amounts borrowed, and (2) obtaining cash from stockholders and providing them with a return on their investment.

4. **Significant noncash transactions** will include the conversion of bonds into common stock and the acquisition of assets through the issuance of bonds or capital stock. These transactions are individually reported at the bottom of the statement of cash flows or they may appear in a separate note or Supplementary Schedule to the financial statements.

General Format

5. The three classes of activities constitute the general **format** of the statement with the operating activities section appearing first, followed by the investing activities and financing activities sections.
    a. The **net cash** provided or used by each activity is totaled to show the **net increase (decrease) in cash** for the period.
    b. The net change in cash for the period is then added to or subtracted from the beginning-of-the-period cash balance.
    c. Finally, any significant noncash investing and financing activities are reported in a **separate schedule** at the bottom of the statement.

6. The statement of cash flows is not prepared from the adjusted trial balance. The information to prepare this statement usually comes from three sources: (a) a comparative balance sheet, (b) the current income statement, and (c) additional information.

The Major Steps

7. The **major steps** in preparing the statement are:
    Step 1: **Determine net cash provided/used by operating activities.** This step involves analyzing not only the current year's income statement, but also comparative balance sheets and selected additional data.
    Step 2: **Determine net cash provided/used by investing and financing activities.** All other changes in the balance sheet accounts must be analyzed to determine their effect on cash.
    Step 3: Compare the net change in cash on the statement of cash flows with the change in the cash account reported on the balance sheet to make sure the amounts agree.

8. In performing step 1, the operating activities section must be **converted** from an accrual basis to a cash basis. This may be done by either the **indirect method** or the **direct method.**
    a. Both methods arrive at the same total amount for "net cash provided by operations" but they differ in disclosing the items that comprise the total amount.
    b. The indirect method is used extensively in practice.
    c. The FASB has expressed a preference for the direct method.

The Indirect Method

9. (S.O. 3) The following points 10 through 15 explain and illustrate the indirect method.

The First Step--Indirect

10. The first step is to determine **net cash provided/used** by operating activities.
    a. Under **generally accepted accounting principles** the accrual basis of accounting is used which results in recognizing revenues when earned and expenses when incurred.
    b. In order to determine cash provided from operations it is necessary to report revenues and expenses on a **cash basis.** This is determined by adjusting net income for items that did not affect cash.

11. The operating section of the statement of cash flows should (a) begin with net income, (b) add (or deduct) items not affecting cash, and (c) show net cash provided (or used) by operating activities.

12. In determining net cash provided by operating activities,
    a. increases in specific current assets other than cash are deducted from net income, and decreases are added to net income.
    b. increases in specific current liabilities are added to net income, and decreases are deducted from net income.
    c. expenses for depreciation, amortization, and depletion and a loss on a sale of equipment are added to net income, and a gain on a sale of equipment is deducted from net income.

The Second Step--Indirect

13. The second step, **net cash provided/used by investing and financing activities** is generally determined from changes in noncurrent accounts reported in the comparative balance sheet and selected additional data.
    a. If the account, Land, increases $50,000 and the transaction data indicates that land was purchased for cash, a cash outflow from an investment activity has occurred.

b.   If the account, Common Stock, increases $100,000 and the transaction data indicates that additional capital stock was issued for cash, a cash inflow from a financing activity has resulted.

14.   The redemption of debt and the retirement or reacquisition of capital stock are cash outflows from financing activities.

The Third Step--Indirect

15.   The third step is to determine the net change in cash on the statement of cash flows with the change in the cash account reported on the balance sheet to make sure the amounts agree.

Analysis of the Statement of Cash Flows

16.   (S.O. 4)   **Free cash flow** describes the cash remaining from operations after adjustment for capital expenditures and dividends. The formula for free cash flow is:
Free Cash Flow = Cash Provided by Operations – Capital Expenditures – Cash Dividends.

Use of a Worksheet

*17.   (S.O. 5) A **worksheet** may be used to assemble and classify the data that will appear on the statement of cash flows. The worksheet is divided into two parts:
a.   Balance sheet accounts with columns for (1) end of last year balances, (2) reconciling items (debit and credit), and end of current year balances.
b.   Statement of cash flows effects with debit and credit columns. This part of the worksheet consists of the operating, investing, and financing sections.

*18.   The following **guidelines** are important in **using** a worksheet.
a.   In the **balance sheet section,** accounts with debit balances are listed separately from those with credit balances.
b.   In the **cash flow effects section,** inflows of cash are entered as debits in the reconciling columns and outflows of cash are entered as credits in the reconciling columns.
c.   The reconciling items shown in the worksheet are not entered in any journal or posted to any account.

*19.   The steps in preparing a worksheet are:
a.   Enter the balance sheet accounts and their beginning and ending balances in the balance sheet accounts section.
b.   Enter the data that explains the changes in the balance sheet accounts (other than cash) and their effects on the statement of cash flows in the reconciling columns of the worksheet.
c.   Enter the increase or decrease in cash on the Cash line and at the bottom of the worksheet. This entry should enable the totals of the reconciling columns to be in agreement.

*20.   The statement of cash flows is prepared entirely from the data that appears in the worksheet under Statement of Cash Flows Effects.

Preparing the Statement of Cash Flows--

The Direct Method

*21. (S.O. 6) The following points 22 through 29 explain and illustrate the direct method.

The First Step--Direct

*22. The first step is to determine net cash provided/used by operating activities by adjusting each item in the income statement from the accrual basis to the cash basis.
  a. If the income statement shows revenue of $120,000 and accounts receivable (net) increased $20,000 during the year, cash revenue is $100,000 ($120,000 - $20,000).
  b. If the income statement reports operating expenses of $60,000 but accounts payable have increased $12,000 during the year, cash operating expenses are $48,000 ($60,000 - $12,000).

*23. In the operating activities section, only **major classes** of cash receipts and cash payments are reported as follows:
  a. **Cash receipts** from (1) sales of goods and services to customers and (2) interest and dividends on loans and investments.
  b. **Cash payments** (1) to suppliers, (2) to employees, (3) for operating expenses, (4) for interest, and (5) for taxes.

*24. The formula for computing **cash receipts from customers** is:

$$\text{Revenue from sales} \quad \begin{bmatrix} + & \text{Decrease in accounts receivable} \\ & \text{or} \\ - & \text{Increase in accounts receivable} \end{bmatrix}$$

*25. The formula for computing **cash payments to suppliers** is:

$$\text{Cost of goods sold} \quad \begin{bmatrix} + & \text{Increase in inventory} \\ & \text{or} \\ - & \text{Decrease in inventory} \end{bmatrix} \quad \begin{bmatrix} + & \text{Decrease in accounts payable} \\ & \text{or} \\ - & \text{Increase in accounts payable} \end{bmatrix}$$

*26. The formula for computing **cash payments for operating expenses** is:

$$\text{Operating expenses (exclusive of depreciation expense)} \quad \begin{bmatrix} + & \text{Increase in prepaid expenses} \\ & \text{or} \\ - & \text{Decrease in prepaid expenses} \end{bmatrix} \quad \begin{bmatrix} + & \text{Decrease in accrued expenses payable} \\ & \text{or} \\ - & \text{Increase in accued expenses payable} \end{bmatrix}$$

*27. The formula for computing **cash payments for income taxes** is:

$$\text{Income tax expense} \quad \begin{bmatrix} + & \text{Decrease in income taxes payable} \\ & \text{or} \\ - & \text{Increase in income taxes payable} \end{bmatrix}$$

The Second Step--Direct

*28. The second step, **net cash provided/used by investing and financing activities** is generally determined from changes in noncurrent accounts reported in the comparative balance sheet and selected additional data.

The Third Step--Direct

*29. The third step is to determine the net increase or decrease in cash by determining the difference between cash at the beginning of the year and cash at the end of the year.

DEMONSTRATION PROBLEM (S.O. 3 and *6)

Presented below is the comparative balance sheet for Kinports Company as of December 31, 2011 and 2010, and the income statement for 2011:

KINPORTS COMPANY
Comparative Balance Sheet
December 31

Assets	2011	2010
Cash	$ 52,000	$ 63,000
Accounts receivable (net)	64,000	75,000
Inventory	193,000	179,000
Prepaid expenses	21,000	27,000
Land	95,000	120,000
Equipment	277,000	221,000
Accumulated depreciation—equipment	(51,000)	(42,000)
Building	300,000	300,000
Accumulated depreciation—building	(100,000)	(75,000)
	$851,000	$868,000

Liabilities and Stockholders' Equity	2011	2010
Accounts payable	$ 34,000	$ 77,000
Bonds payable	245,000	290,000
Common stock, $1 par	275,000	230,000
Retained earnings	297,000	271,000
	$851,000	$868,000

KINPORTS COMPANY
Income Statement
For the Year Ended December 31, 2011

Sales		$600,000
Less:		
Cost of goods sold	$380,000	
Operating expenses	90,000	
Loss on sale of equipment	2,000	
Income tax expense	27,000	499,000
Net income		$101,000

Additional information:
1. Operating expenses include depreciation expense of $54,000.
2. Land was sold at book value.
3. Cash dividends of $75,000 were declared and paid.
4. Equipment was purchased for $82,000. In addition, equipment costing $26,000 with a book value of $6,000 was sold for $4,000.
5. Bonds with a face value of $45,000 were converted into 45,000 shares of $1 par value common stock.
6. Accounts payable pertain to merchandise suppliers.

Instructions
(a) Prepare a statement of cash flows for the year ended December 31, 2011 using the indirect method.
(b) Prepare a statement of cash flows for the year ended December 31, 2011 using the direct method.

Kinports

The Navigator

SOLUTION TO DEMONSTRATION PROBLEM

(a)
KINPORTS COMPANY
Statement of Cash Flows
For the Year Ended December 31, 2011

Cash flows from operating activities		
Net income		$101,000
Adjustments to reconcile net income to net cash provided by operating activities		
Depreciation expense	$ 54,000	
Loss on sale of equipment	2,000	
Decrease in accounts receivable	11,000	
Increase in inventory	(14,000)	
Decrease in prepaid expenses	6,000	
Decrease in accounts payable	(43,000)	16,000
Net cash provided by operating activities		117,000
Cash flows from investing activities		
Sale of equipment	4,000	
Sale of land	25,000	
Purchase of equipment	(82,000)	
Net cash used by investing activities		(53,000)
Cash flows from financing activities		
Cash dividend to stockholders		(75,000)
Net decrease in cash		(11,000)
Cash at beginning of period		63,000
Cash at end of period		$ 52,000
Noncash investing and financing activities		
Conversion of bonds into common stock		$ 45,000

(b)
KINPORTS COMPANY
Statement of Cash Flows
For the Year Ended December 31, 2011

Cash flows from operating activities		
Cash receipts from customers (1)		$611,000
Cash payments		
To suppliers (2)..	$437,000	
For operating expenses (3).............................	30,000	
For income taxes	27,000	(494,000)
Net cash provided by operating activities		117,000
Cash flows from investing activities		
Sale of equipment...	4,000	
Sale of land...	25,000	
Purchase of equipment......................................	(82,000)	
Net cash used by investing activities		(53,000)
Cash flows from financing activities		
Cash dividend to stockholders............................		(75,000)
Net decrease in cash		(11,000)
Cash at beginning of period		63,000
Cash at end of period...		$ 52,000
Noncash investing and financing activities		
Conversion of bonds into common stock.............		$ 45,000

(1)   Cash receipts from customers:

Sales per income statement	$600,000
Add: Decrease in accounts receivable	11,000
Cash receipts from customers	$611,000

(2)   Cash payments to suppliers:

Cost of goods sold per income statement	$380,000
Add: Increase in inventory	14,000
Purchases	394,000
Add: Decrease in accounts payable	43,000
Cash payments to suppliers	$437,000

(3)   Cash payments for operating expenses:

Operating expenses per income statement		$90,000
Deduct: Depreciation expense	$54,000	
Decrease in prepaid expenses	6,000	(60,000)
Cash payments for operating expenses		$30,000

REVIEW QUESTIONS AND EXERCISES

TRUE—FALSE

Indicate whether each of the following is true (T) or false (F) in the space provided.

___F___   1.   (S.O. 1)   The statement of cash flows is an optional financial statement.

___T___   2.   (S.O. 1)   The primary purpose of the statement of cash flows is to provide information about the cash receipts and cash payments of an entity during a period.

___F___   3.   (S.O. 2)   The statement of cash flows classifies cash receipts and cash payments into two categories: operating activities and nonoperating activities.

___F___   4.   (S.O. 2)   Investing activities pertain only to cash flows from acquiring and disposing of investments and productive long-lived assets.

___T___   5.   (S.O. 2)   Financing activities include the obtaining of cash from issuing debt and repaying the amounts borrowed.

___T___   6.   (S.O. 2)   A cash inflow from the sale of equity securities of another entity is an investing activity.

___T___   7.   (S.O. 2)   Cash outflows to pay employees for services rendered are an operating activity.

___T___   8.   (S.O. 2)   A significant noncash transaction occurs when plant assets are acquired by issuing bonds.

___F___   9.   (S.O. 2)   Significant noncash transactions are reported in the statement of cash flows in a separate section entitled Significant Noncash Transactions.

___F___   10.   (S.O. 2)   In the statement of cash flows, the operating activities section is presented last.

___T___   11.   (S.O. 2)   The statement of cash flows helps investors assess the company's ability to pay cash dividends.

___F___   12.   (S.O. 2)   The adjusted trial balance is the only item needed to prepare the Statement of Cash Flows.

___T___   13.   (S.O. 2)   The indirect method is used more often in practice than the direct method.

___T___   14.   (S.O. 2)   In determining net cash provided by operating activities, accrual basis net income is converted to cash basis net income.

___F___   15.   (S.O. 3)   Under the indirect method, retained earnings is adjusted for items that affected reported net income but did **not** affect cash.

____T____ 16. (S.O. 3) Under the indirect method, noncash charges in the income statement are added back to net income.

____F____ 17. (S.O. 3) Under the indirect method, in determining net cash provided by operating activities, an increase in accounts receivable and an increase in accounts payable are added to net income.

____T____ *18. (S.O. 5) The worksheet for the statement of cash flows contains a balance sheet accounts section and a statement of cash flows effects section.

____F____ *19. (S.O. 5) The reconciling items shown on the worksheet are journalized and posted to the accounts.

____T____ *20. (S.O. 5) The reconciling entry for depreciation expense in a worksheet is a credit to Accumulated Depreciation and a debit to Operating-Depreciation Expense.

____F____ *21. (S.O. 6) Under the direct method of determining net cash provided by operating activities, cash revenues and cash expenses are computed.

____F____ *22. (S.O. 6) Under the direct method, the formula for computing cash collections from customers is sales revenues plus the increase in accounts receivable or minus the decrease in accounts receivable.

____T____ *23. (S.O. 6) Under the direct method, cash payments for operating expenses is computed by adding increases in prepaid expenses and decreases in accrued expenses payable to operating expenses.

MULTIPLE CHOICE

Circle the letter that best answers each of the following statements.

1. (S.O. 1) The primary purpose of the statement of cash flows is to:
    a. distinguish between debits and credits to the cash account.
    b. provide information about the cash receipts and cash payments of an entity during a period.
    c. provide an analysis of the different cash accounts.
    d. provide information about the cash available at a particular time.

2. (S.O. 2) Financing activities involve:
    a. lending money to other entities and collecting on those loans.
    b. cash receipts from sales of goods and services.
    c. acquiring and disposing of productive long-lived assets.
    d. long-term liability and owners' equity items.

3. (S.O. 2) Investing activities include all of the following **except** cash:
    a. inflows from the sale of debt securities of other entities.
    b. outflows to redeem the entity's long-term debt.
    c. outflows to purchase property, plant, and equipment.
    d. outflows to make loans to other entities.

4. (S.O. 2) Which of the following statements about significant noncash transactions is **incorrect?**
    a. The reporting of these transactions in the financial statements or notes is optional.
    b. The conversion of bonds into common stock is an example of a significant noncash transaction.
    c. These transactions can be individually reported in a separate note.
    d. These transactions can be reported in a separate section at the bottom of the statement of cash flows.

5. (S.O. 2) The statement of cash flows is prepared from all of the following **except**:
    a. the adjusted trial balance.
    b. comparative balance sheets.
    c. selected transaction data.
    d. current income statement.

6. (S.O. 2) Which of the following steps is **not** required in preparing the statement of cash flows?
    a. Determine the change in cash.
    b. Determine net cash provided by operating activities.
    c. Determine cash from investing and financing activities.
    d. Determine the change in current assets.

7. (S.O. 2) In determining net cash provided by operating activities it is **incorrect** to:
    a. eliminate noncash revenues from net income.
    b. eliminate noncash expenses from net income.
    c. include the issuance of the company's bonds for cash.
    d. convert accrual based net income to a cash basis.

8. (S.O. 2) The information in a statement of cash flows will **not** help investors to assess the entity's ability to:
    a. generate future cash flows.
    b. obtain favorable borrowing terms at a bank.
    c. pay dividends.
    d. pay its obligations when they become due.

9. (S.O. 3) In the Ulen Company, net income is $65,000. If accounts receivable increased $35,000 and accounts payable decreased $10,000, net cash provided by operating activities using the indirect method is:
    a. $20,000.
    b. $40,000.
    c. $90,000.
    d. $110,000.

10. (S.O. 3) Under the indirect method, when accounts receivable decrease during the period,
    a. to convert net income to net cash provided by operating activities, the decrease in accounts receivable must be added to net income.
    b. revenues on a cash basis are less than revenues on an accrual basis.
    c. to convert net income to net cash provided by operating activities, the decrease in accounts receivable must be subtracted from net income.
    d. revenues on an accrual basis are greater than revenues on a cash basis.

11. (S.O. 3) Which of the following is the correct treatment for changes in current liabilities in the cash flow statement using the indirect method?

	Add to Net Income	Deduct from Net Income
a.	Decreases	Increases
b.	Decreases	Decreases
c.	Increases	Decreases
d.	Increases	Increases

12. (S.O. 3) In the Freyfogle Company, land decreased $75,000 because of a cash sale for $75,000, the equipment account increased $30,000 as a result of a cash purchase, and Bonds Payable increased $100,000 from an issuance for cash at face value. The net cash provided by investing activities is:
    a. $75,000.
    b. $145,000.
    c. $45,000.
    d. $70,000.

13. (S.O. 3) In the Tabb Company, Treasury Stock increased $15,000 from a cash purchase, and Retained Earnings increased $40,000 as a result of net income of $62,000 and cash dividends paid of $22,000. Net cash used by financing activities is:
    a. $15,000.
    b. $22,000.
    c. $55,000.
    d. $37,000.

14. (S.O. 3) In converting net income to net cash provided by operating activities, under the indirect method:
    a. decreases in accounts receivable and increases in prepaid expenses are added.
    b. decreases in inventory and increases in accrued liabilities are added.
    c. decreases in accounts payable and decreases in inventory are deducted.
    d. increases in accounts receivable and increases in accrued liabilities are deducted.

15. (S.O. 3) In the Hayes Company, there was an increase in the land account during the year of $24,000. Analysis reveals that the change resulted from a cash sale of land at cost $55,000, and a cash purchase of land for $79,000. In the statement of cash flows, the change in the land account should be reported in the investment section:
    a. as a net purchase of land, $24,000.
    b. only as a purchase of land $79,000.
    c. as a purchase of land $79,000 and a sale of land $55,000.
    d. only as a sale of land $55,000.

16. (S.O. 3) In the Merrit Company, machinery with a book value of $8,000 is sold for $5,000 cash. In the statement of cash flows, the cash proceeds are reported in the:
    a. investing section and the loss is added to net income in the operating section.
    b. financing section and the loss is added to net income in the operating section.
    c. investing section and no adjustment is made to net income.
    d. financing section and no adjustment is made to net income.

*17. (S.O. 5) When a worksheet is used, all but one of the following statements is correct. The **incorrect** statement is:
   a. Reconciling items on the worksheet are not journalized or posted.
   b. The bottom portion of the worksheet shows the statement of cash flows effects.
   c. The balance sheet accounts portion of the worksheet is divided into two parts: assets, and liabilities and stockholders' equity.
   d. Each line pertaining to a balance sheet account should foot across.

*18. (S.O. 5) In the Nowak Company, the beginning and ending balances in Land were $132,000 and $160,000 respectively. During the year, land costing $30,000 was sold for $30,000 cash, and land costing $58,000 was purchased for cash. The entries in the reconciling columns of the worksheet will include a:
   a. credit to Land $30,000 and a debit to Sale of Land $30,000 under investing activities.
   b. debit to Land $58,000 and a credit to Purchase of Land $58,000 under financing activities.
   c. net debit to Land $28,000 and a credit to Purchase of Land $28,000 under investing activities.
   d. credit to Land $30,000 and a debit to Sale of Land $30,000 under financing activities.

*19. (S.O. 6) In the Phander Corporation, cash receipts from customers were $92,000, cash payments for operating expenses were $68,000, and one-third of the company's $4,200 of income taxes were paid during the year. Net cash provided by operating activities is:
   a. $24,000.
   b. $19,800.
   c. $22,600.
   d. $21,200.

*20. (S.O. 6) The Rotunda Company uses the direct method in determining net cash provided by operating activities. If reported cost of goods sold is $140,000, inventory increased $20,000, and accounts payable increased $15,000, cash payments to suppliers are:
   a. $135,000.
   b. $145,000.
   c. $175,000.
   d. $105,000.

*21. (S.O. 6) The Cribbets Company uses the direct method in determining net cash provided by operating activities. During the year operating expenses were $260,000, prepaid expenses increased $20,000, and accrued expenses payable increased $30,000. Cash payments for operating expenses were:
   a. $210,000.
   b. $310,000.
   c. $270,000.
   d. $250,000.

*22. (S.O. 6) The Bainbridge Company uses the direct method in determining net cash provided by operating activities. The income statement shows income tax expense $70,000. Income taxes payable were $25,000 at the beginning of the year and $18,000 at the end of the year. Cash payments for income taxes are:
  a. $63,000.
  b. $70,000.
  c. $77,000.
  d. none of the above.

MATCHING

The Ross Company had the following transactions. In the space provided, classify each transaction by using the following code letters: (O) Operating activity (indirect method), (I) Investing activity, (F) Financing activity, and (N) significant noncash investing and financing activity. (Note: a transaction may be reported in more than one section.)

_F_   1.   Payment of cash dividends to stockholders.

_I_   2.   Sale of land for cash at cost.

_F_   3.   Purchase of treasury stock for cash.

_F_   4.   Issuance of long-term bonds for cash.

_N_   5.   Exchange of equipment for a patent.

_O_   6.   Payment of cash to lenders for interest.

_I_   7.   Loan of money to a supplier.

_I_   8.   Purchase of equity securities of another entity for cash.

_O_   9.   Cash payments to the IRS for income taxes.

_F_   10.   Redemption of bonds at book value.

_O_   11.   Receipt of cash dividends from another entity.

_F_   12.   Sale of treasury stock above its cost.

_I_   13.   Sale of equity securities of another entity at book value for cash.

_I_   14.   Collection of loan made to a supplier.

_O_   15.   Collection from customers for sales of goods.

_N_   16.   Conversion of bonds into common stock.

_O_   17.   Cash payments to employees for services.

_I_   18.   Purchase of land for cash.

_O_   19.   Cash payments to suppliers for inventory.

_O_   20.   Receipt of interest on loans to another entity.

EXERCISES

EX. 17-1 (S.O. 3 and *6) Lafave Inc., a service company, has the following selected information at December 31, 2011.

Balance Sheets	**2011**	**2010**
Cash	$ 83,000	$ 61,000
Accounts receivable	78,000	86,000 *8000*
Prepaid expenses	12,000	6,000 *-6000*
Accounts payable	92,000	87,000 *5000*
Income taxes payable	17,000	13,000 *4000*

Income statement for 2011	
Sales revenues	$173,000
Operating expenses	160,000
Income before income taxes	13,000
Income tax expense	6,000
Net income	$ 7,000

Operating expenses include $4,000 of depreciation expense.

Instructions

(a) Using the direct method, prepare the operating activities section of the statement of cash flows for 2011.

(b) Using the indirect method, prepare the operating activities section of the statement of cash flows for 2011.

(a)   Cash flows from operating activities using the direct method.

(b) Cash flows from operating activities using the indirect method.

EX. 17-2   (S.O. 3 and *6) Illini Law Company reports the following condensed balance sheets at December 31:

Assets	2011	2010	
Cash	$ 53,000	$ 38,000	
Accounts receivable	72,000	76,000	4000
Inventory	65,000	58,000	(7000)
Property, plant and equipment (net)	196,000	172,000	24000
Total	$386,000	$344,000	

Liabilities and Stockholders' Equity	2011	2010	
Accounts payable	$ 48,000	$ 52,000	(4000)
Notes payable, long-term	83,000	71,000	
Common stock	212,000	180,000	
Retained earnings	43,000	41,000	
Total	$386,000	$344,000	

Other information:
1. Net income was $10,000 in 2011 and $25,000 in 2010.
2. Depreciation expense was $8,000 in 2011 and $10,000 in 2010.
3. Machinery costing $62,000 was purchased for cash in 2011.
4. Dividends of $8,000 were paid during 2011.
5. Equipment was sold for cash during 2011 at $2,000 below its book value of $30,000.
6. A $12,000, long-term note payable was issued for cash in 2011.
7. Common stock of $32,000 was issued for cash in 2011.
8. Sales revenue per the income statement was $150,000 in 2011.
9. Cost of goods sold per the 2011 income statement was $110,000.
10. Operating expenses (all paid in cash) per the 2011 income statement were $20,000, excluding depreciation expense.
11. Accounts payable pertain to suppliers.

Instructions
(a)   Prepare a statement of cash flows for 2011 using the indirect method.
(b)   Prepare a statement of cash flows for 2011 using the direct method.

(a)

ILLINI LAW COMPANY
Statement of Cash Flows
For the Year Ended December 31, 2011

(b)

ILLINI LAW COMPANY
Statement of Cash Flows
For the Year Ended December 31, 2011

SOLUTIONS TO REVIEW QUESTIONS AND EXERCISES

TRUE-FALSE

1. (F) The statement of cash flows is the fourth basic financial statement that companies are required to prepare.
2. (T)
3. (F) The statement classifies cash receipts and cash payments into three categories of activity: operating, investing, and financing.
4. (F) Investing activities also include lending money and collecting on these loans.
5. (T)
6. (T)
7. (T)
8. (T)
9. (F) The section is entitled noncash investing and financing activities.
10. (F) The operating section is always listed first followed by the investing and finance sections.
11. (T)
12. (F) The statement of cash flows requires detailed information concerning the changes in account balances.
13. (T)
14. (T)
15. (F) It is net income and not retained earnings that is adjusted under the indirect method.
16. (T)
17. (F) An increase in accounts receivable is deducted from net income.
*18. (T)
*19. (F) Reconciling items are not journalized or posted to any account.
*20. (T)
*21. (T)
*22. (F) Increases in accounts receivable are deducted and decreases in accounts receivable are added.
*23. (T)

MULTIPLE CHOICE

1. (b) The primary purpose of the statement of cash flows is to provide information about the cash receipts and cash payments of an entity during a period.

2. (d) Financing activities involve long-term liability and owners' equity items and include (1) obtaining cash from issuing debt and repaying the amounts borrowed, and (2) obtaining cash from stockholders and providing them with a return on their investment. Answers (a) and (c) are investing activities and answer (b) is an operating activity.

3. (b) Cash outflows to redeem the entity's long-term debt are a financing activity.

4. (a) The reporting of significant noncash transactions in the financial statements or notes is required because they represent significant financing and investing activities that merit disclosure.

5. (a) The statement is not prepared from an adjusted trial balance.

6. (d) It is not necessary to determine the change in current assets because the statement pertains to cash flows.

7. (c) The issuance of a company's bonds is a financing transaction that is not included in determining cash provided by operations.

8. (b) Information in the statement does not permit an assessment of an entity's credit rating or the borrowing terms at a bank.

9. (a) The computation is:

Net income			$65,000
Deduct:	Increase in accounts receivable	$35,000	
	Decrease in accounts payable	10,000	(45,000)
Net cash provided by operations			$20,000

10. (a) To convert net income to net cash provided by operating activities, a decrease in accounts receivable must be added to net income. Also, a decrease in accounts receivable results in revenues on a cash basis being higher than revenues on an accrual basis.

11. (c) In determining net cash from operating activities under the indirect method, when there is an increase in current liabilities the amount is added to net income; and when there is a decrease, the amount is subtracted from net income.

12. (c) The issuance of bonds is a financing activity. The sale of land and the purchase of equipment are investing activities. Therefore, net cash provided by investing activities is $45,000 ($75,000 - $30,000).

13. (d) Net income is an operating activity. The other transactions are financing activities. Thus, net cash used by financing activities is $37,000 ($15,000 + $22,000).

14. (b) Increases in prepaid expenses are deducted (a). Decreases in inventory are added (c). Increases in accrued liabilities are added (d).

15. (c) Both the gross cash inflow, $55,000 and the gross cash outflow $79,000 should be reported.

16. (a) The sale of machinery is an investing activity and the cash proceeds of $5,000 should be reported in this section. The $3,000 loss is a noncash charge that must be added back to net income in the operating section.

*17. (c) The balance sheet accounts are divided into two parts. However, the parts are debit balance accounts and credit balance accounts.

*18. (a) The entries in the reconciling columns are: (1) Cr. Land $30,000 and Dr. Sale of Land $30,000 under investing activities, and (2) Dr. Land $58,000 and Cr. Purchase of Land $58,000 under investing activities.

*19. (c) Cash receipts were $92,000 and cash payments for operating expenses and income taxes were $69,400 ($68,000 + $1,400) or a difference of $22,600.

*20.   (b)   An increase in inventory is added and an increase in accounts payable is deducted. Thus $140,000 + $20,000 - $15,000 = $145,000.

*21.   (d)   An increase in prepaid expenses is added and an increase in accrued expenses payable is deducted. Thus, $260,000 + $20,000 - $30,000 = $250,000.

*22.   (c)   A decrease in income taxes payable is added to income tax expense. Thus $70,000 + $7,000 = $77,000.

MATCHING

1.	F	6.	O	11.	O	16.	N
2.	I	7.	I	12.	F	17.	O
3.	F	8.	I	13.	I	18.	I
4.	F	9.	O	14.	I	19.	O
5.	N	10.	F	15.	O	20.	O

EXERCISES

EX. 17-1

(a)   Cash flows from operating activities

Cash receipts from customers (1)	$181,000
Cash payments for operating expenses (2)	(157,000)
Cash payments for income taxes (3)	(2,000)
Net cash provided by operations	$ 22,000

(1)   Computation of cash receipts from customers:

Sales revenues per income statement	$173,000
Add: Decrease in receivables (net)	8,000
Cash receipts from revenues	$181,000

(2)   Computation of cash payments for operating expenses:

Operating expense per income statement	$160,000
Deduct: Depreciation expense	(4,000)
Deduct: Increase in accounts payable	(5,000)
Add: Increase in prepaid expenses	6,000
Cash payments for operating expenses	$157,000

(3)   Computation of cash payments for income taxes:

Income taxes per income statement	$ 6,000
Deduct: Increase in income taxes payable	(4,000)
Cash payments for income taxes	$ 2,000

(b)   Cash flows from operating activities

Net income		$ 7,000
Add (deduct) items not affecting cash		
Depreciation expense	$ 4,000	
Decrease in accounts receivable	8,000	
Increase in prepaid expense	(6,000)	
Increase in accounts payable	5,000	
Increase in taxes payable	4,000	15,000
Cash provided by operations		$22,000

EX. 17-2

(a)

ILLINI LAW COMPANY
Statement of Cash Flows
For the Year Ended December 31, 2011

Cash flows from operating activities		
Net income		$10,000
Adjustments to reconcile net income to net cash		
provided by operating activities		
Depreciation expense	$ 8,000	
Decrease in accounts receivable	4,000	
Increase in inventory	(7,000)	
Decrease in accounts payable	(4,000)	
Loss on sale of equipment	2,000	3,000
Net cash provided by operating activities		13,000
Cash flows from investing activities		
Sale of equipment	$ 28,000	
Purchase of machinery	(62,000)	
Cash used by investing activities		(34,000)
Cash flows from financing activities		
Issuance of long-term note payable	12,000	
Issuance of common stock	32,000	
Payment of cash dividends	(8,000)	
Cash provided by financing activities		36,000
Net increase in cash		15,000
Cash balance at beginning of period		38,000
Cash balance at end of period		$53,000

(b)
ILLINI LAW COMPANY
Statement of Cash Flows
For the Year Ended December 31, 2011

Cash flows from operating activities		
Cash receipts from customers (1)..		$154,000
Cash payments		
To suppliers (2)...	$121,000	
For operating expenses..	20,000	(141,000)
Net cash provided by operating activities		13,000
Cash flows from investing activities		
Sale of equipment...	$ 28,000	
Purchase of machinery	(62,000)	
Net cash used by investing activities		(34,000)
Cash flows from financing activities		
Issuance of long-term note payable.......................................	12,000	
Issuance of common stock	32,000	
Payment of cash dividends	(8,000)	
Net cash provided by financing activities........................		36,000
Net increase in cash		15,000
Cash balance at beginning of period		38,000
Cash balance at end of period...		$53,000

(1)   Computation of cash receipts from customers:

Sales revenue per income statement	$150,000
Add: Decrease in receivables	4,000
Cash receipts from receivables	$154,000

(2)   Computation of cash payments to suppliers:

Cost of goods sold per income statement	$110,000
Add: Increase in inventory	7,000
Add: Decrease in accounts payable	4,000
Cash payments to suppliers	$121,000

Chapter 18

FINANCIAL STATE-MENT ANALYSIS

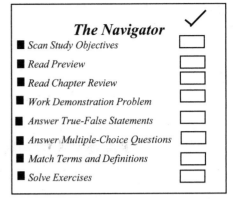

The Navigator ✓
- Scan Study Objectives ☐
- Read Preview ☐
- Read Chapter Review ☐
- Work Demonstration Problem ☐
- Answer True-False Statements ☐
- Answer Multiple-Choice Questions ☐
- Match Terms and Definitions ☐
- Solve Exercises ☐

CHAPTER STUDY OBJECTIVES

After studying this chapter, you should be able to:
1. Discuss the need for comparative analysis.
2. Identify the tools of financial statement analysis.
3. Explain and apply horizontal analysis.
4. Describe and apply vertical analysis.
5. Identify and compute ratios used in analyzing a firm's liquidity, profitability and solvency.
6. Understand the concept of earning power, and indicate how irregular items are presented.
7. Understand the concept of quality of earnings.

The Navigator

PREVIEW OF CHAPTER 18

Financial statement analysis, the topic of this chapter, enhances the usefulness of published financial statements in making decisions about a company. The content and organization of this chapter are shown below.

Financial Statement Analysis

Basics of Financial Statement Analysis	Horizontal and Vertical Analysis	Ratio Analysis	Earning Power and Irregular Items	Quality of Earnings
▶ Need for comparative analysis ▶ Tools of analysis	▶ Balance sheet ▶ Income statement ▶ Retained earnings statement	▶ Liquidity ▶ Profitability ▶ Solvency ▶ Summary	▶ Discontinued operations ▶ Extraordinary items ▶ Changes in accounting principles ▶ Comprehensive income	▶ Alternative accounting methods ▶ Pro forma income ▶ Improper recognition

The Navigator

CHAPTER REVIEW

Characteristics

1. **Financial statement analysis** enables the financial statement user to make informed decisions about a company.

2. When analyzing financial statements, three major characteristics of a company are generally evaluated: (a) liquidity, (b) profitability, and (c) solvency.

3. (S.O. 1) Comparative analysis may be made on a number of different bases.
    a. **Intracompany basis**—Compares an item or financial relationship within a company in the current year with the same item or relationship in one or more prior years.
    b. **Industry averages**—Compares an item or financial relationship of a company with industry averages.
    c. **Intercompany basis**—Compares an item or financial relationship of one company with the same item or relationship in one or more competing companies.

Tools of Financial Analysis

4. (S.O. 2) There are three **basic tools** of analysis: (a) horizontal, (b) vertical, and (c) ratio.

Horizontal Analysis

5. (S.O. 3) **Horizontal analysis,** also called **trend analysis,** is a technique for evaluating a series of financial statement data over a period of time to determine the increase or decrease that has taken place, expressed as either an amount or a percentage. In horizontal analysis, a base year is selected and changes are expressed as percentages of the base year amount.

Vertical Analysis

6. (S.O. 4) **Vertical analysis,** also called **common size analysis**, expresses each item within a financial statement as a percent of a base amount. Generally, the base amount is total assets for the balance sheet, and net sales for the income statement. For example, it may be determined that current assets are 22% of total assets, and selling expenses are 15% of net sales.

Ratio Analysis

7. (S.O. 5) A **ratio** expresses the mathematical relationship between one quantity and another as either a percentage, rate, or proportion. Ratios can be classified as:
    a. **Liquidity ratios**—measures of the short-term debt-paying ability.
    b. **Profitability ratios**—measures of the income or operating success of an enterprise for a given period of time.
    c. **Solvency ratios**—measures of the ability of the enterprise to survive over a long period of time.

8. There are four **liquidity ratios:** the current ratio, the acid test ratio, receivables turnover, and inventory turnover.

9. The **current ratio** expresses the relationship of current assets to current liabilities. It is a widely used measure for evaluating a company's liquidity and short-term debt paying ability. The formula for this ratio is:

$$\text{Current ratio} = \frac{\text{Current assets}}{\text{Current liabilities}}$$

10. The **acid-test** or **quick ratio** relates cash, short-term investments, and net receivables to current liabilities. This ratio indicates a company's immediate liquidity. It is an important complement to the current ratio. The formula for the acid-test ratio is:

$$\text{Acid-test ratio} = \frac{\text{Cash + short-term investments + receivables (net)}}{\text{Current liabilities}}$$

11. The **receivables turnover ratio is** used to assess the liquidity of the receivables. This ratio measures the number of times, on average, receivables are collected during the period. The formula for the ratio is:

$$\text{Receivables turnover} = \frac{\text{Net credit sales}}{\text{Average net receivables}}$$

Average net receivables can be computed from the beginning and ending balances of the net receivables. A popular variant of the receivables turnover ratio is to convert it into an average collection period in terms of days. This is done by dividing the turnover ratio into 365 days.

12. **Inventory turnover** measures the number of times, on average, the inventory is sold during the period. It indicates the liquidity of the inventory. The formula for the ratio is:

$$\text{Inventory turnover} = \frac{\text{Cost of goods sold}}{\text{Average inventory}}$$

Average inventory can be computed from the beginning and ending inventory balances. A variant of the inventory turnover ratio is to compute the **average days to sell the inventory.** This is done by dividing the inventory turnover ratio into 365 days.

13. There are nine **profitability ratios**: the profit margin ratio, asset turnover ratio, return on assets ratio, return on common stockholders' equity ratio, earnings per share, price-earnings ration and the payout ratio.

14. The **profit margin ratio** is a measure of the percentage of each sales dollar that results in net income. The formula is:

$$\text{Profit margin on sales} = \frac{\text{Net income}}{\text{Net sales}}$$

15. **Asset turnover** measures how efficiently a company uses its assets to generate sales. The formula for this ratio is:

$$\text{Asset turnover} = \frac{\text{Net sales}}{\text{Average assets}}$$

16. **Return on assets** is an overall measure of profitability. It measures the rate of return on each dollar invested in assets. The formula is:

$$\text{Return on assets} = \frac{\text{Net income}}{\text{Average assets}}$$

17. **Return on common stockholders' equity** measures profitability from the common stockholders' viewpoint. The ratio shows the dollars of income earned for each dollar invested by the owners. The formula is:

$$\text{Return on common stockholders' equity} = \frac{\text{Net income}}{\text{Average common stockholders' equity}}$$

   a. When preferred stock is present, preferred dividend requirements are deducted from net income to compute income available to common stockholders. Similarly, the par value of preferred stock (or call price, if applicable) must be deducted from total stockholders' equity to arrive at the amount of common stock equity used in this ratio.

   b. Leveraging or trading on the equity at a gain means that the company has borrowed money through the issuance of bonds or notes at a lower rate of interest than it is able to earn by using the borrowed money. A comparison of the rate of return on total assets with the rate of interest paid for borrowed money indicates the profitability of trading on the equity.

18. **Earnings per share** measures the amount of net income earned on each share of common stock. The formula is:

$$\text{Earnings per share} = \frac{\text{Net income}}{\text{Weighted average common shares outstanding}}$$

Any preferred dividends declared for the period must be subtracted from net income.

19. The **price-earnings ratio** measures the ratio of market price per share of common stock to earnings per share. It is an oft-quoted statistic that reflects investors' assessments of a company's future earnings. The formula for the ratio is:

$$\text{Price-earnings ratio} = \frac{\text{Market price per share of stock}}{\text{Earnings per share}}$$

20. The **payout ratio** measures the percentage of earnings distributed in the form of cash dividends. The formula is:

$$\text{Payout ratio} = \frac{\text{Cash dividends}}{\text{Net income}}$$

Companies with high growth rates generally have low payout ratios because they reinvest most of their income into the business.

21. There are two **solvency** ratios: debt to total assets and times interest earned.

22. The **debt to total assets ratio** measures the percentage of total assets provided by creditors. The formula for this ratio is:

$$\text{Debt to total assets} = \frac{\text{Total debt}}{\text{Total assets}}$$

The adequacy of this ratio is often judged in the light of the company's earnings. Companies with relatively stable earnings, such as public utilities, have higher debt to total assets ratios than cyclical companies with widely fluctuating earnings, such as many high-tech companies.

23. The **times interest earned ratio** measures a company's ability to meet interest payments as they become due. The formula is:

$$\text{Times interest earned} = \frac{\text{Income before income taxes and interest expense}}{\text{Interest expense}}$$

Discontinued Operations

24. (S.O. 6) **Discontinued operations** refers to the disposal of a significant component of a business, such as eliminating an entire activity or eliminating a major class of customers.
    a. When the disposal occurs, the income statement should report both income from continuing operations and income (loss) from discontinued operations.
    b. The income (loss) from discontinued operations consists of (1) income (loss) from operations and (2) gain (loss) on disposal of the segment.
    c. Both components are reported net of applicable taxes in a section entitled Discontinued Operations, which follows income from continuing operations.

Extraordinary Items

25. **Extraordinary items** are events and transactions that meet two conditions: (a) unusual in nature and (b) infrequent in occurrence.
    a. To be **"unusual,"** the item should be abnormal and only incidentally related to customary activities of the entity.
    b. To be **"infrequent,"** the item should not be reasonably expected to recur in the foreseeable future.

c.   Extraordinary items are reported net of taxes in a separate section of the income statement immediately below discontinued operations.

Changes in Accounting Principle

26.   A **change in an accounting principle** occurs when the principle used in the current year is different from the one used in the preceding year. Companies report most changes in accounting principle retroactively. That is, they report both the current period and previous periods using the new principle.

Income Statement with Nontypical Items

27.   A partial income statement showing the additional sections and the material items not typical of regular operations is as follows:

Income Statement (partial)

Income before income taxes		$XXX
Income tax expense		XXX
Income from continuing operations		XXX
Discontinued operations:		
Loss from operations of discontinued segment, net of $XXX income tax savings	$XXX	
Gain on disposal of segment, net of $XXX income taxes	XXX	XXX
Income before extraordinary item		XXX
Extraordinary item:		
Gain or loss, net of $XXX income taxes		XXX
Net Income		$XXX

28.   **Comprehensive income** includes all changes in stockholders' equity during a period except those resulting from investments by stockholders and distributions to stockholders.

Quality of Earnings

29.   (S.O. 7) In evaluating the financial performance of a company, the quality of a company's earnings is of extreme importance to analysts. A company that has a high **quality of earnings** provides full and transparent information that will not confuse or mislead users of financial statements.

30.   Variations among companies in the application of generally accepted accounting principles— **alternative accounting methods**—may hamper comparability and reduce quality of earnings.

31.   In recent years, many companies have been also reporting a second measure of income called **pro forma income**—which excludes items that the company thinks are unusual or nonrecurring. Because many companies have abused the flexibility that pro forma numbers allow, it is an area that will probably result in new rule-making.

The Navigator

DEMONSTRATION PROBLEM No. 1 (S.O. 5)

The condensed financial statements of Carpenter Company for the years 2011 and 2010 are presented below:

CARPENTER COMPANY
Balance Sheet
December 31

Assets

	(In thousands)	
	2011	**2010**
Current assets		
Cash and short-term investments	$ 276	$ 232
Accounts receivable (net)	523	379
Inventories	438	382
Prepaid expenses	97	81
Total current assets	1,334	1,074
Property, plant and equipment (net)	3,251	2,799
Intangibles and other assets	177	251
Total assets	$4,762	$4,124

Liabilities and Stockholders' Equity

	2011	**2010**
Current liabilities	$1,994	$1,621
Long-term liabilities	793	752
Stockholders' equity	1,975	1,751
Total liabilities and stockholders' equity	$4,762	$4,124

CARPENTER COMPANY
Income Statement
For the Year Ended December 31

	(In thousands)	
	2011	**2010**
Revenues	$5,194	$4,873
Expenses		
Cost of goods sold	2,596	2,364
Selling and administrative expenses	1,963	1,732
Interest expense	52	46
Total expenses	4,611	4,142
Income before income taxes	583	731
Income tax expense	175	219
Net income	$ 408	$ 512

Instructions
Compute the following ratios for Carpenter for 2011 and 2010.

(a) Current ratio.

(b) Receivables turnover
     (Receivables 12/31/09, $373).

(c) Profit margin ratio.

(d) Rate of return on assets
     (Assets 12/31/09, $3,926).

(e) Return on common stockholders' equity
     (Equity 12/31/09, $1,492).

(f) Debt to total assets

(g) Times interest earned.

(h) Acid-test ratio.

(i) Asset turnover.

The
Navigator

SOLUTION TO DEMONSTRATION PROBLEM

		2011	**2010**
(a)	Current ratio:		
	$1,334 ÷ $1,994 =	.67 : 1	
	$1,074 ÷ $1,621 =		.66 : 1
(b)	Receivables turnover:		
	$5,194 ÷ [($523 + $379) ÷ 2] =	11.52 times	
	$4,873 ÷ [($379 + $373) ÷ 2] =		12.96 times
(c)	Profit margin ratio:		
	$408 ÷ $5,194 =	7.9%	
	$512 ÷ $4,873 =		10.5%
(d)	Rate of return on assets:		
	$408 ÷ [$4,762 + $4,124) ÷ 2] =	9.2%	
	$512 ÷ [$4,124 + $3,926) ÷ 2] =		12.7%
(e)	Return on common stockholders' equity:		
	$408 ÷ [($1,975 + $1,751) ÷ 2] =	21.9%	
	$512 ÷ [($1,751 + $1,492) ÷ 2] =		31.6%
(f)	Debt to total assets:		
	$2,787 ÷ $4,762 =	58.5%	
	$2,373 ÷ $4,124 =		57.5%
(g)	Times interest earned:		
	($583 + $52) ÷ $52 =	12.21 times	
	($731 + $46) ÷ $46 =		16.89 times
(h)	Acid-test ratio:		
	($276 + $523) ÷ $1,994 =	.40 : 1	
	($232 + $379) ÷ $1,621 =		.38 : 1
(i)	Asset turnover:		
	$5,194 ÷ [($4,762 + $4,124) ÷ 2] =	1.17 times	
	$4,873 ÷ [($4,124 + $3,926) ÷ 2] =		1.21 times

DEMONSTRATION PROBLEM No. 2 (S.O. 6)

The Julitta Company has income from continuing operations of $180,000 for the year ended December 31, 2011. It also has the following items (before considering income taxes): (1) an extraordinary flood loss of $37,000, and (2) a gain of $45,000 on the discontinuance of a division. Assume all items are subject to income taxes at a 30% tax rate.

Instructions
Prepare an income statement, beginning with income from continuing operations.

The Navigator

SOLUTION TO DEMONSTRATION PROBLEM

JULITTA COMPANY
Income Statement (partial)
For the Year Ended December 31, 2011

Income from continuing operations...	$180,000
Discontinued operations:	
Gain on disposal of division, net of $13,500 income taxes	31,500
Income before extraordinary item	211,500
Extraordinary item:	
Loss from flood, net of $11,100 taxes	(25,900)
Net income...	$185,600

REVIEW QUESTIONS AND EXERCISES

TRUE—FALSE

Indicate whether each of the following is true (T) or false (F) in the space provided.

_T_ 1. (S.O. 2) Comparative analysis may be made on an intracompany basis, an intercompany basis, and on the basis of industry averages.

_T_ 2. (S.O. 2) The three basic tools of analysis are horizontal analysis, vertical analysis, and ratio analysis.

_F_ 3. (S.O. 3) Trend analysis and vertical analysis mean the same thing.

_T_ 4. (S.O. 3) Horizontal analysis involves determining percentage increases or decreases in financial statement data over a period of time.

_F_ 5. (S.O. 3) A percentage change can be computed only if the base amount is zero or positive.

_T_ 6. (S.O. 4) In vertical analysis, the base amount in an income statement is usually net sales.

_F_ 7. (S.O. 5) A short-term creditor is primarily interested in the solvency of a company.

_T_ 8. (S.O. 5) A long-term creditor is interested in the profitability and solvency of a company.

_F_ 9. (S.O. 5) Profitability ratios measure the ability of the enterprise to survive over a long period of time.

_T_ 10. (S.O. 5) Liquidity ratios include the current ratio, the acid-test ratio, receivables turnover, and inventory turnover.

_F_ 11. (S.O. 5) Solvency ratios include debt to total assets, the price-earnings ratio, and times interest earned.

_F_ 12. (S.O. 5) The formula for the current ratio is current liabilities divided by current assets.

_T_ 13. (S.O. 5) The formula for the acid-test ratio is the sum of cash, short-term investments, and receivables (net) divided by current liabilities.

_T_ 14. (S.O. 5) The receivables turnover ratio indicates how quickly receivables can be converted to cash.

_F_ 15. (S.O. 5) The average days to sell inventory is computed by multiplying the inventory turnover ratio by 365.

___F___ 16.   (S.O. 5)   The formula for the profit margin ratio is net income divided by average assets.

___F___ 17.   (S.O. 5)   The asset turnover ratio is an overall measure of profitability.

___T___ 18.   (S.O. 5)   Preferred dividend requirements must be subtracted from net income when computing the rate of return on common stockholders' equity.

___F___ 19.   (S.O. 5)   Trading on the equity at a gain means that the company's rate of return on total assets is less than the rate of interest paid for borrowed money.

___T___ 20.   (S.O. 5)   The payout ratio measures the percentage of earnings distributed in the form of cash dividends.

___F___ 21.   (S.O. 6) The phasing out of a product line because of a changing market or technological improvements is considered a disposal of a segment.

___T___ 22.   (S.O. 6) When the disposal of a significant component occurs, the income statement should report both income from continuing operations and income (loss) from discontinued operations.

___F___ 23.   (S.O. 6) Extraordinary items are changes in accounting principles that are infrequent in occurrence.

___F___ 24.   (S.O. 6) An employee labor strike would be considered an extraordinary item.

___T___ 25.   (S.O. 6) Extraordinary items are reported net of applicable taxes in a separate section of the income statement.

___T___ 26.   (S.O. 6) A change from the declining-balance method of depreciation to the straight-line method would be considered a change in accounting principle.

___T___ 27.   (S.O. 6) Companies report most changes in accounting principle retroactively.

The Navigator

MULTIPLE CHOICE

Circle the letter that best answers each of the following statements.

1. (S.O. 1) Comparisons of data within a company are an example of the following compara-
    tive basis:
    a. Industry averages.
    b. Intercompany.
    c. Intracompany.
    d. None of the above.

2. (S.O. 3) Horizontal analysis is also known as:
    a. trend analysis.
    b. vertical analysis.
    c. ratio analysis.
    d. common-size analysis.

3. (S.O. 3) Silva Corporation reported net sales of $200,000, $350,000, and $450,000 in the
    years 2009, 2010, and 2011 respectively. If 2009 is the base year, what is the trend
    percentage for 2011?
    a. 129%.
    b. 135%.
    c. 164%.
    d. 225%.

4. (S.O. 3) Evans Enterprises reported current assets of $50,000 at December 31, 2010 and
    $40,000 at December 31, 2011. If 2010 is the base year, this is a percentage increase
    (decrease) of:
    a. (25%).
    b. (20%).
    c. 25%.
    d. 80%.

5. (S.O. 4) When performing vertical analysis, the base amount for administrative expense is
    generally:
    a. administrative expense in a previous year.
    b. net sales.
    c. gross profit.
    d. fixed assets.

6. (S.O. 4) When performing vertical analysis, the base amount for cash is:
    a. Cash in a previous-year balance sheet.
    b. Total current assets.
    c. Total liabilities.
    d. Total assets.

7. (S.O. 4) Vertical analysis facilitates comparison of:
    a. companies of different size in the same industry.
    b. the income statement to the balance sheet.
    c. different years for the same company.
    d. more than one of the above.

8.   (S.O. 5) A ratio can be expressed as a:
    a.   percentage.
    b.   rate.
    c.   proportion.
    d.   all of the above.

9.   (S.O. 5) What type of ratios best measure the short-term ability of the enterprise to pay its maturing obligations and to meet unexpected needs for cash?
    a.   Leverage.
    b.   Solvency.
    c.   Profitability.
    d.   Liquidity.

10.   (S.O. 5) Profitability ratios measure an enterprise's:
    a.   ability to survive over a long period of time.
    b.   short-term ability to meet its obligations.
    c.   income or operating success for a given period of time.
    d.   short-term ability to meet unexpected needs for cash.

11.   (S.O. 5) Which of the following is **not** a liquidity ratio?
    a.   Acid-test ratio.
    b.   Inventory turnover.
    c.   Payout ratio.
    d.   Receivables turnover.

12.   (S.O. 5) The acid-test ratio is also known as the:
    a.   current ratio.
    b.   quick ratio.
    c.   fast ratio.
    d.   times interest earned ratio.

13.   (S.O. 5) Cash, marketable securities, and receivables (net) are included in the acid-test ratio because they are:
    a.   highly liquid.
    b.   not readily saleable.
    c.   not transferable to others.
    d.   included in the current asset section.

14.   (S.O. 5) Avanti Corporation had beginning inventory $50,000, cost of goods purchased $350,000, and ending inventory $100,000. What was Avanti's inventory turnover?
    a.   3 times.
    b.   4 times.
    c.   5.33 times.
    d.   6 times.

15.   (S.O. 5) The average net receivables for Merchant Company was $40,000, and net credit sales were $400,000. What was the average collection period?
    a.   10 days.
    b.   36.5 days.
    c.   70 days.
    d.   Cannot be computed from the information given.

16. (S.O. 5) Reams Corporation reported net income $36,000, net sales $300,000, and average assets $600,000 for 2011. The 2011 profit margin was:
    a. 6%.
    b. 12%.
    c. 50%.
    d. 200%.

17. (S.O. 5) Perez Company reports the following amounts for 2011:

Net income	$ 100,000
Average stockholders' equity	1,000,000
Preferred dividends	28,000
Par value preferred stock	200,000

    The 2011 rate of return on common stockholders' equity is:
    a. 7.2%.
    b. 9.0%.
    c. 10.0%.
    d. 12.5%.

18. (S.O. 5) The debt to total assets ratio:
    a. is a solvency ratio.
    b. is computed by dividing total assets by total debt.
    c. measures the total assets provided by stockholders.
    d. is a profitability ratio.

19. (S.O. 5) In 2011 Johnson Corporation reported income from operations $225,000, interest expense $75,000, and income tax expense $120,000. Johnson's times interest earned ratio was:
    a. 1.4 times.
    b. 2.5 times.
    c. 3 times.
    d. 4 times.

20. (S.O. 6) The Heather Corporation has income before income taxes of $300,000 and an extraordinary loss from a hurricane of $100,000. Both the extraordinary loss and taxable income are subject to a 30% tax rate. The extraordinary loss should be reported as follows:
    a. Extraordinary loss from hurricane—$100,000.
    b. Extraordinary loss from hurricane, net of $30,000 income tax loss—$130,000.
    c. Extraordinary loss from hurricane, net of $60,000 income tax loss—$160,000.
    d. Extraordinary loss from hurricane, net of $30,000 income tax savings—$70,000.

21. (S.O. 6) A loss from the disposal of a segment of a business enterprise should be reported separately in the income statement:
    a. after cumulative effect of changes in accounting principle and before extraordinary items.
    b. before cumulative effect of changes in accounting principle and after extraordinary items.
    c. after extraordinary items and cumulative effect of changes in accounting principle.
    d. before extraordinary items and cumulative effect of changes in accounting principle.

22.   (S.O. 6)   Galileo, Inc. decides on January 1 to discontinue its telescope manufacturing division.   On July 1, the division's assets with a book value of $420,000 are sold for $300,000.   Operating income from January 1 to June 30 for the division amounted to $50,000.   Ignoring income taxes, what total amount should be reported on Galileo's income statement for the current year under the caption, Discontinued Operations?
      a. $50,000.
      b. $70,000 loss.
      c. $120,000 loss.
      d. $170,000.

23.   (S.O. 6)   An extraordinary item is one that:
      a.   occurs infrequently and is uncontrollable in nature.
      b.   occurs infrequently and is unusual in nature.
      c.   is material and is unusual in nature.
      d.   is material and is uncontrollable in nature.

24.   (S.O. 6)   An earthquake destroyed Hooke Company's operating plant, resulting in a loss of $2,200,000.   Hooke's income tax rate is 30%.   In Hooke's income statement, the net effect of the extraordinary loss should be reported at:
      a. $0.
      b. $660,000.
      c. $1,540,000.
      d. $2,200,000.

25.   (S.O. 6)   When there has been a change in an accounting principle,
      a.   the old principle should be used in reporting the results of operations for the current year.
      b.   the cumulative effect of the change should be reported in the current year's retained earnings statement.
      c.   the change should be reported retroactively.
      d.   the new principle should be used in reporting the results of operations of the current year, but their is no change to prior years.

The
Navigator

MATCHING—TERMS

Match each term with its definition by writing the appropriate letter in the space provided. The definitions may be used more than once.

		Terms
_c_	1.	Liquidity ratios.
_i_	2.	Trend analysis.
_f_	3.	Profitability ratios.
_h_	4.	Common size analysis.
_j_	5.	Solvency ratios.
_i_	6.	Horizontal analysis.
_A_	7.	Trading on the equity.
_H_	8.	Vertical analysis.
_d_	9.	Ratio.
_A_	10.	Leveraging.
_g_	11.	Change in accounting principle.
_B_	12.	Discontinued operations.
_e_	13.	Extraordinary item.

Definitions

a. Borrowing money at a rate of interest lower than the rate of return earned by using the borrowed money.

b. The disposal of a significant segment of the business such as the cessation of an entire activity or the elimination of a major class of customers.

c. Measures of the short-term ability of the enterprise to pay its maturing obligations and to meet unexpected needs for cash.

d. An expression of the mathematical relationship between one quantity and another that may be expressed as a percentage, a rate, or a simple proportion.

e. Events and transactions that are unusual in nature and infrequent in occurrence.

f. Measures of the income or operating success of an enterprise for a given period of time.

g. The use of a principle in the current year that is different from the one used in the preceding year.

h. A technique for evaluating financial statement data that expresses each item within a financial statement as a percent of a base amount within the statement.

i A technique for evaluating a series of financial statement data over a period of time to determine the amount and/or percentage increase (decrease) that has taken place, expressed as either an amount or a percentage.

j. Measures of the ability of the enterprise to survive over a long period of time.

MATCHING—RATIOS

Match each ratio with its formula by writing the appropriate letter in the space provided.

	Ratios		Formulas
_K_	1. Current ratio.	a.	$\dfrac{\text{Net income}}{\text{Net sales}}$
_H_	2. Inventory turnover.	b.	$\dfrac{\text{Income before income taxes and interest expense}}{\text{Interest expense}}$
_M_	3. Return on assets.	c.	$\dfrac{\text{Net sales}}{\text{Average assets}}$
_G_	4. Price-earnings ratio.		
_b_	5. Times interest earned.	d.	$\dfrac{\text{Cash + short-term investments + receivables (net)}}{\text{Current liabilities}}$
_d_	6. Acid-test ratio.	e.	$\dfrac{\text{Cash dividends}}{\text{Net income}}$
_a_	7. Profit margin.		
_f_	8. Return on common stock-holders' equity.	f.	$\dfrac{\text{Net income}}{\text{Average common stockholders' equity}}$
_e_	9. Payout ratio.	g.	$\dfrac{\text{Market price of stock}}{\text{Earnings per share}}$
_J_	10. Receivables turnover.	h.	$\dfrac{\text{Cost of goods sold}}{\text{Average inventory}}$
_C_	11. Asset turnover.		
_I_	12. Earnings per share.	i.	$\dfrac{\text{Net income}}{\text{Weighted average common shares outstanding}}$
_L_	13. Debt to total assets.	j.	$\dfrac{\text{Net credit sales}}{\text{Average net receivables}}$
		k.	$\dfrac{\text{Current assets}}{\text{Current liabilities}}$
		l.	$\dfrac{\text{Total debt}}{\text{Total assets}}$
		m.	$\dfrac{\text{Net income}}{\text{Average assets}}$

The Navigator

EXERCISES

EX. 18-1   (S.O. 3) Using horizontal analysis, compute the percentage increase or decrease for Stevens Co. for each current asset and for current assets in total.

Current Assets	2011	2010	Increase or (Decrease) Amount	Percentage
Cash	$ 50,000	$ 40,000	10,000	25%
Receivables (net)	54,000	72,000	(18,000)	25%
Inventories	90,000	100,000	(10,000)	(10%)
Prepaid expenses	42,000	35,000	7000	20%
Total	$236,000	$247,000	(11,000)	4%

EX. 18-2   (S.O. 4) Using vertical analysis, prepare a common-size income statement for Larry Budd, using net sales as the base.

LARRY BUDD CORPORATION
Condensed Income Statement
For the Year Ended December 2011

	Amount	Percent
Net sales	$780,000	100%
Cost of goods sold	470,000	60%
Gross profit	310,000	40%
Operating expenses	140,000	18%
Income from operations	170,000	22%
Interest expense	16,000	2%
Income before income taxes	154,000	20%
Income tax expense	62,000	8%
Net income	$ 92,000	12%

EX. 18-3 (S.O. 5) Letterman Corporation decides to expand its operations by issuing $500,000 of 10% bonds. As a result of the additional financing, income from operations is expected to increase $70,000. Financial data prior to and after the expansion are as follows:

	Before Expansion	After Expansion
Total assets	$2,000,000	$2,514,000
Total liabilities	700,000	1,200,000
Total common stock equity	1,300,000	1,314,000
	$2,000,000	$2,514,000
Income from operations	$ 550,000	$ 620,000
Interest expense	50,000	100,000
Income before income taxes	500,000	520,000
Income tax expense (30%)	150,000	156,000
Net income	$ 350,000	$ 364,000

Instructions
Compute the following ratios before and after expansion. Assume year-end balance sheet amounts are representative of average balances.
1. Return on assets.
2. Return on common stockholders' equity.
3. Debt to total assets.
4. Times interest earned.

Ratio	Before Expansion	After Expansion
1. Return on assets.		
2. Return on common stockholders' equity.		
3. Debt to total assets.		
4. Times interest earned.		

EX. 18-4   (S.O. 6) On December 31, 2011 Fortcamp Company's controller accumulated the following data before considering income taxes of 30%.

Extraordinary gains resulting from a condemnation award by a state government $50,000.

Loss on disposal of Division B, $60,000.

Income before income taxes $500,000.

Instructions

Prepare a partial income statement beginning with income before income taxes.

FORTCAMP COMPANY
Income Statement (partial)
For the Year Ended December 31, 2011

The Navigator

SOLUTIONS TO REVIEW QUESTIONS AND EXERCISES

TRUE-FALSE

1.   (T)
2.   (T)
3.   (F)   Trend analysis and horizontal analysis mean the same thing.
4.   (T)
5.   (F)   A percentage change can be computed only if the base year amount is positive.
6.   (T)
7.   (F)   A short-term creditor is primarily interested in the liquidity of a company.
8.   (T)
9.   (F)   Profitability ratios measure the income or operating success of the enterprise for a given period of time.
10.   (T)
11.   (F)   The price-earnings ratio is a profitability ratio.
12.   (F)   The current ratio is current assets divided by current liabilities.
13.   (T)
14.   (T)
15.   (F)   The average days to sell inventory is computed by dividing 365 by the inventory turnover ratio.
16.   (F)   The formula for the profit margin ratio is net income ÷ net sales.
17.   (F)   The asset turnover ratio measures how efficiently a company uses its assets to generate sales. It is the return on assets ratio that is an overall measure of profitability.
18.   (T)
19.   (F)   Trading on the equity at a gain means that the company's rate of return on total assets exceeds the rate of interest paid for borrowed money.
20.   (T)
21.   (F)   A disposal of a segment refers to the disposal of a significant segment of the business such as the cessation of an entire activity or the elimination of a major class of customers.
22.   (T)
23.   (F)   Extraordinary items are events and transactions that are: (a) unusual in nature, and (b) infrequent in occurrence.
24.   (F)   Losses attributable to labor strikes are not considered extraordinary.
25.   (T)
26.   (T)
27.   (T)

MULTIPLE CHOICE

1. (c)   Comparisons of data within a company are an example of the intracompany basis of comparison.

2. (a)   Vertical analysis (b) is also known as common-size analysis (d). Ratio analysis (c) is different from both horizontal analysis and vertical analysis.

3. (d)   In trend analysis, the base year is assigned a value of 100%. The amounts for the other years are divided by the amount in the base year and expressed as a percentage. The percentage for 2011 is 225% ($450,000 ÷ $200,000).

4. (b)   Current assets decreased by $10,000 from $50,000 to $40,000. This is a percentage decrease of 20% ($10,000 ÷ $50,000).

5. (b)   When performing vertical analysis, the base amount for income statement items is that year's net sales. Answer (a), administrative expense in a previous year, would be the correct answer for horizontal analysis.

6. (d)   When performing vertical analysis, the base amount for balance sheet items is that year's total assets. Answer (a), cash in a previous-year balance sheet, would be the correct answer for horizontal analysis.

7. (a)   Vertical analysis would facilitate comparison of two companies in the same industry by making companies of different sizes comparable. Horizontal analysis would be best for comparing different years for the same company (c).

8. (d)   A ratio expresses the mathematical relationship between one quantity and another, and can be expressed as either a percentage, a rate, or a proportion.

9. (d)   Solvency ratios (b) measure the ability of the enterprise to survive over a long period of time. Profitability ratios (c) measure the operating success (ability to earn income) of the enterprise for a given period of time. Leverage ratios (a) are not a type of ratio.

10. (c)   Choice (a) refers to solvency ratios. Choices (b) and (d) pertain to liquidity ratios.

11. (c)   The payout ratio is a profitability ratio.

12. (b)   The acid-test ratio is also known as the quick ratio.

13. (a)   The acid-test ratio measures a company's immediate ability to pay its short-term debt. The assets in the numerator are highly liquid (quickly convertible into cash) and therefore are immediately available to pay short-term debt.

14. (b)   Cost of goods sold is $300,000 ($50,000 + $350,000 - $100,000). Average inventory is $75,000 [($50,000 + $100,000) ÷ 2]. Thus, the ratio is 4 times ($300,000 ÷ $75,000).

15. (b)   Receivables turnover is 10 times ($400,000 ÷ $40,000). The average collection period is 36.5 days (365 ÷ 10).

16.   (b)   The profit margin is net income ($36,000) divided by net sales ($300,000) or 12%.

17.   (b)   The basic computation for the rate of return on common stockholders' equity is net income divided by average common stockholders' equity. When preferred stock is present, preferred dividends must be subtracted from the numerator and the par value of preferred stock must be subtracted from the denominator.

The result is: $\dfrac{\$100,000 \ - \ \$28,000}{\$1,000,000 \ - \ \$200,000} = 9\%.$

18.   (a)   The debt to total assets ratio is computed by dividing total debt by total assets (b). It measures the total assets provided by creditors (c), and it is not a profitability ratio (d).

19.   (d)   The formula for times interest earned is income before income taxes and interest expense divided by interest expense. The numerator is $300,000 ($225,000 + $75,000). Thus, the times interest earned is 4 ($300,000 ÷ $75,000).

20.   (d)   The tax rate of 30% is applied to income before income taxes of $300,000 to show income taxes of $90,000, and the extraordinary item of $100,000 is reported net of the $30,000 tax savings.

21.   (d)   A loss from the disposal of a segment of a business enterprise should be reported separately immediately following income from continuing operations and before the other additional sections.

22.   (b)   Within the "Discontinued Operations" section both the operating income and the loss on the disposal are reported ($120,000 loss - $50,000 income from operations = $70,000 loss).

23.   (b)   An extraordinary item is one that occurs infrequently and is unusual in nature.

24.   (c)   Extraordinary items should be reported net of income taxes [$2,200,000 X 1 - .30)].

25.   (c)   When there has been a change in an accounting principle the change should be reported retroactively.

MATCHING—TERMS

1.	c	8.	h
2.	i	9.	d
3.	f	10.	a
4.	h	11.	g
5.	j	12.	b
6.	i	13.	e
7.	a		

MATCHING—RATIOS

1.	k	8.	f
2.	h	9.	e
3.	m	10.	j
4.	g	11.	c
5.	b	12.	i
6.	d	13.	l
7.	a		

EXERCISES

EX. 18-1

Current Assets	2011	2010	Increase or (Decrease) Amount	Percentage
Cash	$ 50,000	$ 40,000	$ 10,000	25.0%
Receivables (net)	54,000	72,000	(18,000)	(25.0%)
Inventories	90,000	100,000	(10,000)	(10.0%)
Prepaid expenses	42,000	35,000	7,000	20.0%
Total	$236,000	$247,000	$(11,000)	(4.5%)

EX. 18-2

LARRY BUDD CORPORATION
Condensed Income Statement
For the Year Ended December 31, 2011

	Amount	Percent
Net sales	$780,000	100.0%
Cost of goods sold	470,000	60.3%
Gross profit	310,000	39.7%
Operating expenses	140,000	17.9%
Income from operations	170,000	21.8%
Interest expense	16,000	2.1%
Income before income taxes	154,000	19.7%
Income tax expense	62,000	7.9%
Net income	$ 92,000	11.8%

EX. 18-3

Ratio	Before Expansion	After Expansion
1. Return on assets.	$\dfrac{\$350,000}{\$2,000,000} = 17.5\%$	$\dfrac{\$364,000}{\$2,514,000} = 14.5\%$
2. Return on common stockholders' equity.	$\dfrac{\$350,000}{\$1,300,000} = 26.9\%$	$\dfrac{\$364,000}{\$1,314,000} = 27.7\%$
3. Debt to total assets.	$\dfrac{\$700,000}{\$2,000,000} = 35\%$	$\dfrac{\$1,200,000}{\$2,514,000} = 47.7\%$
4. Times interest earned.	$\dfrac{\$500,000 + \$50,000}{\$50,000} = 11 \text{ times}$	$\dfrac{\$520,000 + \$100,000}{\$100,000} = 6.2 \text{ times}$

EX. 18-4

FORTCAMP COMPANY
Income Statement (partial)
For the Year Ended December 31, 2011

Income before income taxes	$500,000
Income tax expense (30%)	150,000
Income from continuing operations	350,000
Discontinued operations	
Loss on disposal of Division B, net of $18,000 income tax saving	(42,000)
Income before extraordinary item	308,000
Extraordinary item	
Condemnation award, net of $15,000 income tax expense	35,000
Net income	$343,000

Chapter 19

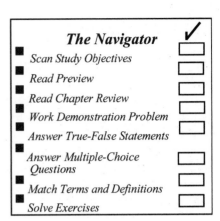

The Navigator ✓
- Scan Study Objectives ☐
- Read Preview ☐
- Read Chapter Review ☐
- Work Demonstration Problem ☐
- Answer True-False Statements ☐
- Answer Multiple-Choice Questions ☐
- Match Terms and Definitions ☐
- Solve Exercises ☐

MANAGERIAL ACCOUNTING

CHAPTER STUDY OBJECTIVES

After studying this chapter, you should be able to:
1. Explain the distinguishing features of managerial accounting.
2. Identify the three broad functions of management.
3. Define the three classes of manufacturing costs.
4. Distinguish between product and period costs.
5. Explain the difference between a merchandising and a manufacturing income statement.
6. Indicate how cost of goods manufactured is determined.
7. Explain the difference between a merchandising and a manufacturing balance sheet.
8. Identify trends in managerial accounting.

The Navigator

PREVIEW OF CHAPTER 19

Beginning with this chapter, we turn our attention to issues such as the costs of material, labor, and overhead and the relationship between costs and profits. The remaining chapters in this textbook focus primarily on the preparation of reports for internal users, such as the managers and officers of a company. These reports are the principal product of managerial accounting. The content and organization of this chapter are as follows:

Managerial Accounting			
Managerial Accounting Basics	**Managerial Cost Concepts**	**Manufacturing Costs in Financial Statements**	**Managerial Accounting Today**
▶ Comparing managerial and financial accounting	▶ Manufacturing costs	▶ Income statement	▶ Service-industry trends
▶ Management functions	▶ Product vs. period costs	▶ Balance sheet	▶ Managerial accounting practices
▶ Business ethics		▶ Cost concepts – A review	

The Navigator

CHAPTER REVIEW

Managerial Accounting Basics

1.   (S.O. 1) **Managerial accounting** is a field of accounting that provides economic and financial information for managers and other internal users. Managerial accounting applies to all types of businesses—service, merchandising, and manufacturing—and to all forms of business organizations—proprietorships, partnerships and corporations. Not-for-profit entities as well as profit-oriented enterprises need managerial accounting.

Comparing Managerial and Financial Accounting

2.   There are both similarities and differences between managerial and financial accounting.
     a.   Both fields of accounting deal with the economic events of a business and require that the results of that company's economic events be quantified and communicated to interested parties.
     b.   The principal differences are the (1) primary users of reports, (2) types and frequency of reports, (3) purpose of reports, (4) content of reports, and (5) verification process.

3.   The role of the managerial accountant has changed in recent years. Whereas in the past their primary concern used to be collecting and reporting costs to management, today they also evaluate how well the company is using its resources and providing information to cross-functional teams comprised of personnel from production, operations, marketing, engineering, and quality control.

Management Functions

4.   (S.O. 2) Managers perform three broad functions within an organization:
     a.   Planning requires managers to look ahead and to establish objectives.
     b.   Directing involves coordinating a company's diverse activities and human resources to produce a smooth-running operation.
     c.   Controlling is the process of keeping the firm's activities on track.

Organizational Structure

5.   In order to assist in carrying out management functions, most companies prepare **organization charts** to show the interrelationships of activities and the delegation of authority and responsibility with the company.

     Stockholders own the corporation but manage the company through a **board of directors**. The **chief executive officer (CEO)** has overall responsibility for managing the business. The **chief financial officer (CFO)** is responsible for all of the accounting and finance issues the company faces. The CFO is supported by the **controller** and the **treasurer**.

Business Ethics

6.   All employees are expected to act ethically in their business activities and an increasing number of organizations provide their employees with a code of business ethics.

7.   Due to many fraudulent activities, U.S. Congress passed the Sarbanes-Oxley Act of 2002 which resulted in many implications for managers and accountants. CEOs and CFOs must certify the fairness of financial statements, top management must certify they maintain an adequate system of internal controls, and other matters.

Manufacturing Costs

8. (S.O. 3) **Manufacturing** consists of activities and processes that convert raw materials into finished goods.

9. Manufacturing costs are typically classified as either (a) direct materials, (b) direct labor or (c) manufacturing overhead.

10. **Direct materials** are raw materials that can be physically and conveniently associated with the finished product during the manufacturing process. **Indirect materials** are materials that (a) do not physically become a part of the finished product or (b) cannot be traced because their physical association with the finished product is too small in terms of cost. Indirect materials are accounted for as part of manufacturing overhead.

11. The work of factory employees that can be physically and conveniently associated with converting raw materials into finished goods is considered **direct labor**. In contrast, the wages of maintenance people, timekeepers, and supervisors are usually identified as **indirect labor** because their efforts have no physical association with the finished product, or it is impractical to trace the costs to the goods produced. Indirect labor is classified as manufacturing overhead.

12. **Manufacturing overhead** consists of costs that are indirectly associated with the manufacture of the finished product. Manufacturing overhead includes items such as indirect materials, indirect labor, depreciation on factory buildings and machines, and insurance, taxes, and maintenance on factory facilities.

Product Versus Period Costs

13. (S.O. 4) **Product costs** are costs that are a necessary and integral part of producing the finished product. **Period costs** are costs that are matched with the revenue of a specific time period rather than included as part of the cost of a salable product. These are nonmanufacturing costs. Period costs include selling and administrative expenses.

Manufacturing Income Statement

14. (S.O. 5) The income statements of a merchandising company and a manufacturing com-pany differ in the cost of goods sold section.

15. The cost of goods sold section of the income statement for a manufacturing company shows:

Beginning Finished Goods Inventory	+	Cost of Goods Manufactured	−	Ending Finished Goods Inventory	=	Cost of Goods Sold

Determining Cost of Goods Manufactured

16. (S.O. 6) The determination of the cost of goods manufactured consists of the following:

    a.

Beginning Work in Process Inventory	+	Total Current Manufacturing Costs	=	Total Cost of Work in Process

    b.

Total Cost of Work in Process	−	Ending Work in Process Inventory	=	Cost of Goods Manufactured

17. The costs assigned to the beginning work in process inventory are the manufacturing costs incurred in the prior period.

18. Total manufacturing costs is the sum of the direct materials costs, direct labor costs, and manufacturing overhead incurred in the current period.

19. Because a number of accounts are involved, the determination of costs of goods manufactured is presented in a Cost of Goods Manufactured Schedule. The cost of goods manufactured schedule shows each of the cost factors above. The format for the schedule is:

Beginning work in process		$XXXX
Direct materials used	$XXXX	
Direct labor...	XXXX	
Manufacturing overhead	XXXX	
Total manufacturing costs...		XXXX
Total cost of work in process		XXXX
Less: Ending work in process		XXXX
Cost of goods manufactured...		$XXXX

Manufacturing Balance Sheet

20. (S.O. 7) The balance sheet for a manufacturing company may have three inventory accounts: finished goods inventory, work in process inventory, and raw materials inventory.

21. The manufacturing inventories are reported in the current asset section of the balance sheet.
    a. The inventories are generally listed in the order of their expected realization in cash.
    b. Thus, finished goods inventory is listed first.

22. Each step in the accounting cycle for a merchandising company is applicable to a manufacturing company.
    a. For example, prior to preparing financial statements, adjusting entries are required.
    b. Adjusting entries are essentially the same as those of a merchandising company.
    c. The closing entries for a manufacturing company are also similar to those of a merchandising company.

Contemporary Developments

23. (S.O. 8) Contemporary developments in managerial accounting involve: (a) a U.S. economy that has in general shifted toward an emphasis on providing services, rather than goods; and (b) efforts to manage the value chain and supply chain.

24. Many companies have significantly lowered inventory levels and costs using **just-in-time (JIT)** inventory methods. Under a just-in-time method, goods are manufactured or purchased just in time for use. In addition, many companies have installed **total quality management (TQM)** systems to reduce defects in finished products.

25. **Activity-based costing (ABC)** is a popular method for allocating overhead that obtains more accurate product costs. The **theory of constraints** is a specific approach used to identify and manage constraints in order to achieve the company goals. The **balanced scorecard** is a performance-measurement approach that uses both financial and nonfinancial measures to evaluate all aspects of a company's operations in an integrated fashion.

The
Navigator

DEMONSTRATION PROBLEM (S.O. 6)

Indicate the missing amounts for the incomplete manufacturing costs, expenses, and selling data for the following four cases:

	Case 1	Case 2	Case 3	Case 4
Direct Materials	$ 7,250	$ 5,500	$ 4,000	Q *[6300]*
Direct Labor	1,500	G *[6900]*	3,600	5,000
Manufacturing Overhead	3,700	11,000	L *[5400]*	5,700
Total Manufacturing Costs	A *[12450]*	23,400	13,000	17,000
Beginning Work in Process Inventory	3,200	H *[2000]*	2,600	R *[4700]*
Ending Work in Process Inventory	B *[1250]*	7,000	1,100	1,900
Sales	24,000	23,000	21,700	S *[46090]*
Sales Discounts	2,300	5,000	M *[2750]*	1,400
Cost of Goods Manufactured	14,400	18,400	N *[14500]*	19,800
Beginning Finished Goods Inventory	C *[5100]*	1,500	1,250	1,490
Goods Available for Sale	19,500	19,900	15,750	T
Cost of Goods Sold	D *[18200]*	14,500	O *[14450]*	U
Ending Finished Goods Inventory	1,300	I *[5400]*	1,300	2,000
Gross Profit	E *[3500]*	J *[3500]*	P *[4500]*	25,400
Operating Expenses	3,400	2,900	2,100	V
Net Income	F *[100]*	K *[600]*	2,400	2,700

The Navigator

SOLUTION TO DEMONSTRATION PROBLEM

A = $12,450 ($7,250 + $1,500 + $3,700).

B = $1,250 ($3,200 + $12,450 - $14,400).

C = $5,100 ($19,500 - $14,400).

D = $18,200 ($19,500 - $1,300).

E = $3,500 ($24,000 - $2,300 - $18,200).

F = $100 ($3,500 - $3,400).

G = $6,900 ($23,400 - $5,500 - $11,000).

H = $2,000 ($18,400 + $7,000 - $23,400).

I = $5,400 ($19,900 - $14,500).

J = $3,500 ($23,000 - $5,000 - $14,500).

K = $600 ($3,500 - $2,900).

L = $5,400 ($13,000 - $4,000 - $3,600).

M = $2,750 [$21,700 - ($14,450 + $4,500)].

N = $14,500 ($13,000 + $2,600 - $1,100).

O = $14,450 ($15,750 - $1,300).

P = $4,500 ($2,400 + $2,100).

Q = $6,300 ($17,000 - $5,000 - $5,700).

R = $4,700 ($19,800 - $17,000 + $1,900).

S = $46,090 ($25,400 + $19,290 + $1,400).

T = $21,290 ($19,800 + $1,490).

U = $19,290 ($21,290 - $2,000).

V = $22,700 ($25,400 - $2,700).

REVIEW QUESTIONS AND EXERCISES

TRUE—FALSE

Indicate whether each of the following is true (T) or false (F) in the space provided.

_____ 1. (S.O. 1) Managerial accounting is primarily concerned with managers and external users.

_____ 2. (S.O. 1) Managerial accountants assist management in evaluating how well the company is employing its resources.

_____ 3. (S.O. 2) Managerial reports are required to follow generally accepted accounting principles.

_____ 4. (S.O. 2) Planning involves coordinating the diverse activities and human resources of a company to produce a smooth running operation.

_____ 5. (S.O. 2) Control involves performance evaluation by management.

_____ 6. (S.O. 2) Directing involves coordinating the diverse activities and human resources of a company to produce a smooth running operation.

_____ 7. (S.O. 3) When the physical association of raw materials with the finished product is too small to trace in terms of cost they are usually classified as indirect materials.

_____ 8. (S.O. 3) The wages of maintenance employees, timekeepers, and supervisors are usually classified as direct labor.

_____ 9. (S.O. 3) Manufacturing overhead consists of any costs that are directly associated with the manufacture of the finished goods.

_____ 10. (S.O. 4) Product costs are also called inventoriable costs.

_____ 11. (S.O. 4) Period costs are costs that are matched with the revenue of a specific time period.

_____ 12. (S.O. 4) Product costs include selling and administrative expenses.

_____ 13. (S.O. 5) The three components in determining cost of goods sold in a manufacturing company are beginning finished goods inventory, cost of goods manufactured, and ending finished goods inventory.

_____ 14. (S.O. 5) Direct materials become a cost of the finished goods manufactured when they are acquired, not when they are used.

_____ 15. (S.O. 5) In a manufacturing company, the calculation of cost of goods sold is the beginning finished goods inventory plus the cost of goods manufactured less the ending finished goods inventory.

_____ 16. (S.O. 6) The sum of the direct materials costs, direct labor costs, and beginning work in process is the total manufacturing costs for the year.

_____ 17. (S.O. 6) Beginning work in process inventory plus total current manufacturing costs incurred less ending work in process inventory equals the cost of goods manufactured.

_____ 18. (S.O. 6) The costs assigned to beginning work in process inventory are based on the manufacturing costs incurred in the prior period.

_____ 19. (S.O. 7) Raw Materials Inventory shows the cost of completed goods on hand.

_____ 20. (S.O. 7) In a manufacturing company balance sheet, manufacturing inventories are reported in the current asset section in the order of their expected use in production.

The Navigator

MULTIPLE CHOICE

Circle the letter that best answers each of the following statements.

1. (S.O. 1) Which of the following would **not** describe managerial accounting reports?
    a. They are internal reports.
    b. They provide general purpose information for all users.
    c. They are issued as frequently as the need arises.
    d. The reporting standard is relevance to the decision to be made.

2. (S.O. 1) Financial and managerial accounting are similar in that both:
    a. have the same primary users.
    b. produce general-purpose reports.
    c. have reports that are prepared quarterly and annually.
    d. deal with the economic events of an enterprise.

3. (S.O. 2) The function of coordinating the diverse activities and human resources of a company to produce a smooth running operation is:
    a. planning.
    b. directing.
    c. controlling.
    d. accounting.

4. (S.O. 2) The function that pertains to keeping the activities of the enterprise on track is:
    a. planning.
    b. directing.
    c. controlling.
    d. accounting.

5. (S.O. 2) The function that involves looking ahead and establishing objectives by management is:
    a. planning.
    b. directing.
    c. controlling.
    d. accounting.

6. (S.O. 4) Direct materials are a:

	Product Cost	Period Cost
a.	No	Yes
b.	Yes	Yes
c.	No	No
d.	Yes	No

7. (S.O. 4) Direct labor is a(n):
    a. nonmanufacturing cost.
    b. indirect cost.
    c. product cost.
    d. period cost.

8. (S.O. 4) For a manufacturing company, which of the following is an example of a period cost rather than a product cost?
    a. Depreciation on factory equipment.
    b. Wages of salespersons.
    c. Wages of machine operators.
    d. Insurance on factory equipment.

9. (S.O. 4) Property taxes on a manufacturing plant are an element of:

	Product Cost	Period Cost
a.	Yes	No
b.	Yes	Yes
c.	No	Yes
d.	No	No

10. (S.O. 4) The salary of a plant manager would be considered a:

	Product Cost	Period Cost
a.	Yes	Yes
b.	Yes	No
c.	No	Yes
d.	No	No

11. (S.O. 5) For the year, Mahatma Company has cost of goods manufactured $325,000, beginning finished goods inventory $150,000, and ending finished goods inventory $175,000. The cost of goods sold is:
    a. $275,000.
    b. $300,000.
    c. $325,000.
    d. $350,000.

12. (S.O. 5) If the cost of goods manufactured is less than the cost of goods sold, which of the following is correct?
    a. Finished Goods Inventory has increased.
    b. Work in Process Inventory has increased.
    c. Finished Goods Inventory has decreased.
    d. Work in Process Inventory has decreased.

13. (S.O. 6) The account that shows the cost of production for those units that have been started in the manufacturing process, but that are **not** complete at the end of the accounting period is:
a. Raw Materials Inventory.
b. Work in Process Inventory.
c. Finished Goods Inventory.
d. Cost of Goods Sold.

14. (S.O. 6) Nehru Company has beginning and ending raw materials inventories of $32,000 and $40,000, respectively. If direct materials used were $130,000, what was the cost of raw materials purchased?
a. $130,000.
b. $140,000.
c. $122,000.
d. $138,000.

15. (S.O. 6) Ghindia Company has beginning and ending work in process inventories of $52,000 and $58,000 respectively. If total current manufacturing costs are $248,000, what is the total cost of work in process?
a. $300,000.
b. $306,000.
c. $242,000.
d. $254,000.

16. (S.O. 6) Mura Company has beginning work in process inventory of $72,000 and total current manufacturing costs of $318,000. If cost of goods manufactured is $320,000, what is the cost of the ending work in process inventory?
a. $60,000.
b. $74,000.
c. $80,000.
d. $70,000.

17. (S.O. 6) If the total manufacturing costs are greater than the cost of goods manufactured, which of the following is correct?
a. Work in Process Inventory has increased.
b. Finished Goods Inventory has increased.
c. Work in Process Inventory has decreased.
d. Finished Goods Inventory has decreased.

18. (S.O. 7) The inventory accounts that show the cost of completed goods on hand and the costs applicable to production that is only partially completed are, respectively
a. Work in Process Inventory and Raw Materials Inventory.
b. Finished Goods Inventory and Raw Materials Inventory.
c. Finished Goods Inventory and Work in Process Inventory.
d. Raw Materials Inventory and Work in Process Inventory.

19. (S.O. 7) In the current asset section of a balance sheet, manufacturing inventories are listed in the following sequence:

	Raw Materials Inventory	Work in Process Inventory	Finished Goods Inventory
a.	1	2	3
b.	2	3	1
c.	3	1	2
d.	3	2	1

20. (S.O. 8) When companies allocate overhead based on each product's use of activities in making the product, this is known as:
   a.   Just-in-time (JIT) inventory.
   b.   Value chain allocation.
   c.   Activity-based costing.
   d.   total quality management.

The
Navigator

MATCHING

Match each term with its definition by writing the appropriate letter in the space provided.

Terms		Definitions

Terms

_____ 1. Direct labor.

_____ 2. Period costs.

_____ 3. Indirect labor.

_____ 4. Managerial accounting.

_____ 5. Direct materials.

_____ 6. Product costs.

_____ 7. Indirect materials.

_____ 8. Manufacturing overhead.

_____ 9. Value chain.

_____ 10. Just-in-time inventory.

_____ 11. Activity-based costing.

_____ 12. Total quality management.

_____ 13. Balanced scorecard.

Definitions

a. Costs that are matched with the revenue of a specific time period and charged to expense as incurred.

b. A method of allocating overhead based on each product's use of activities in making the product.

c. A field of accounting that provides economic and financial information for managers and other internal users.

d. A performance-measurement approach that uses both financial and nonfinancial measures, tied to company objectives, to evaluate a company's operations in an integrated fashion.

e. Work of factory employees that has no physical association with the finished product, or it is impractical to trace the costs to the goods produced.

f. Systems implemented to reduce defects in finished products with the goal of achieving zero defects.

g. Manufacturing costs that are indirectly associated with the manufacture of the finished product.

h. All activities associated with providing a product or service.

i. The work of factory employees that can be physically and conveniently associated with converting raw materials into finished goods.

j. Raw materials that do not physically become part of the finished product or cannot be traced because their physical association with the finished product is too small.

k. Inventory system in which goods are manufactured or purchased just-in-time for use.

l. Costs that are a necessary and integral part of producing the finished product.

m. Raw materials that can be physically and conveniently associated with manufacturing the finished product.

The Navigator

EXERCISES

EX. 19-1   (S.O. 6) At the end of 2010, the following information pertains to Norman Company:

Factory repairs	$10,000
Factory utilities	8,000
Factory insurance	7,500
Factory depreciation	6,000
Factory property taxes	5,500
Indirect labor	9,000
Raw Materials Inventory	
January 1	15,000
December 31	20,000
Direct labor	25,000
Work in Process Inventory	
January 1	32,000
December 31	30,000
Purchases of raw materials	48,000

Instructions
Prepare a Cost of Goods Manufactured Schedule for Norman Company.

NORMAN COMPANY
Cost of Goods Manufactured Schedule
For the Year Ended December 31, 2010

EX. 19-2   (S.O. 3 and 4) The Svengooli Company specializes in manufacturing woodchuck traps. The company has a large number of orders to keep the factory production at 10,000 per month. Svengooli's monthly manufacturing costs and other expense data are as follows:

1.	Rent on factory equipment	$ 6,000
2.	Advertising for the traps	8,000
3.	Insurance on factory building	2,000
4.	Raw materials	24,000
5.	Supplies for the general office	500
6.	Wages for assembly line workers	39,700
7.	Depreciation on office equipment	800
8.	Miscellaneous factory materials	400
9.	Company president's salary	2,700
10.	Utility costs for the factory	900
11.	Maintenance costs for the factory	400
12.	Factory supervisor's salary	1,500
13.	Sales commissions	3,700
14.	Depreciation on factory building	900

Instructions
Enter each item and place an "X" mark under each of the following column headings.

Cost Item	Product Cost			Period Costs
	Direct Materials	Direct Labor	Manufacturing Overhead	
1.				
2.				
3.				
4.				
5.				
6.				
7.				
8.				
9.				
10.				
11.				
12.				
13.				
14.				

The Navigator

SOLUTIONS TO REVIEW QUESTIONS AND EXERCISES

TRUE-FALSE

1. (F) Managerial accounting relates primarily to managers and other internal users.
2. (T)
3. (F) The reporting standard for internal reports is relevance to the decision being made.
4. (F) Planning requires management to look ahead and to establish objectives. The statement given relates to the function of directing.
5. (T)
6. (T)
7. (T)
8. (F) The wages of these employees are usually identified as indirect labor because their efforts either have no physical association with the finished product or it is impractical to trace the costs to the goods produced.
9. (F) Manufacturing overhead consists of costs that are indirectly associated with the manufacture of the finished product.
10. (T)
11. (T)
12. (F) Period costs include selling and administrative expenses.
13. (T)
14. (F) Direct materials become a cost of the finished goods manufactured when they are used, not when they are acquired.
15. (T)
16. (F) The sum of the direct materials costs, direct labor costs, and manufacturing overhead incurred is the total manufacturing costs for the year.
17. (T)
18. (T)
19. (F) Raw Materials Inventory shows the cost of raw materials on hand. Finished Goods Inventory shows the cost of completed goods on hand.
20. (F) Manufacturing inventories are reported in the current asset section in order of their expected realization in cash.

MULTIPLE CHOICE

1. (b) Managerial accounting reports are special-purpose reports for a particular user for a specific decision.

2. (d) Financial reports are for external users and managerial reports are for internal users (a). Financial reports are usually identified as general-purpose reports and managerial reports are for specific purposes (b). The financial reports are prepared quarterly and annually and managerial reports are issued as frequently as the need arises (c).

3. (b) Directing involves coordinating the diverse activities and human resources of a company in a manner that results in a smooth running operation.

4. (c) Controlling is the process of keeping the activities of the enterprise on track. Management determines whether planned goals are being met and what changes are necessary when there are deviations from targeted objectives.

5.   (a)   Planning requires management to look ahead and to establish future goals and objectives.

6.   (d)   Direct materials, direct labor, and manufacturing overhead are all referred to as manufacturing costs; and as such are also known as product costs.

7.   (c)   Direct labor is a product cost.

8.   (b)   Period costs are costs that are matched with the revenue of a specific time period rather than with production of a product. Therefore, the wages of salespersons are a period cost. The other answer choices are product costs.

9.   (a)   Property taxes on the manufacturing plant are considered a part of manufacturing overhead. Therefore, they are a product cost but not a period cost.

10.   (b)   The salary of a plant manager would be a part of manufacturing overhead and a product cost.

11.   (b)   The cost of goods sold is:

Beginning finished goods inventory	$150,000
Cost of goods manufactured	325,000
Cost of goods available for sale	475,000
Ending finished goods inventory	175,000
Cost of goods sold	$300,000

12.   (c)   For cost of goods manufactured to be less than cost of goods sold, the beginning inventory of finished goods must be greater than the ending inventory of finished goods.

13.   (b)   The Work in Process Inventory account represents the cost of production for those units that have been started in the manufacturing process, but which are not complete at the end of the accounting period.

14.   (d)   Ending inventory $40,000 plus direct materials used $130,000 equals total cost of materials available for use, $170,000. $170,000 less the beginning inventory, $32,000 equals the cost of materials purchased, $138,000.

15.   (a)   The total cost of work in process is the beginning work in process inventory $52,000 plus the total current manufacturing costs $248,000.

16.   (d)   The cost of the ending work in process is the total cost of work in process $390,000 ($72,000 + $318,000) minus the cost of goods manufactured $320,000.

17.   (a)   For total current manufacturing costs to be greater than the cost of goods manufactured, the beginning inventory of work in process must be less than the ending inventory of work in process.

18.   (c)   Finished goods Inventory shows the cost of completed goods on hand. Work in Process Inventory shows the costs applicable to production that is only partially completed.

19. (d)   Manufacturing inventories are listed in the current asset section in the order of their expected realization in cash. Thus, the order is finished goods, work in process, and raw materials.

20. (c)   When companies allocate overhead based on each product's use of activities in making the product, this is known as activity-based costing.

MATCHING

1.	i	9.	h
2.	a	10.	k
3.	e	11.	b
4.	c	12.	f
5.	m	13.	d
6.	l		
7.	j		
8.	g		

EXERCISES

EX. 19-1

NORMAN COMPANY
Cost of Goods Manufactured Schedule
For the Year Ended December 31, 2010

Work in process, January 1			$ 32,000
Direct materials			
Raw materials inventory, January 1	$15,000		
Raw materials purchases....................................	48,000		
Total raw materials available for use.................	63,000		
Less: Raw materials inventory December 31....	20,000		
Direct materials used		$43,000	
Direct labor...		25,000	
Manufacturing overhead			
Factory repairs	10,000		
Indirect labor	9,000		
Factory utilities	8,000		
Factory insurance...	7,500		
Factory depreciation.......................................	6,000		
Factory property taxes	5,500		
Total manufacturing overhead..................		46,000	
Total manufacturing costs..			114,000
Total cost of work in process			146,000
Less: Work in process, December 31			30,000
Cost of goods manufactured...................................			$116,000

EX. 19-2

Cost Item	Direct Materials	Direct Labor	Manufacturing Overhead	Period Costs
		Product Cost		
1.			X	
2.				X
3.			X	
4.	X			
5.				X
6.		X		
7.				X
8.			X	
9.				X
10.			X	
11.			X	
12.			X	
13.				X
14.			X	

Chapter 20

The Navigator ✓

■ Scan Study Objectives ☐

■ Read Preview ☐

■ Read Chapter Review ☐

■ Work Demonstration Problem ☐

■ Answer True-False Statements ☐

■ Answer Multiple-Choice Questions ☐

■ Match Terms and Definitions ☐

■ Solve Exercises ☐

JOB ORDER COSTING

CHAPTER STUDY OBJECTIVES

After studying this chapter, you should be able to:

1. Explain the characteristics and purposes of cost accounting.
2. Describe the flow of costs in a job order costing system.
3. Explain the nature and importance of a job cost sheet.
4. Indicate how the predetermined overhead rate is determined and used.
5. Prepare entries for jobs completed and sold.
6. Distinguish between under- and overapplied manufacturing overhead.

The Navigator

PREVIEW OF CHAPTER 20

This chapter illustrates how manufacturing costs are assigned to specific jobs. We begin the discussion in this chapter with an overview of the flow of costs in a job order cost accounting system. We then use a case study to explain and illustrate the documents, entries, and accounts in this type of cost accounting system. The content and organization of this chapter are as follows:

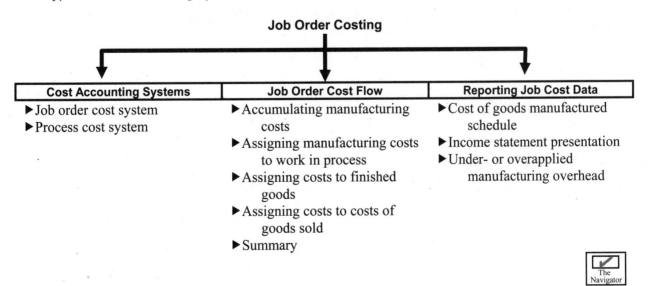

Job Order Costing

Cost Accounting Systems	Job Order Cost Flow	Reporting Job Cost Data
▶ Job order cost system	▶ Accumulating manufacturing costs	▶ Cost of goods manufactured schedule
▶ Process cost system	▶ Assigning manufacturing costs to work in process	▶ Income statement presentation
	▶ Assigning costs to finished goods	▶ Under- or overapplied manufacturing overhead
	▶ Assigning costs to costs of goods sold	
	▶ Summary	

The Navigator

CHAPTER REVIEW

Cost Accounting Systems

1. (S.O. 1) **Cost accounting** involves the measuring, recording, and reporting of product costs. From the data accumulated, both the total cost and unit cost of each product is determined.

2. A **cost accounting system** consists of accounts for the various manufacturing costs. These accounts are fully integrated into the general ledger of a company. An important feature of a cost accounting system is the use of a perpetual inventory system. Such a system provides information immediately on the cost of a product. The two basic types of cost accounting systems are (a) a job order cost system and (b) a process cost system.

3. Under a **job order cost system,** costs are assigned to each job or to each batch of goods.

4. A **process cost system** is used when a large volume of similar products are manufactured. Process costing accumulates product-related costs for a period of time instead of assigning costs to specific products or job orders.

Job Order Cost Flow

5. (S.O. 2) The **flow of costs** in job order cost accounting parallels the physical flow of the materials as they are converted into finished goods. There are two major steps in the flow of costs: (a) accumulating the manufacturing costs incurred and (b) assigning the accumulated costs to the work done.

6. No effort is made when costs are incurred to associate the costs with specific jobs.

7. The **assignment of manufacturing costs** involves entries to Work in Process Inventory, Finished Goods inventory, and Cost of Goods Sold.

8. The costs of raw materials purchased are debited to **Raw Materials Inventory** when materials are received. This account is a **control account.** The subsidiary ledger consists of individual **materials inventory records** (stores ledger cards) for each item of raw materials.

9. **Factory labor costs** are debited to **Factory Labor** when they are incurred. The cost of factor labor consists of (1) gross earnings of factory workers, (2) employer payroll taxes on the earnings, and (3) fringe benefits incurred by the employer. Factory Labor is not a control account.

10. Manufacturing overhead costs are recognized daily as incurred and periodically through adjusting entries. The costs are debited to **Manufacturing Overhead** which is a control account. The subsidiary ledger consists of individual accounts for each type of cost.

Assigning Manufacturing Costs to Work in Process

11. (S.O. 3) The assignment of manufacturing overhead costs to work in process involves debits to Work in Process Inventory and credits to:
    a. Raw Materials Inventory based on **materials requisition slips.**
    b. Factory Labor based on **time tickets.**
    c. Manufacturing Overhead based on a predetermined overhead rate.

Job Cost Sheet

12. A **job cost sheet** is a form used to record the costs chargeable to a specific job and to determine the total and unit cost of the completed job. A separate job cost sheet is kept for each job. Each entry to Work in Process Inventory must be accompanied by a corresponding posting to one or more job cost sheets.

13. Raw materials costs are assigned when the materials are issued by the storeroom. Work in Process Inventory is debited for direct materials used, Manufacturing Overhead is debited for indirect materials used, and Raw Materials Inventory is credited.

14. Factory Labor costs are assigned to jobs on the basis of time tickets prepared when the work is performed. Work in Process Inventory is debited for direct labor costs, Manufacturing Overhead is debited for indirect labor costs, and Factory Labor is credited.

Manufacturing Overhead Costs

15. (S.O. 4) Manufacturing overhead relates to production operations as a whole and therefore cannot be assigned to specific jobs on the basis of actual costs incurred. Instead, manufacturing overhead is assigned to work in process and to specific jobs on an estimated basis through the use of a predetermined overhead rate.

16. The **predetermined overhead rate** is based on the relationship between estimated annual overhead costs and expected annual operating activity. This relationship is expressed in terms of a common activity base such as direct labor costs, direct labor hours, or machine hours.
    a. The formula for the predetermined overhead rate is:

$$\begin{matrix} \text{Estimated} \\ \text{Annual} \\ \text{Overhead Costs} \end{matrix} \div \begin{matrix} \text{Expected} \\ \text{Annual Operating} \\ \text{Activity} \end{matrix} = \begin{matrix} \text{Predetermined} \\ \text{Overhead Rate} \end{matrix}$$

    b. The use of a predetermined overhead rate enables the company to determine the approximate total cost of each job when the job is completed.
    c. In recent years, there has been a trend toward use of **machine hours** as the activity base due to increased reliance on automation in manufacturing operations.

17. At the end of each month, the balance in Work in Process Inventory should equal the sum of the costs shown on the job cost sheets for unfinished jobs.

Assigning Costs to Finished Goods

18. (S.O. 5) When a job is completed, the total cost is debited to Finished Goods Inventory and credited to Work in Process Inventory. Finished Goods Inventory is a control account that controls individual finished goods records in a finished goods subsidiary ledger.

19. **Cost of goods sold** is recognized when the sale occurs by a debit to Cost of Goods Sold and a credit to Finished Goods Inventory.

20. At the end of a period, financial statements are prepared that present aggregate data on all jobs manufactured and sold.
    a. The cost of goods manufactured schedule has one new feature: in determining total manufacturing costs, **manufacturing overhead applied** is used instead of actual overhead costs.
    b. The cost of goods manufactured schedule is prepared directly from the Work in Process Inventory account.

Under- or Overapplied Manufacturing Overhead

21. (S.O. 6) Manufacturing Overhead may be under- or overapplied. When Manufacturing Overhead has a **debit balance,** overhead is said to be underapplied. **Underapplied overhead** means that the overhead assigned to work in process is less than the overhead incurred. When manufacturing overhead has a credit balance, overhead is overapplied. **Overapplied overhead** means that the overhead assigned to work in process is greater than the overhead incurred.

22. At the **end of the year,** any balance in Manufacturing Overhead is eliminated through an adjusting entry, usually to Cost of Goods Sold.
    a. Underapplied overhead is debited to Cost of Goods Sold.
    b. Overapplied overhead is credited to Cost of Goods Sold.

The
Navigator

DEMONSTRATION PROBLEM (S.O. 2, 3, 4, 5, and 6)

During April, Pam Lee Company works on two jobs: Numbers 101 and 102. Summary data concerning these jobs are as follows:

Manufacturing Costs Incurred
Purchased $68,000 of raw materials on account.
Factory labor of $100,000 plus $6,000 employer payroll taxes.
Manufacturing overhead exclusive of indirect materials and indirect labor of $72,500.

Assignment of Costs
Direct materials: Job 101-$36,000, Job 102-$30,000
Indirect materials: $4,000
Direct labor: Job 101-$68,000, Job 102-$34,500
Indirect labor: $3,500
Manufacturing overhead rate 70% of direct labor costs.

Job 101 was completed and sold on account for $184,000. Job 102 was only partially completed.

Instructions
(a)   Journalize the April transactions in the sequence followed in the chapter.
(b)   What was the amount of under- or overapplied manufacturing overhead?

SOLUTION TO DEMONSTRATION PROBLEM

(a) 1.   Raw Materials Inventory 68,000
             Accounts Payable   68,000
             (Purchase of raw materials on account)

    2.   Factory Labor.. 106,000
             Factory Wages Payable...   100,000
             Payroll Taxes Payable   6,000
             (To record factory labor costs)

    3.   Manufacturing Overhead 72,500
             Accounts Payable, Accumulated Depreciation,
               and Prepaid Insurance..   72,500
             (To record overhead costs)

    4.   Work in Process Inventory... 66,000
        Manufacturing Overhead 4,000
             Raw Materials Inventory   70,000
             (To assign raw materials to production)

    5.   Work in Process Inventory... 102,500
        Manufacturing Overhead 3,500
             Factory Labor...   106,000
             (To assign factory labor to production)

    6.   Work in Process Inventory... 71,750
             Manufacturing Overhead   71,750
             (To assign overhead to jobs: $102,500 X 70%)

    7.   Finished Goods Inventory... 151,600
             Work in Process Inventory   151,600
             [To record completion of Job 101: $36,000 +
               $68,000 + (68,000 X 70%)]

    8.   Accounts Receivable 184,000
        Cost of Goods Sold.. 151,600
             Sales...   184,000
             Finished Goods Inventory.......................................   151,600
             (To record sale of Job 101)

(b)   Manufacturing Overhead has a debit balance of $8,250 as shown below:

Manufacturing Overhead			
(3)	72,500	(6)	71,750
(4)	4,000		
(5)	3,500		
Bal.	8,250		

The manufacturing overhead is underapplied during the month.

REVIEW QUESTIONS AND EXERCISES

TRUE—FALSE

Indicate whether each of the following is true (T) or false (F) in the space provided.

_____   1. (S.O. 1) Cost accounting involves the measuring, recording, and reporting of product costs and period costs.

_____   2. (S.O. 1) A cost accounting system consists of manufacturing cost accounts that are fully integrated into the general ledger of a company.

_____   3. (S.O. 1) An important feature of a cost accounting system is the use of a periodic inventory system.

_____   4. (S.O. 1) A process cost system is best used when each job (or batch) has its own distinguishing characteristics.

_____   5. (S.O. 1) A company **cannot** use both a job order system and a process cost system.

_____   6. (S.O. 2) The flow of costs in job order cost accounting parallels the physical flow of the materials as they are converted into finished goods.

_____   7. (S.O. 2) The cost of raw materials purchased is credited to Raw Materials Inventory when materials are received.

_____   8. (S.O. 2) Raw materials Inventory is a control account.

_____   9. (S.O. 2) Factory Labor is a control account.

_____ 10. (S.O. 3) A job cost sheet is a requisition form signed by an authorized employee for the issuance of materials.

_____ 11. (S.O. 3) Each entry to Work in Process must be accompanied by a corresponding posting to one or more job cost sheets.

_____ 12. (S.O. 3) Raw materials costs are assigned to Work in Process Inventory when the materials are purchased.

_____ 13. (S.O. 3) Requisitions for direct materials are posted daily to the individual job cost sheets.

_____ 14. (S.O. 3) Factory labor costs are assigned to jobs on the basis of time tickets prepared when work is performed.

_____ 15. (S.O. 4) The predetermined overhead rate is based on the relationship between estimated annual overhead costs and expected annual operating capacity expressed in terms of a common activity base.

_____ 16. (S.O. 4) The use of a predetermined overhead rate enables the company to determine the approximate total cost when the job still is in work in process.

_____ 17. (S.O. 5) Recognition of the cost of goods sold is made when each sale occurs.

_____ 18. (S.O. 6) Overapplied manufacturing overhead exists when the overhead assigned to work in process is less than the overhead incurred.

_____ 19. (S.O. 6) At the end of the year, underapplied overhead is usually credited to Cost of Goods Sold.

_____ 20. (S.O. 6) After the entry for underapplied or overapplied overhead is posted, Manufacturing Overhead will have a zero balance.

The Navigator

MULTIPLE CHOICE

Circle the letter that best answers each of the following statements.

1. (S.O. 1) Cost accounting involves the following activities pertaining to product costs:
    a. measuring.
    b. recording.
    c. reporting.
    d. all of the above.

2. (S.O. 1) Job order costing would **not** be used by a company that manufactures:
    a. homes.
    b. motion pictures.
    c. cereal.
    d. bridges.

3. (S.O. 2) In a job order cost system, it would be correct in recording the purchase of raw materials to debit:
    a. Work in Process Inventory.
    b. Work in Process and Manufacturing Overhead.
    c. Raw Materials Inventory.
    d. Finished Goods Inventory.

4. (S.O. 3) In a job order cost system, indirect labor costs are recognized in the ledger by a debit to:
    a. Manufacturing Overhead.
    b. Work in Process Inventory.
    c. Finished Goods Inventory.
    d. Accrued Payroll.

5. (S.O. 3) In job order costing, the basic form to accumulate the cost of each job is the:
   a. materials inventory record.
   b. finished goods inventory record.
   c. cost of goods sold record.
   d. job cost sheet.

6. (S.O. 3) In job order costing, when indirect materials are used in production:
   a. Work in Process Inventory is debited.
   b. Manufacturing Overhead is credited.
   c. Raw Materials Inventory is debited.
   d. Raw Materials Inventory is credited.

7. (S.O. 3) A cost that would **not** be included in the manufacturing overhead account is:
   a. factory utilities.
   b. direct labor.
   c. indirect labor.
   d. depreciation expense on factory machinery.

8. (S.O. 3) Which of the following is **not** a control account?
   a. Raw Materials Inventory.
   b. Factory Labor.
   c. Manufacturing Overhead.
   d. All of the above are control accounts.

9. (S.O. 4) In the Bono Company, the predetermined overhead rate is 70% of direct labor cost. During the month, $250,000 of factory labor costs are incurred of which $180,000 is direct labor and $70,000 is indirect labor. Actual overhead incurred was $130,000. The amount of overhead debited to Work in Process Inventory should be:
   a. $126,000.
   b. $130,000.
   c. $175,000.
   d. $180,000.

10. (S.O. 4) Jinnah Company applies overhead on the basis of 200% of direct labor cost. Job No. 501 is charged with $30,000 of direct materials costs and $40,000 of manufacturing overhead. The total manufacturing costs for Job No. 501 is:
    a. $70,000.
    b. $110,000.
    c. $90,000.
    d. $100,000.

11. (S.O. 4) Patel Company manufactures customized chairs. The following pertains to Job 276:

Direct materials used	$4,200
Direct labor hours worked	300
Direct labor rate per hour	$ 8.00
Machine hours used	200
Applied factory overhead rate	
per machine hour	$15.00

What is the total manufacturing cost for Job 276?
a. $8,800.
b. $9,600.
c. $10,300.
d. $11,100.

12. (S.O. 4) Ambedkar Inc. applies overhead to production at a predetermined rate of 90% based on direct labor cost. Job No. 343, the only job still in process at the end of August, has been charged with manufacturing overhead of $2,250. What was the amount of direct materials charged to Job 343 assuming the balance in Work in Process Inventory is $9,000?
a. $2,250.
b. $2,500.
c. $4,250.
d. $9,000.

13. (S.O. 5) When a job is finished, the journal entry will include a:
a.   credit to Finished Goods Inventory.
b.   debit to Work in Process Inventory.
c.   debit to Manufacturing Overhead.
d.   debit to Finished Goods Inventory.

14. (S.O. 5) When the units are sold, the journal entry will include a:
a.   credit to Finished Goods Inventory.
b.   debit to Work in Process Inventory.
c.   debit to Manufacturing Overhead.
d.   credit to Cost of Goods Sold.

15. (S.O. 6) The Edge Company uses a predetermined overhead rate of $5 per direct labor hour. In December, actual overhead amounted to $650,000 and actual direct labor hours were 132,000. For the month, overhead was:
a. $50,000 overapplied.
b. $50,000 underapplied.
c. $10,000 overapplied.
d. $10,000 underapplied.

16. (S.O. 6) Mountbatten Co. uses a predetermined overhead rate of $3 per direct labor hour. In July, actual overhead amounted to $325,000 and actual direct labor hours were 100,000. For the month, overhead was:
a. $30,000 overapplied.
b. $30,000 underapplied.
c. $25,000 overapplied.
d. $25,000 underapplied.

17. (S.O. 6) Overapplied manufacturing overhead exists when overhead assigned to work in process is:
    a. more than overhead incurred and there is a debit balance in Manufacturing Overhead at the end of a period.
    b. less than overhead incurred and there is a debit balance in Manufacturing Overhead at the end of a period.
    c. more than overhead incurred and there is a credit balance in Manufacturing Overhead at the end of a period.
    d. less than overhead incurred and there is a credit balance in Manufacturing Overhead at the end of a period.

18. (S.O. 6) At the end of the year, to transfer underapplied overhead to cost of goods sold, the journal entry will include a:
    a. credit to Cost of Goods Sold.
    b. debit to Cost of Goods Sold.
    c. debit to Manufacturing Overhead.
    d. debit to Factory Labor.

19. (S.O. 6) At the end of the year, to transfer overapplied overhead to cost of goods sold, the journal entry will include a:
    a. debit to Manufacturing Overhead.
    b. credit to Manufacturing Overhead.
    c. credit to Factory Labor.
    d. debit to Work in Process Inventory.

20. (S.O. 6) Which of the following statements about under- or overapplied manufacturing overhead is correct?
    a. After the entry to transfer over- or under-applied overhead to Cost of Goods Sold is posted, Manufacturing Overhead will have a zero balance.
    b. When Manufacturing Overhead has a credit balance, overhead is said to be underapplied.
    c. At the end of the year, under- or overapplied overhead is eliminated by a closing entry.
    d. When annual financial statements are prepared, overapplied overhead is reported in current liabilities.

The Navigator

MATCHING

Match each term with its definition by writing the appropriate letter in the space provided.

Terms

_____ 1. Time ticket.

_____ 2. Job order cost system.

_____ 3. Cost accounting.

_____ 4. Cost accounting system.

_____ 5. Job cost sheet.

_____ 6. Materials requisition slip.

_____ 7. Predetermined overhead rate.

_____ 8. Underapplied overhead.

_____ 9. Overapplied overhead.

Definitions

a. An area of accounting that involves the measuring, recording, and reporting of product costs.

b. A rate based on the relationship between estimated annual overhead costs and expected annual operating activity expressed in terms of a common activity base.

c. Manufacturing cost accounts that are fully integrated into the general ledger of a company.

d. Overhead assigned to work in process is less than the overhead incurred.

e. A form used to record the costs chargeable to a job and to determine the total and unit cost of the completed job.

f. A document authorizing the issuance of raw materials from the storeroom to production.

g. Overhead assigned to work in process is greater than the overhead incurred.

h. A cost accounting system in which costs are assigned to each job or batch.

i. A document indicating the time worked by an employee and the account and job to be charged.

The
Navigator

EXERCISES

EX. 20-1　(S.O. 2, 3, 4, 5, and 6)　McEllen Company uses job order costing. Manufacturing overhead is applied to production at a predetermined rate of 150% of direct labor cost. Additional information is available as follows:

- Job 201 was the only job in process at January 31, 2010, with accumulated costs as follow:

Direct materials	$4,000
Direct labor	2,000
Manufacturing overhead	3,000
	$9,000

- Jobs 202, 203, and 204 were started during February.
- Direct materials requisitioned for February totaled $26,000.
- Direct labor cost of $20,000 was incurred for February.
- Actual manufacturing overhead was $32,000 for February.
- The only job still in process at February 28, 2010, was Job 204, with costs of $2,800 for direct materials and $1,800 for direct labor.

Instructions
(a)　Make the journal entry to record materials used.
(b)　Make the journal entry to assign factory labor to production.
(c)　Make the journal entry to assign overhead to jobs.
(d)　Make a combined journal entry to record the completion of Jobs No. 201, 202, and 203.
(e)　Prove the agreement of Work in Process Inventory with the costs of Job 204.

General Journal			J1
Date	Account Title	Debit	Credit

EX. 20-2   (S.O. 2, 4, 5, and 6)   Selected account balances as of January 1 for Remmers Company are: Raw Materials Inventory $220,000, Work in Process Inventory $160,000, and Finished Goods Inventory $350,000.

During 2010, the following transactions took place:

1.   Purchased $820,000 of raw materials.
2.   Incurred $680,000 of factory labor costs of which $630,000 relate to wages payable and $50,000 to employer payroll taxes payable.
3.   Incurred overhead costs of $174,000 (Credit Accounts Payable $124,000 and Cash $50,000).
4.   Used direct materials of $600,000 and indirect materials of $200,000.
5.   Used direct labor of $650,000 and indirect labor of $30,000.
6.   Applied overhead at 30% of direct labor cost.
7.   Completed jobs totaling $1,100,000.
8.   Sold jobs costing $1,000,000 for $1,400,000, on account.

Instructions
(a)   Prepare the entries for Remmers Company for the above transactions assuming a job order cost accounting system is used. (Omit explanations.)
(b)   At December 31, the ledger of Remmers Company shows underapplied manufacturing overhead of $5,000. Prepare the entry to transfer this balance to Cost of Goods Sold.

General Journal			J1
Date	Account Title	Debit	Credit

General Journal			J
Date	Account Title	Debit	Credit

The Navigator

SOLUTIONS TO REVIEW QUESTIONS AND EXERCISES

TRUE-FALSE

1. (F) Cost accounting does not generally pertain to period costs.
2. (T)
3. (F) An important feature of a cost accounting system is the use of a perpetual inventory system.
4. (F) A job order cost system is best used when each job (or batch) has its own distinguishing characteristics.
5. (F) A company can use both a job order system and a process cost system as General Motors does with different types of automobiles.
6. (T)
7. (F) The cost of raw materials purchased is **debited** to Raw Materials Inventory when materials are received.
8. (T)
9. (F) Factory Labor is not a control account.
10. (F) A job cost sheet is a form used to record the costs chargeable to a specific job and to determine the total and unit cost of the job.
11. (T)
12. (F) Raw materials costs are assigned to Work in Process Inventory when the materials are issued by the storeroom.
13. (T)
14. (T)
15. (T)
16. (F) The use of a predetermined overhead rate enables the company to determine the approximate total cost of each job when the job is completed.
17. (T)
18. (F) Overapplied manufacturing overhead exists when the overhead assigned to work in process is greater than the overhead incurred.
19. (F) At the end of the year, underapplied overhead is usually debited to Cost of Goods Sold, and overapplied overhead is credited to Cost of Goods Sold.
20. (T)

MULTIPLE CHOICE

1. (d) Cost accounting involves the measuring, recording, and reporting of product costs.

2. (c) Job order costing would be used by a company that manufactures many jobs with distinguishing characteristics such as homes (a), motion pictures (b), and bridges (d). Process costing would be used for a homogeneous product such as cereal.

3. (c) Finished Goods Inventory is only debited for the cost of the completed job. The usual entry for the purchase of raw materials is Dr. Raw Materials Inventory, and Cr. Accounts Payable.

4. (a) Indirect labor costs are recorded by a debit to manufacturing overhead.

5. (d) A job cost sheet is a form used to record the cost charged to a specific job and to determine the total and unit cost of the completed job. Answers (a) and (b) pertain to subsidiary ledgers for raw materials and finished goods inventories. There is no cost of goods sold record (c).

6. (d) When indirect materials are used in production the following entry is made:

Manufacturing Overhead..	XXX	
Raw Materials Inventory...................................		XXX

7. (b) Factory utilities (a), indirect labor (c), and depreciation expense on factory machinery (d) are all included in the manufacturing overhead account. Direct labor is assigned directly to Work in Process Inventory.

8. (b) Raw Materials Inventory (a) and Manufacturing Overhead (c) are both control accounts. Factory Labor is not a control account.

9. (a) The debit to Work in Process Inventory is direct labor cost ($180,000) times the predetermined overhead rate of 70%.

10. (c) Manufacturing overhead is 200% of direct labor cost. Thus, direct labor cost is $20,000 ($40,000 ÷ 200%) and total costs are $90,000 ($30,000 + $20,000 + $40,000).

11. (b) The total manufacturing cost is calculated as follows:

Direct materials used...	$4,200
Direct labor (300 X $8.00)	2,400
Manufacturing overhead (200 X $15.00)...........	3,000
Total manufacturing cost.................................	$9,600

12. (c) If manufacturing overhead was $2,250, direct labor was $2,500 ($2,250 ÷ 90%). Therefore, direct materials must equal $4,250 [$9,000 - ($2,250 + $2,500)].

13. (d) When a job is finished, the following journal entry is made:

Finished Goods Inventory	XXX	
Work in Process Inventory................................		XXX

14. (a) When units are sold, the following journal entries are made:

Cost of Goods Sold	XXX	
Finished Goods Inventory................................		XXX

Accounts Receivable...	XXX	
Sales..		XXX

15. (c) The amount of overhead applied was $660,000 ($5 X 132,000). Therefore, there is $10,000 of overapplied overhead ($660,000 - $650,000).

16. (d) The amount of overhead applied was $300,000 ($3.00 X 100,000). Therefore, there is $25,000 of underapplied overhead ($325,000 - $300,000).

17. (c) Overapplied manufacturing overhead exists when overhead assigned to work in process is more than overhead incurred and results in a credit balance in Manufacturing Overhead at the end of the period.

18. (b) To transfer underapplied overhead to Cost of Goods Sold, the following entry is made:

Cost of Goods Sold   XXX
      Manufacturing Overhead   XXX

19. (a) To transfer overapplied overhead to Cost of Goods Sold, the following entry is made:

Manufacturing Overhead...   XXX
      Cost of Goods Sold   XXX

20. (a) Answer (b) is incorrect because when Manfacturing Overhead has a credit balance, overhead is said to be overapplied. At the end of the year, under- or overapplied overhead is eliminated by an adjusting entry (c), and it is not reported in the balance sheet (d).

MATCHING

1.	i	6.	f
2.	h	7.	b
3.	a	8.	d
4.	c	9.	g
5.	e		

EXERCISES

EX. 20-1

<table>
<tr>
<td colspan="5" align="center">**General Journal**</td>
</tr>
<tr>
<td colspan="4"></td>
<td align="right">**J1**</td>
</tr>
<tr>
<td align="center">**Date**</td>
<td align="center">**Account Title**</td>
<td align="center">**Debit**</td>
<td align="center">**Credit**</td>
</tr>
<tr>
<td>(a)</td>
<td>Work in Process Inventory</td>
<td>26,000</td>
<td></td>
</tr>
<tr>
<td></td>
<td>   Raw Materials Inventory</td>
<td></td>
<td>26,000</td>
</tr>
<tr>
<td></td>
<td>   (To record materials used)</td>
<td></td>
<td></td>
</tr>
<tr>
<td></td>
<td></td>
<td></td>
<td></td>
</tr>
<tr>
<td>(b)</td>
<td>Work in Process Inventory</td>
<td>20,000</td>
<td></td>
</tr>
<tr>
<td></td>
<td>   Factory Labor</td>
<td></td>
<td>20,000</td>
</tr>
<tr>
<td></td>
<td>   (To assign factory labor to production)</td>
<td></td>
<td></td>
</tr>
<tr>
<td></td>
<td></td>
<td></td>
<td></td>
</tr>
<tr>
<td>(c)</td>
<td>Work in Process Inventory</td>
<td>30,000</td>
<td></td>
</tr>
<tr>
<td></td>
<td>   Manufacturing Overhead</td>
<td></td>
<td>30,000</td>
</tr>
<tr>
<td></td>
<td>   (To assign overhead to jobs:</td>
<td></td>
<td></td>
</tr>
<tr>
<td></td>
<td>   150% X $20,000)</td>
<td></td>
<td></td>
</tr>
<tr>
<td>(d)</td>
<td>Finished Goods Inventory</td>
<td>77,700</td>
<td></td>
</tr>
<tr>
<td></td>
<td>   Work in Process Inventory</td>
<td></td>
<td>77,700</td>
</tr>
<tr>
<td></td>
<td>[$9,000 + $26,000 + $20,000 + $30,000 -</td>
<td></td>
<td></td>
</tr>
<tr>
<td></td>
<td>$2,800 - $1,800 - ($1,800 X 150%)]</td>
<td></td>
<td></td>
</tr>
</table>

(e)

```
                Work in Process Inventory
        Bal.        9,000 | (d)        77,700
        (a)        26,000 |
        (b)        20,000 |
        (c)        30,000 |
        Bal.        7,300 |
```

Job 204

Direct materials	2,800
Direct labor	1,800
Manufacturing overhead	2,700*
Total	7,300

*$1800 X 150% = $2,700.

EX. 20-2

Date	Account Title	Debit	Credit
	General Journal		**J1**
(a)	1. Raw Materials Inventory	820,000	
	Accounts Payable		820,000
	2. Factory Labor	680,000	
	Factory Wages Payable		630,000
	Employer Payroll Taxes Payable		50,000
	3. Manufacturing Overhead	174,000	
	Accounts Payable		124,000
	Cash		50,000
	4. Work in Process Inventory	600,000	
	Manufacturing Overhead	200,000	
	Raw Materials Inventory		800,000
	5. Work in Process Inventory	650,000	
	Manufacturing Overhead	30,000	
	Factory Labor		680,000
	6. Work in Process Inventory	195,000	
	Manufacturing Overhead		195,000
	7. Finished Goods Inventory	1,100,000	
	Work in Process Inventory		1,100,000

General Journal			J2
Date	**Account Title**	**Debit**	**Credit**
	8. Accounts Receivable	1,400,000	
	Sales		1,400,000
	Cost of Goods Sold	1,000,000	
	Finished Goods Inventory		1,000,000
(b)	Cost of Goods Sold	5,000	
	Manufacturing Overhead		5,000

Chapter 21

PROCESS COSTING

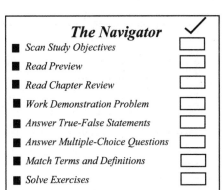

The Navigator ✓
- ■ Scan Study Objectives ☐
- ■ Read Preview ☐
- ■ Read Chapter Review ☐
- ■ Work Demonstration Problem ☐
- ■ Answer True-False Statements ☐
- ■ Answer Multiple-Choice Questions ☐
- ■ Match Terms and Definitions ☐
- ■ Solve Exercises ☐

CHAPTER STUDY OBJECTIVES

After studying this chapter, you should be able to:
1. Understand who uses process cost systems.
2. Explain the similarities and differences between job order cost and process cost systems.
3. Explain the flow of costs in a process cost system.
4. Make the journal entries to assign manufacturing costs in a process cost system.
5. Compute equivalent units.
6. Explain the four steps necessary to prepare a production cost report.
7. Prepare a production cost report.
8. Explain just-in-time (JIT) processing.
9. Explain activity-based costing (ABC).
*10. Apply activity-based costing to specific company data.

*Note: All asterisked (*) items relate to material contained in the Appendix to the chapter.

PREVIEW OF CHAPTER 21

In contrast to job order cost accounting, which focuses on the individual job, process cost accounting focuses on the processes involved in mass-producing products that are identical or very similar in nature. The primary objective of the chapter is to explain and illustrate process cost accounting. At the end of the chapter, two contemporary developments, just-in-time (JIT) processing and activity-based costing (ABC) are considered. The content and organization of this chapter are as follows:

Process Costing

Nature of Process Cost System	Equivalent Units	Comprehensive Example of Process Costing	Contemporary Developments
▶Uses ▶Similarities and differences ▶Process cost flow ▶Assigning manufacturing costs	▶Weighted-average method ▶Refinements ▶Production cost report	▶Physical units ▶Equivalent units of production ▶Unit production costs ▶Cost reconciliation schedule ▶Production cost report ▶Costing systems-final comments	▶Just-in-time processing ▶Activity-based costing

CHAPTER REVIEW

Process Manufacturing and Accounting

1. (S.O. 1) Process cost systems are used to apply costs to similar products that are produced in a continuous fashion, such as the production of ice cream, steel, or soft drinks. In comparison, costs in a job order cost system are assigned to a specific job, such as the construction of a customized home, the making of a motion picture, or the manufacturing of a specialized machine.

2. (S.O. 2) Job order cost and process cost systems are similar in that (a) both use the same three manufacturing cost elements of direct materials, direct labor, and manufacturing overhead; (b) both accumulate costs of raw materials by debiting Raw Materials Inventory, factory labor by debiting Factory Labor, and manufacturing overhead costs by debiting Manufacturing Overhead; and (c) both flow costs to the same accounts of Work in Process, Finished Goods Inventory, and Cost of Goods Sold.

3. The major differences between a job order cost system and a process cost system are as follows:

Feature	Job Order Cost System	Process Cost System
Work in process accounts	One for each job	One for each process
Documents used	Job cost sheets	Production cost reports
Determination of total manufacturing costs	Each job	Each period
Unit-cost computations	Cost of each job ÷ Units produced for the job	Total manufacturing costs ÷ Equivalent units produced during the period

Process Cost Flow

4. (S.O. 3) In the Tyler Company example in the text book, manufacturing consists of two processes: machining and assembly. In the Machining Department, the raw materials are shaped, honed, and drilled. In the Assembly Department, the parts are assembled and packaged.

5. Materials, labor, and manufacturing overhead can be added in both the Machining and Assembly Departments. When the Machining Department finishes its work, the partially completed units are transferred to the Assembly Department. In the Assembly Department, the goods are finished and are then transferred to the finished goods inventory. Upon sale, the goods are removed from the finished goods inventory.

Assignment of Manufacturing Costs

6. (S.O. 4) All raw materials issued for production are a materials cost to the producing department. Materials requisition slips may be used in a process cost system, but fewer requisitions are generally required than in a job order cost system, because the materials are used for processes rather than for specific jobs. The entry to record the materials used is:

Work in Process--Machining	XXXX	
Work in Process--Assembly	XXXX	
Raw Materials Inventory		XXXX

7. Time tickets may be used in determining the cost of labor assignable to the production departments. The labor cost chargeable to a process can be obtained from the payroll register or departmental payroll summaries. All labor costs incurred within a producing department are a cost of processing the raw materials. The entry to assign the labor costs is:

Work in Process--Machining	XXXX	
Work in Process--Assembly	XXXX	
Factory Labor		XXXX

8. The basis for allocating the overhead costs to the production departments in an objective and equitable manner is the activity that "drives" or causes the costs. A primary driver of overhead costs in continuous manufacturing operations is machine time used, not direct labor. Thus, machine hours are widely used in allocating manufacturing overhead costs. The entry to allocate overhead is:

Work in Process--Machining	XXXX	
Work in Process--Assembly	XXXX	
Manufacturing Overhead		XXXX

9. At the end of the period, the following transfer entries are needed:

Work in Process--Assembly	XXXX	
Work in Process--Machining		XXXX
Finished Goods Inventory	XXXX	
Work in Process--Assembly		XXXX
Cost of Goods Sold	XXXX	
Finished Goods Inventory		XXXX

Equivalent Units

10. (S.O. 5) A major step in process cost accounting is the calculation of equivalent units. **Equivalent units of production** measure the work done during the period, expressed in fully completed units. This concept is used to determine the cost per unit of completed product.

11. The formula to compute equivalent units of production is as follows:

$$\text{Units Completed and Transferred Out} + \text{Equivalent Units of Ending Work in Process} = \text{Equivalent Units of Production}$$

12. The method of computing equivalent units here is referred to as the weighted-average method. It considers the degree of completion (weighting) of the units completed and transferred out and the ending work in process.

13. To illustrate the computation of equivalent units using the weighted-average method, assume that materials are entered at the beginning of the process and the following information is provided for the Processing Department of the Silva Company:

		Percentage Complete	
	Physical Units	Materials	Conversion Costs
Work in process, Beg.	2,500	100%	80%
Started into production	4,500		
Total units	7,000		
Units transferred out	6,000		
Work in process, End.	1,000	100%	60%
Total units	7,000		

14. The two equivalent unit computations are as follows:

	Equivalent Units	
	Materials	Conversion Costs
Units transferred out	6,000	6,000
Work in process, End		
1,000 X 100%	1,000	
1,000 X 60%		600
Total equivalent units	7,000	6,600

Production Cost Report

15. (S.O. 6) A **production cost report** is the key document used by management to understand the activities in a department because it shows the production quantity and cost data related to that department. In order to be ready to complete a production cost report, the company must perform four steps:
   a. Compute the physical unit flow.
   b. Compute the equivalent units of production.
   c. Compute unit production costs.
   d. Prepare a cost reconciliation schedule.

16. The **computation of physical units** involves:
   a. adding the units started (or transferred) into production during the period to the units in process at the beginning of the period to determine the **total units to be accounted for**; and
   b. accounting for these units by determining the **output** for the period—which consists of units transferred out during the period and units in process at the end of the period.
   In the example above, the **total units to be accounted for** and the **units accounted for** are both equal to 7,000 units for the Silva Company.

17. In computing unit costs, production costs are expressed in terms of equivalent units of production. When equivalent units are different for materials and conversion costs, the formulas for computing unit costs are as follows:

$$\begin{array}{ccc}\text{Total Materials} & & \text{Equivalent Units} & & \text{Unit Materials} \\ \text{Cost} & \div & \text{of Materials} & = & \text{Cost}\end{array}$$

$$\begin{array}{ccc}\text{Total Conversion} & & \text{Equivalent Units} & & \text{Unit Conversion} \\ \text{Costs} & \div & \text{of Conversion Costs} & = & \text{Cost}\end{array}$$

$$\begin{array}{ccc}\text{Unit Materials} & & \text{Unit Conversion} & & \text{Total Manufacturing} \\ \text{Cost} & + & \text{Cost} & = & \text{Cost per Unit}\end{array}$$

18. The **cost reconciliation schedule** shows that the total costs accounted for equal the **total costs to be accounted for** as follows:

Costs to be accounted for		
Transferred out		$XXXX
Work in process, End		
Materials	$XXXX	
Conversion costs	<u>XXXX</u>	<u>XXXX</u>
Total costs		<u>$XXXX</u>

19. (S.O. 7) Assume the Processing Department of the Silva Company has the following additional cost information:

Work in process, Beg.	
Direct materials: 100% complete	$ 24,000
Conversion costs: 80% complete	<u>19,620</u>
Cost of work in process, Beg.	<u>$ 43,620</u>
Costs incurred during production	
Direct materials	$200,000
Conversion costs	<u>150,000</u>
Costs incurred	<u>$350,000</u>

20. The Silva Company's Processing Department Production Cost Report at the end of the period is as follows:

Processing Department
Production Cost Report
For the Period Ended

| | | Equivalent Units | |
| | Physical | | Conversion |
	Units	Materials	Costs
QUANTITIES			
Units to be accounted for			
Work in process, Beg.	2,500		
Started into production	4,500		
Total units	7,000		
Units accounted for			
Transferred out	6,000	6,000	6,000
Work in process, End.	1,000	1,000	600 (1,000 x 60%)
Total units	7,000	7,000	6,600

| | | Conversion | |
	Materials	Costs	Total
COSTS			
Unit costs			
Costs during the period	$224,000	$169,620	$393,620
Equivalent units	7,000	6,600	
Unit costs	$32.00	$25.70	$57.70
Costs to be accounted for			
Work in process, Beg.			$ 43,620
Started into production			350,000
Total costs			$393,620
Cost Reconciliation Schedule			
Costs accounted for			
Transferred out (6,000 X $57.70)			$346,200
Work in process, End.			
Materials (1,000 X $32.00)		$32,000	
Conversion costs (600 X $25.70)		15,420	47,420
Total costs			$393,620

Operations Costing

21. Companies often use a combination of a process cost and a job order cost system, called **operations costing.** Operations costing is similar to process costing in that standardized methods are used to manufacture the product. At the same time, the product may have some customized, individual features that require the use of a job order cost system.

Just-in-Time Processing

22. (S.O. 8) **Just-in-Time (JIT) processing** is dedicated to producing the right products (or parts) at the right time as they are needed. Raw materials are received just in time for use in production, subassembly parts are completed just in time for use in finished goods, and finished goods are completed just in time to be sold.

23. The **major** benefits of JIT processing are:
    a. Manufacturing inventories are significantly reduced or eliminated.
    b. Product quality is enhanced.
    c. Rework costs and inventory storage costs are reduced or eliminated.
    d. Production cost savings are realized from the improved flow of goods through the processes.

24. Under JIT the raw materials and work in process inventory accounts are combined into one Raw and In-Process Inventory account.

Activity-Based Costing

25. (S.O. 10) **Activity-based costing (ABC)** is a method of product costing that focuses on the activities performed to produce specific products. An ABC system is similar to conventional costing systems in accounting for direct materials and direct labor but differs in regard to manufacturing overhead.

26. In ABC, the cost of a product is equal to the sum of the costs of all activities performed to manufacture it. In selecting a basis, ABC seeks to identify the cost drivers that measure the activities performed on the product. For example, a possible cost driver for ordering raw materials is the number of times an order is placed.

*27. (S.O. 10) ABC involves the following steps:
    a. Identify the major activities that pertain to the manufacture of specific products.
    b. Accumulate manufacturing overhead costs by activities.
    c. Identify the cost driver(s) that accurately measure(s) each activity's contribution to the finished product.
    d. Assign manufacturing overhead costs for each activity to products using the cost driver(s).

*28. ABC provides the following benefits:
    a. More accurate product costing.
    b. Control over overhead costs is enhanced.
    c. Better management decisions can be made.

The Navigator

DEMONSTRATION PROBLEM (S.O. 5 and 6)

Assume data for the Stuart Cox Company for the Cutting Department for the month of November is as follows:

Units:
Work in process, Nov. 1	21,000
Direct materials: 100% complete	
Conversion costs: 40% complete	
Units started into production during Nov.	500,000
Units completed and transferred out	450,000
Work in process, Nov. 30	71,000
Direct materials: 100% complete	
Conversion costs: 20% complete	

Costs:
Work in process, Nov. 1	
Direct materials: 100% complete	$ 18,000
Conversion costs: 40% complete	16,600
Cost of work in process, Nov. 1	$ 34,600
Costs incurred during production in Nov.	
Direct materials	$262,000
Conversion costs	555,280
Costs incurred Nov.	$817,280

Instructions
Compute the physical unit flow, the equivalent units of production and unit production costs.

SOLUTION TO DEMONSTRATION PROBLEM

Cutting Department

	Physical Units
Units to be accounted for	
Work in process, Nov. 1	21,000
Started (transferred) into production	500,000
Total units	521,000
Units accounted for	
Completed and transferred out	450,000
Work in process, Nov. 30	71,000
Total units	521,000

	Equivalent Units	
	Materials	Conversion Costs
Units transferred out	450,000	450,000
Work in process, Nov. 30		
71,000 X 100%	71,000	
71,000 X 20%		14,200
Total equivalent units	521,000	464,200

Unit Materials Cost = ($18,000 + $262,000) ÷ 521,000 = $0.54
Unit Conversion Cost = ($16,600 + $555,280) ÷ 464,200 = $1.23

REVIEW QUESTIONS AND EXERCISES

TRUE—FALSE

Indicate whether each of the following is true (T) or false (F) in the space provided.

_____ 1. (S.O. 1)   Process cost accounting focuses on the individual job as opposed to job order costing which focuses on homogeneous products.

_____ 2. (S.O. 1)   In continuous process manufacturing, generally once the production begins, it continues until the finished product emerges.

_____ 3. (S.O. 1)   In process costing, there is usually only one work in process account.

_____ 4. (S.O. 2)   One similarity of process cost accounting with job order cost accounting is that both determine total manufacturing costs after each job.

_____ 5. (S.O. 2)   One difference of process costing when compared with job order cost accounting is that they both track different manufacturing cost elements.

_____ 6. (S.O. 3)   The flow of costs in a process costing system require that materials be added in one department, labor added in another department and manufacturing overhead in a third department.

_____ 7. (S.O. 4)   Raw materials are usually added to production at the beginning of the first process.

_____ 8. (S.O. 4)   In process cost accounting, manufacturing costs are accumulated by debits to Raw Materials Inventory, Factory Labor, and Manufacturing Overhead.

_____ 9. (S.O. 4)   In process costing, there are usually more requisition slips because the materials are used for processes rather than jobs.

_____ 10. (S.O. 4)   The primary driver of overhead costs in continuous manufacturing operations is machine time used.

_____ 11. (S.O. 4)   When finished goods are sold, the entry to record the cost of goods sold is a debit to Finished Goods Inventory and a credit to Cost of Goods Sold.

_____ 12. (S.O. 5)   When computing physical units, the beginning inventory plus units started equals the units transferred out plus ending inventory.

_____ 13. (S.O. 5)   Equivalent units of production are a measure of the work done during the period.

_____ 14. (S.O. 5)   Equivalent Units of Production are equal to the Units Completed and Transferred Out and Equivalent Units of Ending Work in Process.

_____ 15. (S.O. 5)   When there is no beginning work in process and materials are entered at the beginning of the process, equivalent units of materials are the same as the units started into production.

_____ 16. (S.O. 5)   If 15,000 units are completed and transferred out and there are 5,000 units in ending inventory 60% complete, the equivalent units for conversion costs are 18,000.

_____ 17. (S.O. 5)   The unit conversion cost is equal to the total conversion costs divided by equivalent units of materials.

_____ 18. (S.O. 6)   A production cost report shows both production quantity and cost data for a production department.

_____ 19. (S.O. 6) In order to compute the physical unit flow, a company must first compute unit production costs.

_____ 20. (S.O. 7)   When calculating equivalent units of production, beginning work in process is generally included in the units "transferred out."

_____ 21. (S.O. 8)   A primary objective of just-in-time manufacturing is the creation of large inventories.

_____ 22. (S.O. 9) In activity-based costing the focus is on the activities performed to produce specific products.

_____ 23. (S.O. 9) Activity-based costing seeks to identify the cost driver that measures the activities performed on the product.

The
Navigator

MULTIPLE CHOICE

Circle the letter that best answers each of the following statements.

1. (S.O. 1) Which of the following is an **incorrect** statement concerning process cost accounting?
    a.   Individual work in process accounts are maintained for each production department or manufacturing process.
    b.   The summarization of manufacturing costs is performed on production cost reports.
    c.   The focus is on the individual job.
    d.   The system is used by companies that manufacture products through a series of continuous processes or operations.

2. (S.O. 2) Which of the following is considered a difference between a job order cost and a process cost system?
    a.   The manufacturing cost elements.
    b.   Documents used to track costs.
    c.   The accumulation of the costs of materials, labor, and overhead.
    d.   The flow of costs.

3. (S.O. 2) Which of the following is considered a similarity between a job order cost and a process cost system?
    a.   The flow of costs.
    b.   The number of work in process accounts used.
    c.   The point at which costs are totaled.
    d.   Unit cost computations.

4. (S.O. 5) Total physical units to be accounted for are equal to the units:
    a.   started (or transferred) into production.
    b.   started (or transferred) into production plus the units in beginning work in process.
    c.   started (or transferred) into production less the units in beginning work in process.
    d.   completed and transferred out.

5. (S.O. 5) Equivalent units of production are a measure of:
    a.   units completed and transferred out.
    b.   units transferred out.
    c.   units in ending work in process.
    d.   the work done during the period expressed in fully completed units.

6. (S.O. 6) In Saint-Simon, Inc., the Assembly Department started 6,000 units and completed 7,000 units. If beginning work in process was 3,000 units, how many units are in ending work in process?
    a.   0.
    b.   1,000.
    c.   2,000.
    d.   4,000.

7. (S.O. 6) In the Blanc Company, the Cutting Department had beginning work in process of 4,000 units, transferred out 9,000 units, and had an ending work in process of 2,000 units. How many units were started by Blanc during the month?
    a.   6,000.
    b.   7,000.
    c.   9,000.
    d.   11,000.

8. (S.O. 6) In the Camria Company, materials are entered at the beginning of the process. If there is no beginning work in process, but there is an ending work in process inventory, the number of equivalent units as to material costs will be:
    a.   the same as the units started.
    b.   the same as the units completed.
    c.   less than the units started.
    d.   less than the units completed.

9. (S.O. 6) In its first month of operation, the Molding Department started 20,000 units into production. During the month, 18,000 units were transferred out and the 2,000 units in work in process were 100% complete as to materials and 40% complete as to conversion costs. Equivalent units for conversion costs are:
    a.   20,000.
    b.   18,000.
    c.   18,800.
    d.   19,200.

10. (S.O. 6) Equivalent units of production for conversion costs:
    a.   includes all of the beginning work in process units transferred out.
    b.   includes only materials added or conversion costs performed on beginning work in process during the period.
    c.   includes all of the ending work in process units started during the period.
    d.   excludes all of the ending work in process units.

11. (S.O. 6) The Cutting Department for Babeuf Company began the period with 4,000 units that were 75% complete, transferred out 14,000 units, and ended with 6,000 units that were 40% complete. The number of equivalent units of conversion costs is:
    a.   13,400.
    b.   14,600.
    c.   15,400.
    d.   16,400.

12. (S.O. 6) The Molding Department of the Smith Company has the following production data: beginning work in process 20,000 units (60% complete), started into production 340,000 units, completed and transferred out 320,000 units, and ending work in process 40,000 units (40% complete).   Assuming materials are entered at the beginning of the process, equivalent units for materials are:
    a.   360,000.
    b.   300,000.
    c.   320,000.
    d.   380,000.

13. (S.O. 6) Using the data in question 12 and assuming conversion costs are incurred uniformly during the process, the equivalent units for conversion costs are:
    a.   320,000.
    b.   324,000.
    c.   336,000.
    d.   360,000.

14. (S.O. 6) Malthus Company has the following equivalent units for July: materials 10,000 and conversion costs 9,000. Production cost data are:

	Materials	Conversion
Work in process, July 1	$ 9,600	$ 4,500
Costs added in July	75,600	63,000

    The unit production costs for July are:

	Materials	Conversion Costs
a.	$7.56	$7.50
b.	8.52	7.00
c.	7.56	7.00
d.	8.52	7.50

15. (S.O. 6) For the Assembly Department, unit materials cost is $8 and unit conversion cost is $12. If there are 4,000 units in ending work in process 75% complete as to conversion costs, the costs to be assigned to the inventory are:
    a. $80,000.
    b. $68,000.
    c. $60,000.
    d. $72,000.

16. (S.O. 6) In the Shaping Department of the Hendrix Company, the unit materials cost is $5.00 and the unit conversion cost is $3.00. The department transferred out 8,000 units and had 1,000 units in ending work in process 20% complete. If all materials are added at the beginning of the process, what is the total cost to be assigned to the ending work in process?
    a. $1,600.
    b. $5,000.
    c. $5,600.
    d. $8,000.

17. (S.O. 7) In a production cost report, which one of the following sections is **not** shown under Costs?
    a.   Unit costs.
    b.   Costs to be accounted for.
    c.   Costs during the period.
    d.   Units accounted for.

18. (S.O. 7) Which of the following statements about the production cost report is **incorrect?**
    a.   Units accounted for must equal units to be accounted for.
    b.   The report only provides a basis for determining whether unit costs and total costs are correct.
    c.   Total costs should reconcile.
    d.   There are four steps in preparing the report.

19. (S.O. 6)   When materials are added at the beginning of the process and costs are transferred in from another department, unit materials cost is based on the:
    a.   sum of the materials costs in the beginning work in process plus the cost of materials added during the period.
    b.   materials costs added during the period.
    c.   sum of the materials costs in the beginning work in process plus materials costs added during the period plus the costs transferred in.
    d.   costs transferred in.

20. (S.O. 6) The Finishing Department of the Monica Company has 27,500 equivalent units of materials in June. An analysis of the work in process account shows: materials cost in beginning work in process $25,000, materials cost added during the period $50,000, and costs transferred in from assembly $200,000. The unit materials cost for June is:
    a. $10.
    b. $8.
    c. $2.
    d. $3.

21. (S.O. 8)   Which of the following statements is **incorrect** concerning just-in-time (JIT) processing?
    a.   U.S. firms are switching to JIT processing in response to foreign competition.
    b.   JIT manufacturing is dedicated to producing the right products at the right time as they are needed.
    c.   JIT strives to eliminate inventories by using a "push" approach in manufacturing.
    d.   JIT accounting creates a Raw and In-Process Inventory account.

22. (S.O. 9) Which of the following statements is **incorrect** concerning activity-based costing (ABC)?
    a.   ABC may be used with either a job order or process cost accounting system.
    b.   ABC assumes all costs related to the activity should respond proportionally to changes in the activity level of the cost driver.
    c.   The primary benefit of ABC is more accurate and meaningful product costing.
    d.   ABC focuses on units of production.

The
Navigator

MATCHING

Match each term with its definition by writing the appropriate letter in the space provided.

Terms

_____ 1. Production cost report.

_____ 2. Physical units.

_____ 3. Process cost accounting.

_____ 4. Operations costing.

_____ 5. Unit production costs.

_____ 6. Weighted-average method.

_____ 7. Equivalent units of production.

_____ 8. Total units (costs) to be accounted for.

_____ 9. Total units (costs) accounted for.

_____ 10. Activity-based costing.

_____ 11. Just-in-time processing.

Definitions

a. An accounting system used to apply costs to similar products that are mass-produced in a continuous fashion.

b. The sum of the units (costs) started (or transferred) into production during the period plus the units (costs) in process at the beginning of the period.

c. A measure of the work done during the period, expressed in fully completed units.

d. Method used to compute equivalent units of production which considers the degree of completion (weighting) of the units completed and transferred out and the ending work in process.

e. Actual units to be accounted for during a period irrespective of any work performed.

f. Costs expressed in terms of equivalent units of production.

g. An internal report that shows both production quantity and production costs.

h. A combination of a process cost and a job order cost system, in which products are manufactured primarily by standardized methods, with some customization.

i. The sum of the units (costs) transferred out during the period plus the units (costs) in process at the end of the period.

j. A processing system dedicated to producing the right products (or parts) as they are needed.

k. A cost accounting system that focuses on the activities performed in manufacturing a specific product.

EXERCISES

EX. 21-1   Avanti Manufacturing Company has two production departments: Molding and Assembly.   March 1 inventories are Raw Materials $3,600, Work in Process—Molding $2,200, Work in Process—Assembly $8,800 and Finished Goods $26,000.   During March, the following transactions occurred:

1.   Purchased $28,400 of raw materials on account.
2.   Incurred $48,000 of factory labor. (Credit Wages Payable.)
3.   Incurred $62,000 of manufacturing overhead; $39,000 was paid and the remainder is unpaid.
4.   Requisitioned materials for Molding $12,300 and Assembly $7,200.
5.   Used Factory labor for Molding $26,000 and Assembly $22,000.
6.   Applied overhead at the rate of $18 per machine hour. Machine hours were Molding 1,540 and Assembly 1,430.
7.   Transferred goods costing $62,000 from the Molding Department to the Assembly Department.
8.   Transferred goods costing $122,600 from Assembly to Finished Goods.
9.   Sold goods costing $110,000 for $185,000 on account.

Instructions
Journalize the transactions. (Omit explanations.)

EX. 21-2   (S.O. 5 and 6) Sismondi Company has a process cost accounting system. During May, the Assembly and Finishing Departments had the following data concerning physical units:

Assembly:	
Work in process, May 1	3,000
Started into process during the month	65,000
Work in process, May 31	7,000

Finishing:	
Work in process, May 1	6,000
Transferred in from Assembly Department during the month	?
Work in process, May 31	4,000

Instructions
Compute the physical units transferred out and in process for each department.

SISMONDI COMPANY

	Assembly	**Finishing**
Units to be accounted for		
Units accounted for		

EX. 21-3   (S.O. 2 through 8) The Muller Company reports the following physical units for its Polishing Department for the month ended July 31, 2010.

Units to be accounted for	Physical Units
Work in process, July 1	1,000
Transferred in	11,000
Total units	12,000

Units accounted for	
Completed and transferred out	10,500
Work in process, July 31 (30% complete)	1,500
Total units accounted for	12,000

Work in process July 1 was $3,000 for direct materials and $1,920 for conversion costs. Costs incurred in July were: materials $59,400, labor $23,520, and overhead $9,600. The percentage complete refers to conversion costs. Materials and transferred in units are added at the beginning of the process.

Instructions
Prepare the production cost report.

MULLER COMPANY
Polishing Department
Production Cost Report
For the Month Ended July 31, 2010

		Equivalent Units	
QUANTITIES	**Physical Units**	**Materials**	**Conversion Costs**

Units to be accounted for

Units accounted for

COSTS

Unit costs	Materials	Conversion Costs	Total

Costs to be accounted for

Costs Reconciliation Schedule

*EX. 21-4   (S.O. 11) Fastchip, Inc. manufactures two computers: the FC-PC which sells for $2,000, and the FC-laptop, which sells for $4,200. The production cost per unit for each computer in 2010 was as follows:

	FC-PC	FC-laptop
Direct Materials	$1,260	$3,040
Direct labor ($25 per hour)	200	300
Manufacturing overhead ($10 per DLH)	80	120
Total per unit cost	$1,540	$3,460

In 2010, Fastchip manufactured 20,000 units of the FC-PC and 15,000 units of the FC-laptop. The overhead rate of $10 per direct labor hour was determined by dividing the total expected manufacturing overhead of $3,400,000 by the total direct labor hours (340,000) for the two computers.

The gross profit and gross margin on the computers were: FC-PC $460 ($2,000 - $1,540) and 23% ($460/$2,000); and FC-laptop $740 ($4,200 - $3,460) and 17.62% ($740/$4,200). Because of the lower profit margin on the FC-laptop, management is considering phasing out the FC-laptop and increasing the production of the FC-PC.

Before finalizing its decision, management asks the controller of Fastchip to prepare an analysis using activity-based costing. The controller accumulates the following information about overhead for the year ended December 31, 2010:

Activity	Cost Driver	Total Cost	Cost Driver Volume	Overhead Rate
Ordering raw materials	# of orders	$ 100,000	80	$1,250
Receiving raw materials	# of shipments	$ 120,000	75	$1,600
Materials handling	weight of materials	$ 600,000	60,000 lbs.	$ 10
Production scheduling	# of orders	$ 100,000	35,000	$ 2.86
Machining	machine hours	$ 800,000	2,000	$ 400
Quality control inspections	# of inspections	$1,200,000	10,000	$ 120
Factory supervision	# of employees	$ 480,000	250	$1,920

The cost driver volume for each product was:

Cost Driver	FC-PC	FC-laptop	Total
# of orders-r.m.	60	20	80
# of shipments-r.m.	50	25	75
weight of materials	40,000 lbs.	20,000 lbs.	60,000 lbs.
# of orders-prod.	20,000	15,000	35,000
machine hours	1,100	900	2,000
# of inspections	8,000	2,000	10,000
# of employees	150	100	250

Instructions
(a)   Assign the total 2010 manufacturing overhead costs to the two products using activity-based costing (ABC).
(b)   What was the cost per unit, gross profit and gross margin of each model using ABC costing?

SOLUTIONS TO REVIEW QUESTIONS AND EXERCISES

TRUE-FALSE

1. (F)   Job order costing focuses on the individual job, while process cost accounting focuses on the processes involved in producing homogeneous products.
2. (T)
3. (F)   A distinctive feature of process cost accounting is that individual work in process accounts are maintained for each production department or manufacturing process.
4. (F)   Under process cost accounting, the determination of total manufacturing costs is made for each accounting period.
5. (F)   Both job order costing and process costing track the same three manufacturing cost elements—direct materials, direct labor, and manufacturing overhead.
6. (F)   The flow of costs indicates that materials, labor, and manufacturing overhead can be added in any or all departments.
7. (T)
8. (T)
9. (F)   Fewer requisitions are generally required because the materials are used for processes rather than jobs.
10. (T)
11. (F)   When finished goods are sold, the entry to record the cost of goods sold is a debit to Cost of Goods Sold and a credit to Finished Goods Inventory.
12. (T)
13. (T)
14. (T)
15. (T)
16. (T)
17. (F)   The unit conversion cost is equal to the total conversion costs divided by equivalent units of conversion costs.
18. (T)
19. (F)   The order of calculation in a production cost report requires that the computation of the physical unit flow come before the computation of the unit production costs.
20. (T)
21. (F)   A primary objective of just-in-time manufacturing is to eliminate all manufacturing inventories.
22. (T)
23. (T)

MULTIPLE CHOICE

1. (c)   Process cost accounting focuses on the process involved in producing homogeneous products not on individual jobs. Answers (a), (b), and (d) are all correct statements concerning process cost accounting.

2. (b)   One of the differences between a job order cost and a process cost system is the documents used to track costs. Answers a., c., and d., are all considered to be examples of similarities between the two systems.

3. (a)   One of the similarities between a job order cost and a process cost system is the flow of costs. Answers b., c., and d., are all considered to be examples of differences between the two systems.

4. (b) Total physical units are equal to the sum of the units started (or transferred) into production plus the units in beginning work in process.

5. (d) Equivalent units of production are a measure of the work done during the period expressed in fully completed units.

6. (c) The number of units in ending work in process is:

Beginning work in process	3,000
Started	6,000
Total units to be accounted for	9,000
Less: Units completed	7,000
Ending work in process	2,000

7. (b) The number of units started is:

Transferred out	9,000
Ending work in process	2,000
Total units accounted for	11,000
Less: Beginning work in process	4,000
Number of units started	7,000

8. (a) Because the inventory is 100% complete as to materials costs, the number of equivalent units would be equal to the number of units started into production. All of the units started (even units not completed) have 100% of the materials used.

9. (c) Equivalent units are equal to the 18,000 units transferred out plus 800 units of ending work in process (2,000 X 40%).

10. (a) Equivalent units of production for conversion costs includes all the units transferred out which usually includes all of the beginning work in process units.

11. (d) The number of equivalent units is:

Units transferred out	14,000
Ending work in process (6,000 X .40)	2,400
Total equivalent units	16,400

12. (a) Equivalent units for materials are:

Units transferred out	320,000
Ending work in process (40,000 X 100%)	40,000
Total equivalent units	360,000

13. (c) Equivalent units for conversion costs are:

Units transferred out	320,000
Ending work in process (40,000 X 40%)	16,000
Total equivalent units	336,000

14. (d) Total materials cost ($9,600 + $75,600) divided by 10,000 units is $8.52 and total conversion costs ($4,500 + $63,000) divided by 9,000 units is $7.50.

15. (b) The materials cost is $32,000 (4,000 X $8) and the conversion cost is $36,000 (3,000 equivalent units X $12).

16. (c) The total cost to be assigned to the ending work in process is:

Materials	1,000 X 100% X $5.00 =	$5,000
Conversion costs	1,000 X 20% X $3.00 =	600
Total		$5,600

17. (d) Units accounted for are reported under Quantities in the production cost report.

18. (b) The report is generally used for evaluating the productivity of a department.

19. (c) When materials are added at the beginning of the process, transferred in costs are considered to be a materials cost. The base for computing unit materials cost is the sum of the materials cost added during the period plus the costs transferred in.

20. (a) Transferred in costs are considered to be a materials cost. Thus, the total materials cost is $275,000 and the unit materials cost is $10 ($275,000 ÷ 27,500).

21. (c) Just-in-time manufacturing strives to eliminate inventories by using a "pull" approach in manufacturing. Answers a., b., and d. are all correct statements concerning just-in-time manufacturing.

22. (d) Conventional cost systems focus on units of production. ABC focuses on the activities performed to produce specific products. Answers a., b., and c. are all correct statements about ABC.

MATCHING

1.	g		7.	c
2.	e		8.	b
3.	a		9.	i
4.	h		10.	k
5.	f		11.	j
6.	d.			

EXERCISES

EX. 21-1

1.	Raw Materials		28,400	
	Accounts Payable			28,400
2.	Factory Labor		48,000	
	Wages Payable			48,000
3.	Manufacturing Overhead		62,000	
	Cash			39,000
	Accounts Payable			23,000
4.	Work in Process—Molding		12,300	
	Work in Process—Assembly		7,200	
	Raw Materials Inventory			19,500
5.	Work in Process—Molding		26,000	
	Work in Process—Assembly		22,000	
	Factory Labor			48,000
6.	Work in Process—Molding		27,720	
	Work in Process—Assembly		25,740	
	Manufacturing Overhead			53,460
7.	Work in Process—Assembly		62,000	
	Work in Process—Molding			62,000
8.	Finished Goods Inventory		122,600	
	Work in Process—Assembly			122,600
9.	Cost of Goods Sold		110,000	
	Finished Goods Inventory			110,000
	Accounts Receivable		185,000	
	Sales			185,000

EX. 21-2

SISMONDI COMPANY

	Assembly	Finishing
Units to be accounted for		
Beginning work in process	3,000	6,000
Started into production	65,000	61,000
Total units	68,000	67,000
Units accounted for		
Transferred out	61,000	63,000
Ending work in process	7,000	4,000
Total units	68,000	67,000

EX. 21-3

MULLER COMPANY
Polishing Department
Production Cost Report
For the Month Ended July 31, 2010

QUANTITIES	Physical Units	Materials	Conversion Costs	
			Equivalent Units	
Units to be accounted for				
Work in process, July 1	1,000			
Transferred in	11,000			
Total units	12,000			
Units accounted for				
Transferred out	10,500	10,500	10,500	
Work in process, July 31	1,500	1,500	450	(1,500 X 30%)
Total units	12,000	12,000	10,950	

COSTS

Unit costs		Materials	Conversion Costs	Total
Costs in July	(a)	$62,400*	$35,040**	$97,440
Equivalent units	(b)	12,000	10,950	
Unit costs (a) ÷ (b)		$5.20	$3.20	$8.40

Costs to be accounted for	
In process, July 1	$ 4,920
Costs in July	92,520
Total costs charged	$97,440

Costs Reconciliation Schedule

Costs accounted for		
Transferred out (10,500 X $8.40)		$88,200
Work in process, July 30		
Materials (1,500 X $5.20)	7,800	
Conversion costs (450 X $3.20)	1,440	9,240
Total costs accounted for		$97,440

*Work in process $3,000 + materials added $59,400
**Work in process $1,920 + labor $23,520 + overhead $9,600.

*EX. 21-4

(a)

	Rate	FC-PC Number	FC-PC Cost	FC-laptop Number	FC-laptop Cost	Cost
# of orders-r.m.	$1,250	60	$ 75,000	20	$ 25,000	$ 100,000
# of shipments-r.m.	1,600	50	80,000	25	40,000	120,000
weight of materials	10	40,000	400,000	20,000	200,000	600,000
# of orders-prod.	2.86	20,000	57,200	15,000	42,900	100,100*
machine hours	400	1,100	440,000	900	360,000	800,000
# of inspections	120	8,000	960,000	2,000	240,000	1,200,000
# of employees	1,920	150	288,000	100	192,000	480,000
Total assigned costs			$2,300,200		$1,099,900	$3,400,100*
Units produced			20,000		15,000	
Overhead cost per unit			$ 115.01		$ 73.33	

*rounding error of $100.

(b)

	FC-PC	FC-laptop
Direct Materials	$1,260.00	$3,040.00
Direct labor ($25 per hour)	200.00	300.00
Manufacturing overhead	115.01	73.33
Total per unit cost	$1,575.01	$3,413.33

FC-PC

Gross profit: $2,000 - $1,575.01 = $424.99

Gross margin: $424.99/$2,000 = 21.25%

FC-laptop

Gross profit: $4,200 - $3,413.33 = $786.67

Gross margin: $786.67/$4,200 = 18.73%

Chapter 22

COST-VOLUME-PROFIT

The Navigator	✓
■ Scan Study Objectives	☐
■ Read Preview	☐
■ Read Chapter Review	☐
■ Work Demonstration Problem	☐
■ Answer True-False Statements	☐
■ Answer Multiple-Choice Questions	☐
■ Match Terms and Definitions	☐
■ Solve Exercises	☐

CHAPTER STUDY OBJECTIVES

After studying this chapter, you should be able to:
1. Distinguish between variable and fixed costs.
2. Explain the significance of the relevant range.
3. Explain the concept of mixed costs.
4. List the five components of cost-volume-profit analysis.
5. Indicate what contribution margin is and how it can be expressed.
6. Identify the three ways to determine the break-even point.
7. Give the formulas for determining sales required to earn target net income.
8. Define margin of safety, and give the formulas for computing it.
9. Describe the essential features of a cost-volume-profit income statement.
*10. Explain the difference between absorption costing and variable costing.

*Note: All asterisked (*) items relate to material contained in the Appendix to the chapter.

PREVIEW OF CHAPTER 22

Management must understand how costs respond to changes in sales volume and the effect of the interaction of costs and revenues on profits. A prerequisite to understanding cost-volume-profit (CVP) relationships is knowledge of the behavior of costs. In this chapter, we first explain the considerations involved in cost behavior analysis. Then we discuss and illustrate CVP analysis and variable costing. The content and organization of the chapter are as follows:

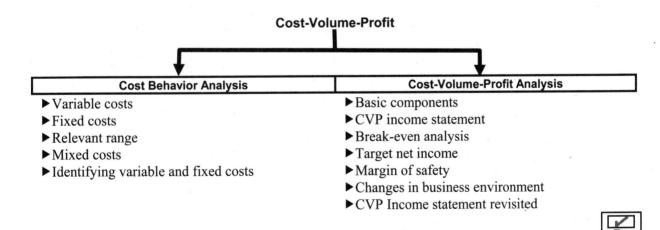

CHAPTER REVIEW

Cost Behavior Analysis

1. **Cost behavior analysis** is the study of how specific costs respond to changes in the level of business activity. A knowledge of cost behavior helps management plan operations and decide between alternative courses of action.

2. The **activity index** identifies the activity that causes changes in the behavior of costs; examples include direct labor hours, sales dollars, and units of output. With an appropriate activity index, costs can be classified as variable, fixed or mixed.

Variable and Fixed Costs

3. (S.O. 1) **Variable costs** are costs that **vary in total** directly and proportionately with changes in the activity level. Examples of variable costs include direct materials and direct labor, sales commissions, and freight out. A variable cost may also be defined as a cost that **remains the same per unit** at every level of activity.

4. **Fixed costs** are costs that remain the same in total regardless of changes in the activity level. Examples include property taxes, insurance, rent, supervisory salaries, and depreciation. Fixed costs per unit vary inversely with activity; as volume increases, unit cost declines and vice versa.

Relevant Range

5. (S.O. 2) The range over which a company expects to operate during the year is called the **relevant range.** Within the relevant range a **straight-line relationship** exists for both variable and fixed costs.

Mixed Costs

6. (S.O. 3) **Mixed costs** contain both a variable element and a fixed element; they increase in total as the activity level increases, but not proportionately. For purposes of CVP analysis, mixed costs must be classified into their fixed and variable elements.

7. The **high-low method** uses the total costs incurred at the high and low levels of activity. The difference in costs represents variable costs, since only the variable cost element can change as activity levels change.

8. The steps in computing fixed and variable costs under the high-low method are:
    a. Determine variable cost per unit from the following formula:

    $$\text{Change in Total Costs} \div \text{High minus Low Activity Level} = \text{Variable Cost per Unit}$$

    b. Determine the fixed cost by subtracting the total variable cost at either the high or the low activity level from the total cost at that activity level.

Cost-Volume-Profit Analysis

9. **Cost-volume-profit (CVP) analysis** is the study of the effects of changes in costs and volume on a company's profits. It is a critical factor in such management decisions as profit planning, setting selling prices, determining the product mix, and maximizing use of production facilities.

10. CVP analysis considers the interrelationships among the following **components**: (a) volume or level of activity, (b) unit selling prices, (c) variable cost per unit, (d) total fixed costs, and (e) sales mix.

Basic CVP Components

11. (S.O. 4) The following **assumptions** underlie each CVP analysis:
     a.   The behavior of both costs and revenues is linear throughout the relevant range of the activity index.
     b.   All costs can be classified with reasonable accuracy as either variable or fixed.
     c.   Changes in activity are the only factors that affect costs.
     d.   All units produced are sold.
     e.   When more than one type of product is sold, the sales mix will remain constant.

Contribution Margin

12. (S.O. 5) **Contribution margin** is the amount of revenue remaining after deducting variable costs. The formula for contribution margin per unit is:

$$\text{Unit Selling Price} - \text{Unit Variable Cost} = \text{Contribution Margin Per Unit}$$

13. Contribution margin per unit indicates the amount available to cover fixed costs and contribute to income. The formula for the **contribution margin ratio** is:

$$\text{Contribution Margin per Unit} \div \text{Unit Selling Price} = \text{Contribution Margin Ratio}$$

The ratio indicates the portion of each sales dollar that is available to apply to fixed costs and to contribute to income.

Break-Even Analysis

14. (S.O. 6) The **break-even point** is the level of activity at which total revenue equals total costs, both fixed and variable. Knowledge of the break-even point is useful to management when it decides whether to introduce new product lines, change sales prices on established products, or enter new market areas.

15. A common equation used for CVP analysis is as follows:

$$\text{Sales} = \text{Variable Costs} + \text{Fixed Costs} + \text{Net Income}$$

16. Under the **contribution margin technique,** the break-even point can be computed by using either the contribution margin per unit or the contribution margin ratio.

17. The formula, using unit contribution margin, is:

$$\text{Fixed Costs} \quad \div \quad \frac{\text{Contribution}}{\text{Margin per Unit}} \quad = \quad \frac{\text{Break-even Point}}{\text{in Units}}$$

18.   The formula using the contribution margin is:

$$\text{Fixed Costs} \quad \div \quad \frac{\text{Contribution}}{\text{Margin Ratio}} \quad = \quad \frac{\text{Break-even Point}}{\text{in Dollars}}$$

19.   A chart (or graph) can also be used as an effective means to determine and illustrate the break-even point. A cost-volume-profit (CVP) graph is as follows:

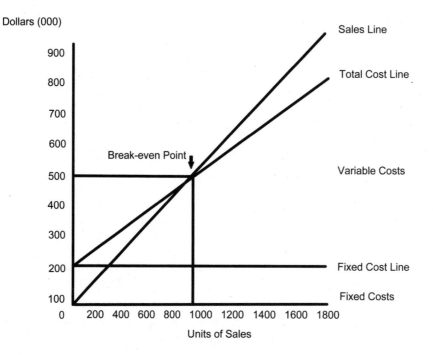

Target Net Income

20.   (S.O. 7) **Target net income** is the income objective for individual product lines. The following equation is used to determine target net income sales:

Required Sales = Variable Costs + Fixed Costs + Target Net Income

Margin of Safety

21.   (S.O. 8) **Margin of safety** is the difference between actual or expected sales and sales at the break-even point.
a.   The formula for stating the margin of safety in dollars is:

$$\frac{\text{Actual (Expected)}}{\text{Sales}} \quad - \quad \text{Break-even Sales} \quad = \quad \frac{\text{Margin of Safety}}{\text{in Dollars}}$$

b.   The formula for determining the margin of safety ratio is:

$$\frac{\text{Margin of Safety}}{\text{in Dollars}} \quad \div \quad \frac{\text{Actual (Expected)}}{\text{Sales}} \quad = \quad \frac{\text{Margin of}}{\text{Safety Ratio}}$$

The higher the dollars or the percentage, the greater the margin of safety.

CVP Income Statement

22. (S.O. 9) The **cost-volume-profit (CVP) income statement** classifies costs and expenses as variable or fixed and specifically reports contribution margin in the body of the statement.

Absorption and Variable Costing

*23. (S.O. 10) There are two approaches to **product costing.**
  a. Under **full or absorption costing** all manufacturing costs are charged to the product.
  b. Under **variable costing,** only direct materials, direct labor, and variable manufacturing overhead costs are product costs; fixed manufacturing overhead costs are recognized as period costs (expenses) when incurred.

*24. The income statement under variable costing is prepared in the cost-volume-profit format.

*25. The effects of the alternative costing methods on income from operations are:

Circumstance	Effects on Income From Operations
Units produced exceed units sold	Income under absorption costing is higher than under variable costing
Units produced are less than units sold	Income under absorption costing is lower than under variable costing
Units produced equal units sold	Income will be equal under both approaches

*26. The use of variable costing in product costing is acceptable only for **internal use by management.** It cannot be used in determining products costs in financial statements prepared in accordance with generally accepted accounting principles because it understates inventory costs.

The Navigator

DEMONSTRATION PROBLEM (S.O. 1, 6, 7, and 8)

The Valley Video Shop has two employees. The manager, J.J., is paid $2,200 per month. The other employee, Bob, is paid $1,200 per month. In addition, Bob is paid a commission of 20 cents per video that is rented. Other monthly costs are: store rent $1,000 plus 10 cents per rented video, depreciation on videos $1,000, utilities $400, and advertising $400. The price of a rented movie is $2.00.

Instructions
(a)   Determine the variable cost per rented video and the total monthly fixed costs.
(b)   Compute the break-even point in units and dollars.
(c)   Determine the margin of safety and margin of safety ratio, assuming 5,000 videos are rented in a month.
(d)   Determine the rentals required to earn net income of $2,000.

SOLUTION TO DEMONSTRATION PROBLEM

(a)   Variable Cost = $0.30 ($0.20 + $0.10)
       Fixed Cost = $6,200 ($2,200 + $1,200 + $1,000 + $1,000 + $400 + $400)

(b)   Break-even Point: $6,200/($2.00 - $0.30) = 3,648 rented videos
                            (3,648 X $2.00) = $7,296 in sales dollars

(c)   (1) $10,000 - $7,296 = $2,704.
       (2) $2,704 ÷ $10,000 = 27.04%

(d)   Required sales: ($6,200 + $2,000) ÷ ($2.00 - $.30) = 4,824 rentals or $9,648.

REVIEW QUESTIONS AND EXERCISES

TRUE—FALSE

Indicate whether each of the following is true (T) or false (F) in the space provided.

_____ 1. (S.O. 1) The activity level is represented by an activity index such as direct labor hours, units of output, or sales dollars.

_____ 2. (S.O. 1) Variable cost per unit changes as the level of activity changes.

_____ 3. (S.O. 1) Fixed costs remain the same in total regardless of changes in the activity index.

_____ 4. (S.O. 1) The trend in most companies is to have more variable costs and fewer fixed costs.

_____ 5. (S.O. 2) Within the relevant range, it is assumed costs are curvilinear.

_____ 6. (S.O. 3) For purposes of CVP analysis, mixed costs must be classified into their fixed and variable elements.

_____ 7. (S.O. 3) The high-low method is a mathematical method that uses total costs incurred at the high and low levels of activity.

_____ 8. (S.O. 3) Under the high-low method, the variable cost per unit is computed by dividing the change in total costs by the high minus low activity level.

_____ 9. (S.O. 4) One assumption of CVP analysis is that changes in activity are **not** the only factors that affect costs.

_____ 10. (S.O. 4) One assumption of CVP analysis is that all costs can be classified as either variable or fixed with reasonable accuracy.

_____ 11. (S.O. 5) The contribution margin per unit is the unit selling price less the fixed costs per unit.

_____ 12. (S.O. 5) The contribution margin ratio of 30% means that 70 cents of each sales dollar is available to cover fixed costs and to produce a profit.

_____ 13. (S.O. 6) If the contribution margin ratio is 60% and the amount of fixed costs are $400,000, then the sales dollars at the break-even point are $666,667.

_____ 14. (S.O. 6) At the break-even point, contribution margin must equal total fixed costs.

_____ 15. (S.O. 6) A cost-volume-profit graph shows the amount of net income or loss at each level of sales.

_____ 16. (S.O. 7) If variable costs per unit are 70% of sales, fixed costs are $290,000, and target net income is $70,000, required sales are $1,200,000.

_____ 17. (S.O. 8) The margin of safety is the difference between fixed costs and variable costs.

_____ 18. (S.O. 8)   The margin of safety ratio is equal to the margin of safety in dollars divided by the actual or (expected) sales.

_____ 19. (S.O. 9)   A CVP income statement classifies expenses by function rather than by cost behavior.

_____ *20. (S.O. 10) Absorption costing and variable costing differ in the treatment of all manu-facturing costs.

_____ *21. (S.O. 10) When units produced exceed units sold, income is lower under absorption costing than under variable costing.

_____ *22. (S.O. 10) When units produced equal units sold, income is the same under both absorption costing and variable costing.

_____ *23. (S.O. 10) The use of variable costing is only acceptable for internal use by manage-ment.

MULTIPLE CHOICE

Circle the letter that best answers each of the following statements.

1. (S.O. 1) Costs that vary in total directly and proportionately with changes in the activity level are:
    a.   variable costs.
    b.   fixed costs.
    c.   mixed costs.
    d.   semivariable costs.

2. (S.O. 1) Fixed costs are costs that:
    a.   remain the same in total regardless of changes in the activity level.
    b.   vary inversely with activity on a per unit basis.
    c.   both (a) and (b).
    d.   neither (a) nor (b).

3. (S.O. 2) Within the relevant range, the variable cost per unit:
    a.   differs at each activity level.
    b.   remains constant at each activity level.
    c.   increases as production increases.
    d.   decreases as production increases.

4. (S.O. 3) In the Gabbana Company, maintenance costs are a mixed cost. At the low level of activity (40 direct labor hours), maintenance costs are $600. At the high level of activity (100 direct labor hours), maintenance costs are $1,100. Using the high-low method, what is the variable maintenance cost per unit and the total fixed maintenance cost?

	Variable Cost Per Unit	Total Fixed Cost
a.	$8.33	$267
b.	$8.33	$500
c.	$11.00	$220
d.	$15.00	$400

5. (S.O. 4) Which of the following is **not** an underlying assumption of cost-volume-profit analysis?
   a. All costs can be classified as either variable or fixed with reasonable accuracy.
   b. When more than one type of product is sold, total sales will be in a constant sales mix.
   c. Changes in activity and other factors affect costs.
   d. The behavior of both costs and revenues is linear throughout the entire range of the activity index.

6. (S.O. 5) The contribution margin ratio increases when:
   a. fixed costs increase.
   b. fixed costs decrease.
   c. variable costs as a percentage of sales decrease.
   d. variable costs as a percentage of sales increase.

7. (S.O. 5) The contribution margin per unit decreases when unit selling price remains the same and:
   a. fixed costs increase.
   b. fixed costs decrease.
   c. variable costs per unit increases.
   d. variable cost per unit decreases.

8. (S.O. 6) A formula for break-even point in sales dollars is:
   a. Contribution margin per unit divided by fixed costs.
   b. Fixed costs divided by contribution margin per unit.
   c. Contribution margin ratio divided by fixed costs.
   d. Fixed costs divided by contribution margin ratio.

9. (S.O. 6) Dolce Company is planning to sell 400,000 hammers for $1.50 per unit. The contribution margin ratio is 20%. If Dolce will break even at this level of sales, what are the fixed costs?
   a. $120,000.
   b. $280,000.
   c. $400,000.
   d. $480,000.

10. (S.O. 6) At the break-even point, fixed costs are:
   a. less than the contribution margin.
   b. equal to the contribution margin.
   c. more than the contribution margin.
   d. indeterminate of the contribution margin.

Items 11 and 12 are based on the following data for the Mizrahi Company.
Sales (50,000 units) $1,000,000, direct materials and direct labor $300,000, other variable costs $50,000, and fixed costs $130,000.

11.   (S.O. 6) What is Mizrahi's break-even point in units?
a.   9,848.
b.   10,000.
c.   18,571.
d.   26,000.

12.   (S.O. 6) What is Mizrahi's contribution margin ratio?
a.   66%.
b.   65%.
c.   59%.
d.   35%.

13.   (S.O. 6) Versace Company is contemplating an expansion program based on expected sales $600,000, variable costs $420,000, and fixed costs $120,000. What is the amount of break-even sales?
a. $400,000.
b. $420,000.
c. $540,000.
d. $660,000.

14.   Mugler Company sells radios for $50 per unit. The fixed costs are $210,000 and the variable costs are 60% of the selling price. As a result of new automated equipment, it is anticipated that fixed costs will increase by $50,000 and variable costs will be 50% of the selling price. The new break-even point in units is:
a.   10,500.
b.   10,400.
c.   10,300.
d.   8,400.

Items 15 and 16 are based on the following data:

Moschino Company sells cassette players for $60 each. Variable costs are $40 per unit, and fixed costs total $30,000.

15.   (S.O. 7) How many cassette players must Moschino sell to earn net income of $70,000?
a.   5,000.
b.   3,500.
c.   2,500.
d.   1,500.

16.   (S.O. 6) What sales are needed by Moschino to break even?
a. $40,000.
b. $75,000.
c. $90,000.
d. $120,000.

17. (S.O. 7) Lagerfeld Company reported the following results from the sale of 5,000 hammers in May: sales $200,000, variable costs $120,000, fixed costs $60,000, and net income $20,000. Assume that Lagerfeld increases the selling price of hammers by 10% on June 1. How many hammers will have to be sold in June to maintain the same level of net income?
    a. 4,000.
    b. 4,300.
    c. 4,500.
    d. 5,000.

18. (S.O. 8) Gaultier Company had actual sales of $800,000 when break-even sales were $600,000. What is the margin of safety ratio?
    a. 25%.
    b. 33%.
    c. 67%.
    d. 75%.

19. (S.O. 9) Givenchy Company sells 100,000 wrenches for $12.00 a unit. Fixed costs are $280,000 and net income is $200,000. What should be reported as variable expenses in the CVP income statement?
    a. $480,000.
    b. $720,000.
    c. $900,000.
    d. $920,000.

*20. (S.O. 10) In the Klein Company, 50,000 units are produced and 40,000 units are sold. Variable manufacturing costs per unit are $8 and fixed manufacturing costs are $160,000. The cost of the ending finished goods inventory under each costing approach is:

	Absorption Costing	Variable Costing
a.	$112,000	$ 80,000
b.	112,000	100,000
c.	120,000	80,000
d.	120,000	100,000

*21. (S.O. 10) When units produced are less than units sold, income under absorption costing will be:
    a. higher than under variable costing.
    b. the same as under variable costing.
    c. lower than under variable costing.
    d. indeterminate compared to variable costing.

*22. (S.O. 10) In the Hermes Company, sales are $800,000, cost of goods under absorption costing is $600,000 and total operating expenses are $120,000. If cost of goods sold is 70% variable and total operating expenses are 60% fixed, what is the contribution margin under variable costing?
    a. $380,000.
    b. $332,000.
    c. $308,000.
    d. $260,000.

*23.   (S.O. 10) Variable costing is:
   a.   not compatible with responsibility accounting.
   b.   acceptable under generally accepted accounting principles.
   c.   acceptable for income tax purposes.
   d.   only acceptable for internal use by management.

MATCHING

Match each term with its definition by writing the appropriate letter in the space provided.

Terms	Definitions
_____ 1. Contribution margin.	a. The study of how specific costs respond to changes in the level of activity.
_____ 2. Relevant range.	b. A costing approach in which all manufacturing costs are charged to the product.
_____ 3. Variable costs.	c. The level of activity at which total revenues equal total costs.
_____ 4. CVP income statement.	d. Costs that contain both variable and a fixed cost element.
_____ 5. Mixed costs.	e. The income objective for individual product lines.
_____ 6. Margin of safety.	f. A statement for internal use that classifies costs and expenses as fixed or variable and reports contribution margin.
_____ 7. Cost behavior analysis.	g. A costing approach in which only variable manufacturing costs are product costs and fixed manufacturing costs are period costs (expenses).
_____ 8. Target net income.	
_____ 9. Absorption costing.	h. The difference between actual or expected sales and sales at the break-even point.
_____ 10. Cost-volume-profit (CVP) analysis.	i. Costs that remain the same in total regardless of changes in the activity level.
_____ 11. Variable costing.	j. The amount of revenue remaining after deducting variable costs.
_____ 12. High-low method.	k. The study of the effects of changes in costs and volume on a company's profits.
_____ 13. Fixed costs.	l. The range of the activity index over which the company expects to operate during the year.
_____ 14. Break-even point.	m. Costs that vary in total directly and proportionately with changes in the activity level.
	n. A mathematical method that uses the total costs incurred at the high and low levels of activity.

EXERCISES

EX. 22-1   (S.O. 3) Galliano Company has accumulated the following information pertaining to maintenance costs for the last eight months.

Month	Direct Labor Hours	Maintenance Cost
January	2,800	$15,000
February	1,000	7,000
March	2,500	13,000
April	4,000	22,000
May	3,000	18,000
June	3,500	19,000
July	1,500	8,000
August	2,000	10,000

Instructions
Using the high-low method, compute (1) variable cost per direct labor hour and (2) the fixed cost per month.

EX. 22-2   (S.O. 5, 6, 7, and 8) Rykiel Company sells radios. For the year its revenues and costs were: sales $550,000 (11,000 units), variable costs $330,000, and fixed costs $150,000.

Instructions
(a)   Compute the contribution margin per unit.
(b)   Compute the contribution margin ratio.
(c)   Compute the break-even point in dollars using the contribution margin ratio.
(d)   Compute the break-even point in units using the unit contribution margin.
(e)   Compute the margin of safety ratio.
(f)   Compute the number of units that must be sold to earn net income of $100,000.

(a)   _____

        _____

        _____

        _____

        _____

        _____

(b)   _____

        _____

        _____

        _____

        _____

        _____

(c)   _____

        _____

        _____

        _____

        _____

        _____

(d)

(e)

(f)

*EX. 22-3   (S.O. 10) During March of 2010 Fendi Company produced 3,000 units but only sold 2,500 units. The company had no beginning inventory. The unit selling price was $4,000. Manufacturing costs were: variable $2,000 per unit produced and fixed $1,800,000. Selling and administrative expenses were: variable $80 per unit of sales and fixed $300,000.

Instructions
(a)   Compute the manufacturing cost of one unit of product using (1) absorption costing and (2) variable costing.
(b)   Prepare an income statement for March using the variable costing approach.

(a)   _____

_____

_____

_____

_____

_____

(b)   _____

_____

_____

_____

_____

_____

_____

_____

_____

_____

_____

_____

_____

The
Navigator

SOLUTIONS TO REVIEW QUESTIONS AND EXERCISES

TRUE-FALSE

1.   (T)
2.   (F)   A variable cost remains the same per unit at every level of activity.
3.   (T)
4.   (F)   Because of increased use of automation and less use of the work force, the trend in most companies is to have more fixed costs and fewer variable costs.
5.   (F)   Within the relevant range, costs are assumed to be linear.
6.   (T)
7.   (T)
8.   (T)
9.   (F)   One assumption of CVP analysis is that changes in activity are the only factors that affect costs.
10. (T)
11. (F)   The contribution margin per unit is the unit selling price less the variable costs per unit.
12. (F)   The contribution margin ratio of 30% means that 30 cents of each sales dollar is available to cover fixed costs and to produce a profit.
13. (T)
14. (T)
15. (T)
16. (T)
17. (F)   The margin of safety is the difference between actual or expected sales and sales at the break-even point.
18. (T)
19. (F)   A CVP income statement classifies expenses by behavior (variable or fixed); a traditional statement classifies expenses by function.
*20. (F) The approaches only differ concerning fixed manufacturing overhead costs which are a product cost under absorption costing and a period cost under variable costing.
*21. (F) In this circumstance, income is higher under absorption costing than under variable costing.
*22. (T)
*23. (T)

MULTIPLE CHOICE

1. (a)   Fixed costs remain the same in total as activity levels change (b). Mixed costs and semivariable costs are the same; they increase in total but not proportionately.

2. (c)   In total, a fixed cost remains the same regardless of changes in the activity level. However, as volume increases, unit cost declines and vice versa.

3. (b)   The variable cost per unit remains constant at different levels of activity. The total variable cost changes in proportion and direction with the change in the activity level.

4. (a)   To determine the variable cost per unit, the following formula is used:

		High minus Low		Variable Cost
Change in Total Costs	÷	Activity Level	=	per Unit
($1,100 - $600)	÷	(100 - 40)	=	$8.33

The fixed cost ($267) is determined by subtracting the total variable cost at either activity level from the total cost at that activity level: High = $1,100 - (100 X $8.33); Low = $600 - (40 X $8.33).

5. (c)   Answers a., b., and d., are all underlying assumptions of cost-volume-profit analysis. Answer (c) is not an underlying assumption because the assumption is that changes in activity are the only factor that affects costs.

6. (c)   The following format can be used to visualize the effect on the contribution margin ratio:

	Dollars	**Percentage**
Sales	$100	100%
Variable costs	60	60%
Contribution margin	$ 40	40%

Thus, if variable costs as a percentage of sales decreases, the contribution margin ratio will increase. The changes in fixed costs are not relevant.

7. (c)   The following format represents the contribution margin per unit of a hypothetical product:

	Per Unit
Sales	$10.00
Variable costs	6.00
Contribution margin	$ 4.00

If the variable cost per unit increases, then the contribution margin decreases. Fixed costs are not a factor in computing contribution margin.

8. (d)   Fixed costs divided by the contribution margin ratio equals the break-even point in dollars. Fixed costs divided by the contribution margin per unit equals the break-even point in units.

9. (a) At the break-even point, fixed costs equal the contribution margin. The contribution margin is $120,000 [20% X (400,000 x $1.50)], which is also the amount of fixed costs.

10. (b) If fixed costs and the contribution margin are not equal, then the net income is not equal to zero and therefore the company is not at break-even point.

11. (b) The contribution per unit is unit selling price $20 ($1,000,000 ÷ 50,000) less unit variable costs $7 [($300,000 + $50,000) ÷ 50,000] or $13. Break-even sales in units equals fixed costs $130,000 ÷ contribution margin per unit $13 or 10,000 units.

12. (b) The contribution margin ratio is equal to the contribution margin per unit $13 divided by unit selling price $20 or 65%.

13. (a) Break-even sales in dollars is equal to fixed costs divided by the contribution margin ratio. The contribution margin ratio is 30% [($600,000 - $420,000) ÷ $600,000]. Therefore, break-even sales are $400,000 ($120,000 ÷ .30).

14. (b) Using the mathematical equation, the computation is: $50X = $25X + $260,000 ($210,000 + $50,000). Therefore,

$$X = 10,400 \text{ units}$$

15. (a) The required unit sales are determined by dividing fixed costs plus target net income by the contribution margin per unit. The contribution margin per unit is $20 ($60 - $40). Therefore, required unit sales are 5,000 ($100,000 ÷ $20).

16. (c) The break-even point in sales dollars is equal to fixed costs divided by the contribution margin ratio. The contribution margin ratio is equal to 33.3% [($60 - $40) ÷ $60]. Therefore, the break-even point is $90,000 ($30,000 ÷ .333).

17. (a) The selling price per unit during the month of May was $40 ($200,000 ÷ 5,000). During June the selling price increases to $44 ($40 X 110%). The variable cost per unit remains the same in June as it was in May, $24 ($120,000 ÷ 5,000). Therefore, during June the contribution margin per unit is equal to $20. Required sales in units is the sum of the fixed costs plus target net income divided by the contribution margin per unit. Thus, the required units are 4,000 [($60,000 + $20,000) ÷ $20].

18. (a) The margin of safety in dollars is equal to actual (expected) sales less break-even sales, $200,000 ($800,000 - $600,000). The margin of safety ratio is equal to the margin of safety in dollars $200,000 divided by actual (expected) sales $800,000, or 25%.

19.   (b)   The CVP income statement is presented as follows:

Sales (100,000 X $12.00)	$1,200,000
Variable expenses	?
Contribution margin	?
Fixed expenses	280,000
Net income	$ 200,000

Thus, contribution margin is equal to $480,000 and variable expenses must equal $720,000.

*20.   (a)   There are 10,000 units in ending inventory. Under absorption costing, unit cost is $11.20 [$8 + ($160,000 ÷ 50,000)]. Total costs are $112,000. Under variable costing, unit cost is $8 and total cost $80,000.

*21.   (c)   When units produced are less than units sold income under absorption costing will be lower than under variable costing.

*22.   (b)   Contribution margin is sales less variable cost of goods sold and variable expenses. Thus, the amount is $800,000 - $420,000 ($600,000 X 70%) - $48,000 ($120,000 X 40%) or $332,000.

*23.   (d)   Variable costing is compatible with responsibility accounting (a.) However, it is not acceptable under generally accepted accounting principles (b.) or for income tax purposes (c.) because it understates inventory costs.

MATCHING

1. j	6. h	11. g
2. l	7. a	12. n
3. m	8. e	13. i
4. f	9. b	14. c
5. d	10. k	

EXERCISES

EX. 22-1

(1)   Variable cost per unit is computed by dividing the change in total costs by the high minus low activity index. ($22,000 - $7,000) ÷ (4,000 - 1,000) = $5.00
(2)   The fixed cost per month can be computed by subtracting the total variable cost at either activity level from the total cost at that activity level.
             Low $ 7,000 - ($5.00 X 1,000) = $2,000.
             High $22,000 - ($5.00 X 4,000) = $2,000.

EX. 22-2

(a) Contribution margin per unit is: $220,000 ÷ 11,000 = $20.
(b) Contribution margin ratio is: $220,000 ÷ $550,000 = 40%.
(c) The break-even point in dollars is: $150,000 ÷ .40 = $375,000.
(d) The break-even point in units is: $150,000 ÷ $20 = 7,500.
(e) The margin of safety is: $550,000 - $375,000 = $175,000.
     The margin of safety ratio is: $175,000 ÷ $550,000 = 32% (rounded).
(f) The number of units to earn net income of $100,000 is: ($150,000 + $100,000) ÷ $20 = 12,500.

EX. 22-3

(a)

Manufacturing Costs	Absorption Costing	Variable Costing
Variable	$2,000	$2,000
Fixed ($1,800,000 ÷ 3,000)	600	
	$2,600	$2,000

(b)

FENDI COMPANY
Income Statement
For the Month Ended March 31, 2010
(Variable Costing)

Sales (2,500 X $4,000)			$10,000,000
Variable expenses			
Variable cost of goods sold			
Inventory, March 1	$ -0-		
Variable manufacturing costs			
(3,000 X $2,000)	6,000,000		
Cost of goods available for sale	6,000,000		
Inventory, March 31, (500 X $2,000)	1,000,000		
Variable cost of goods sold	5,000,000		
Variable selling and administrative expenses			
(2,500 X $80)	200,000		
Total variable expenses			5,200,000
Contribution margin			4,800,000
Fixed expenses			
Manufacturing overhead	1,800,000		
Selling and administrative expenses	300,000		
Total fixed expenses			2,100,000
Income from operations			$ 2,700,000

Chapter 23

BUDGETARY PLANNING

The Navigator ✓

- ■ Scan Study Objectives ☐
- ■ Read Preview ☐
- ■ Read Chapter Review ☐
- ■ Work Demonstration Problem ☐
- ■ Answer True-False Statements ☐
- ■ Answer Multiple-Choice Questions ☐
- ■ Match Terms and Definitions ☐
- ■ Solve Exercises ☐

CHAPTER STUDY OBJECTIVES

After studying this chapter, you should be able to:
1. Indicate the benefits of budgeting.
2. State the essentials of effective budgeting.
3. Identify the budgets that comprise the master budget.
4. Describe the sources for preparing the budgeted income statement.
5. Explain the principal sections of a cash budget.
6. Indicate the applicability of budgeting in nonmanufacturing companies.

The Navigator

PREVIEW OF CHAPTER 23

Our primary focus in this chapter is budgeting—specifically, how budgeting is used as a planning tool by management. Through budgeting, it should be possible for management to maintain enough cash to pay creditors, to have sufficient raw materials to meet production requirements, and to have adequate finished goods to meet expected sales. The content and organization of this chapter are as follows:

Budgetary Planning

Budgetary Basics	Preparing the Operating Budgets	Preparing the Financial Budgets	Budgeting in Non-Manufacturing Companies
▶ Budgeting and accounting ▶ Benefits ▶ Essentials of effective budgeting ▶ Length of budget period ▶ Budgeting process ▶ Budgeting and human behavior ▶ Budgeting and long-Range planning ▶ The master budget	▶ Sales ▶ Production ▶ Direct materials ▶ Direct labor ▶ Manufacturing overhead ▶ Selling and administrative expense ▶ Budgeted income statement	▶ Cash ▶ Budgeted balance sheet	▶ Merchandisers ▶ Service ▶ Not-for-profit

The Navigator

CHAPTER REVIEW

Budgeting Basics

1. (S.O. 1) A **budget** is a formal written statement of management's plans for a specified time period, expressed in financial terms.

2. The **role of accounting** during the budgeting process is to (a) provide historical data on revenues, costs, and expenses, (b) express management's plans in financial terms, and (c) prepare periodic budget reports.

Benefits of Budgeting

3. The primary benefits of budgeting are as follows:
   a. It requires all levels of management to **plan ahead.**
   b. It provides **definite objectives** for evaluating performance.
   c. It creates an **early warning system** for potential problems.
   d. It facilitates the **coordination of activities** within the business.
   e. It results in greater **management awareness** of the entity's overall operations.
   f. It **motivates personnel** throughout the organization.

Essentials of Effective Budgeting

4. (S.O. 2) In order to be effective management tools, budgets must be based upon
   a. A **sound organizational structure** in which authority and responsibility are clearly defined.
   b. **Research and analysis** to determine the feasibility of new products, services, and operating techniques.
   c. **Management acceptance** which is enhanced when all levels of management participate in the preparation of the budget, and the budget has the support of top management.

5. The most common budget period is one year. A **continuous twelve-month budget** results from dropping the month just ended and adding a future month. The annual budget is often supplemented by monthly and quarterly budgets.

6. The responsibility for coordinating the preparation of the budget is assigned to a **budget committee.** The budget committee usually includes the president, treasurer, chief accountant (controller), and management personnel from each major area of the company.

7. A budget can have a significant impact on **human behavior.** A budget may have a strong positive influence on a manager when
   a. Each level of management is invited and encouraged to participate in developing the budget.
   b. Criticism of a manager's performance is tempered with advice and assistance.

8. **Long-range planning** involves the selection of strategies to achieve long-term goals and the development of policies and plans to implement the strategies. Long-range plans contain considerably less detail than budgets.

The Master Budget

9. (S.O. 3) The **master budget** is a set of interrelated budgets that constitutes a plan of action for a specified time period. It is developed within the framework of a sales forecast which shows potential sales for the industry and the company's expected share of such sales.

10. There are **two classes** of budgets in the master budget.
    a. **Operating budgets** are the individual budgets that result in the preparation of the budgeted income statement.
    b. **Financial budgets** focus primarily on the cash resources needed to fund expected operations and planned capital expenditures.

11. The **sales budget** is the first budget prepared. It is derived from the sales forecast, and it represents management's best estimate of sales revenue for the budget period. It is prepared by multiplying the expected unit sales volume for each product by its anticipated unit selling price.

12. The **production budget** shows the units that must be produced to meet anticipated sales. It is derived from the budgeted sales units plus the desired ending finished goods units less the beginning finished goods units.

13. The **direct materials budget** shows both the quantity and cost of direct materials to be purchased. It is derived from the direct materials units required for production plus the desired ending direct materials units less the beginning direct materials units.

14. The **direct labor budget** shows the quantity (hours) and cost of direct labor necessary to meet production requirements. The direct labor budget is critical in maintaining a labor force that can meet expected levels of production.

15. The **manufacturing overhead budget** shows the expected manufacturing overhead costs. The **selling and administrative expense budget** is a projection of anticipated operating expenses. Both budgets distinguish between fixed and variable costs.

Budgeted Income Statement

16. (S.O. 4) The **budgeted income statement** is the important end-product in preparing operating budgets. This budget indicates the expected profitability of operations and it provides a basis for evaluating company performance.
    a. The budget is prepared from the budgets described in review points 11-15.
    b. For example, to find cost of goods sold, it is necessary to determine the total unit cost of a finished product using the direct materials, direct labor, and manufacturing overhead budgets.

Cash Budget

17. (S.O. 5) The **cash budget** shows anticipated cash flows. It contains three sections (cash receipts, cash disbursements, and financing) and the beginning and ending cash balances. Data for preparing this budget are obtained from the other budgets.

18. The **budgeted balance sheet** is a projection of financial position at the end of the budget period. It is developed from the budgeted balance sheet for the preceding year and the budgets for the current year.

Budgeting in Nonmanufacturing Companies

19. (S.O. 6) The major differences in the master budget of a merchandiser and a manufacturing company are that a merchandiser (a) uses a **merchandise purchases budget** instead of a production budget and (b) does not use the manufacturing budgets (direct materials, direct labor, and manufacturing overhead).

20. In service enterprises, the critical factor in budgeting is coordinating professional staff needs with anticipated services. Budget data for service revenue may be obtained from expected **output** or expected **input.**

21. In the budget process for **not-for-profit organizations,** the emphasis is on cash flows rather than on a revenue and expense basis. For governmental units, the budget must be strictly followed and overspending is often illegal.

DEMONSTRATION PROBLEM (S.O. 5)

The Crawford Company begins operations with a cash balance of $60,000 on January 1, 2010. Relevant quarterly budgeted data pertaining to a cash budget for the first two quarters of the year are as follows:

Sales: (1) $140,000, (2) $250,000. All sales are on account; 60% of the sales are expected to be collected in cash in the period of sale, and the balance in the following quarter.

Direct materials purchases: (1) $65,000, (2) $165,000. 40% of each purchase is paid in cash at the time of the purchase, and the balance is paid in the following quarter.

Direct labor: (1) $40,000, (2) $50,000. Wages are paid at the time they are incurred.

Manufacturing overhead: (1) $35,000, (2) $30,000. These costs include depreciation of $3,200 per quarter. All cash overhead costs are paid as incurred.

Selling and administrative expenses: (1) $18,000, (2) $19,000. These expenses include $1,000 of depreciation per quarter. All cash selling and administrative costs are paid when incurred.

The company has a line of credit at a local bank that enables it to borrow up to $30,000 per quarter. Interest on any loans and income taxes may be ignored.

The Crawford Company wants to maintain a minimum quarterly cash balance of $40,000.

Instructions
(a) Prepare schedules for (1) expected collections from customers and (2) expected payments for direct materials purchases.
(b) Prepare a cash budget by quarters for the six months ending June 30, 2010.

SOLUTION TO DEMONSTRATION PROBLEM

(a) (1)   **Schedule of Expected Cash Collections from Customers**

	Quarter	
	1	**2**
First quarter sales ($140,000)	$84,000	$ 56,000
Second quarter sales ($250,000)		150,000
Total collections	$84,000	$206,000

(2)   **Schedule of Expected Payments for Direct Materials**

	Quarter	
	1	**2**
First quarter purchases ($65,000)	$26,000	$ 39,000
Second quarter purchases ($165,000)		66,000
Total payments	$26,000	$105,000

(b)

CRAWFORD COMPANY
Cash Budget
For the 6-months Ending June 30, 2010

	1	**2**	**Total**
Beginning cash balance	$60,000	$ 40,000	$ 60,000
Add: Receipts			
Collections from customers	84,000	206,000	290,000
Total available cash	144,000	246,000	350,000
Less: Disbursements			
Direct materials	26,000	105,000	131,000
Direct labor	40,000	50,000	90,000
Manufacturing overhead	31,800	26,800	58,600
Selling and administrative			
expenses	17,000	18,000	35,000
Total disbursements	114,800	199,800	314,600
Excess (deficiency) of available			
cash over disbursements	29,200	46,200	35,400
Financing			
Borrowings	10,800		10,800
Repayments	-0-	6,200	6,200
Ending cash balance	$ 40,000	$ 40,000	$ 40,000

REVIEW QUESTIONS AND EXERCISES

TRUE—FALSE

Indicate whether each of the following is true (T) or false (F) in the space provided.

_____   1.   (S.O. 1) The budget itself and the administration of the budget are entirely accounting responsibilities.

_____   2.   (S.O. 1) A primary benefit of budgeting is that it provides definite objectives for evaluating subsequent performance at each level of responsibility.

_____   3.   (S.O. 2) If a budget is effective enough, it can be a substitute for management.

_____   4.   (S.O. 2) Management acceptance of budgets occurs more frequently when the flow of input data is from the highest level of responsibility to the lowest level of responsibility.

_____   5.   (S.O. 2) Effective budgeting depends on an organizational structure in which authority and responsibility over all phases of operations are clearly defined.

_____   6.   (S.O. 2) The budget committee is usually made up of people outside the company in order to decrease bias.

_____   7.   (S.O. 2) Financial planning models and statistical and mathematical techniques may be used in forecasting sales.

_____   8.   (S.O. 3) Long-range planning usually emphasizes meeting annual profit objectives.

_____   9.   (S.O. 3) Long-range plans contain considerably less detail than short-term budgets.

_____   10. (S.O. 3) The sales budget is derived from the production budget.

_____   11. (S.O. 3) The production budget shows unit production data as well as cost data.

_____   12. (S.O. 3) The direct materials budget is derived from the direct materials units required for production plus desired ending direct materials units less beginning direct materials units.

_____   13. (S.O. 3) The direct labor budget contains only quantity data (hours) which are derived from the production budget.

_____   14. (S.O. 3) The manufacturing overhead budget shows the expected manufacturing overhead costs.

_____   15. (S.O. 5) The cash budget contains three sections (cash receipts, cash disbursements, and financing) and the beginning and ending cash balances.

_____   16. (S.O. 5) In order to develop a budgeted balance sheet, the previous year's balance sheet is needed.

_____   17.   (S.O. 6)   One difference between the master budget of a merchandising company and a manufacturing company is that the purchases budget is used instead of a production budget.

_____   18.   (S.O. 6)   In service enterprises, the critical factor in budgeting is coordinating materials and equipment with anticipated services.

_____   19.   (S.O. 6)   Not-for-profit organizations usually budget on the basis of cash flows (expenditures and receipts) rather than on a revenue and expense basis.

_____   20.   (S.O. 6)   For governmental units, the budget must be strictly followed and over-spending is often illegal.

The
Navigator

MULTIPLE CHOICE

Circle the letter that best answers each of the following statements.

1.   (S.O. 1)   The responsibility for expressing management's budgeting goals in financial terms is performed by the:
    a.   accounting department.
    b.   top management.
    c.   lower level of management.
    d.   budget committee.

2.   (S.O. 1)   Which of the following would **not** be considered a benefit of budgeting?
    a.   Facilitates the coordination of activities.
    b.   Requires all levels of management to plan ahead.
    c.   Always motivates personnel.
    d.   Results in greater management awareness of the entity's overall operations.

3.   (S.O. 2)   In order for budgets to be effective there must be:
    a.   sound organizational structure.
    b.   research and analysis.
    c.   management acceptance of the budget program.
    d.   all of the above.

4.   (S.O. 2)   For better management acceptance, the flow of input data for budgeting should begin with the:
    a.   accounting department.
    b.   top management.
    c.   lower levels of management.
    d.   budget committee.

5.   (S.O. 2)   Responsibility for coordinating the preparation of the budget is assigned to the:
    a.   accounting department.
    b.   top management.
    c.   lower levels of management.
    d.   budget committee.

6. (S.O. 2) Which of the following is **not** a characteristic of long-range planning?
    a. It encompasses a period of at least five years.
    b. Consideration is given to the economic and political environment.
    c. More detail is presented than in a budget.
    d. It is used to review progress rather than as a basis for control.

7. (S.O. 3) The starting point in preparing the master budget is the:
    a. cash budget.
    b. budgeted income statement.
    c. direct materials budget.
    d. sales budget.

8. (S.O. 3) The Turlington Company has 12,000 units in beginning finished goods. If sales are expected to be 60,000 units for the year and Turlington desires ending finished goods of 15,000 units, how many units must Turlington produce?
    a. 57,000.
    b. 60,000.
    c. 63,000.
    d. 75,000.

9. (S.O. 3) The Evangelista Company has 3,000 units in beginning finished goods. The sales budget shows expected sales to be 12,000 units. If the production budget shows that 14,000 units are required for production, what was the desired ending finished goods?
    a. 1,000.
    b. 3,000.
    c. 5,000.
    d. 9,000.

10. (S.O. 3) In the Campbell Company required production for June is 44,000 units. To make one unit of finished product, three pounds of direct material Z are required. Actual beginning and desired ending inventories of direct material Z are 100,000 and 110,000 pounds, respectively. How many pounds of direct material Z must be purchased?
    a. 126,000.
    b. 132,000.
    c. 136,000.
    d. 142,000.

11. (S.O. 3) Taylor Company determines that 13,500 pounds of direct materials are needed for production in July. There are 800 pounds of direct materials on hand at July 1 and the desired ending inventory is 700 units. If the cost per unit of direct materials is $3, what is the budgeted total cost of direct materials purchases?
    a. $39,600.
    b. $40,200.
    c. $40,800.
    d. $41,400.

12. (S.O. 3) Navia Company is preparing its direct labor budget for May. Projections for the month are that 8,350 units are to be produced and that direct labor time is three hours per unit. If the labor cost per hour is $9, what is the total budgeted direct labor cost for May?
    a. $217,350.
    b. $221,400.
    c. $225,450.
    d. $243,000.

13. (S.O. 3) Porizkova Company requires that ending finished goods inventory for each month be 10% of the next month's budgeted sales. Budgeted sales in units are February 15,000, March 13,000 and April 17,000. What should be the level of production scheduled for March?
    a. 12,800.
    b. 13,000.
    c. 13,400.
    d. 14,700.

14. (S.O. 5) On January 1, Ghauri Company has a beginning cash balance of $21,000. During the year, the company expects cash disbursements of $170,000 and cash receipts of $145,000. If Ghauri requires an ending cash balance of $20,000, the Ghauri Company must borrow:
    a. $16,000.
    b. $20,000.
    c. $24,000.
    d. $46,000.

15. (S.O. 5) The Tennant Company has the following budgeted sales: January $40,000, February $60,000, and March $50,000. 40% of the sales are for cash and 60% are on credit. For the credit sales, 50% are collected in the month of sale, and 50% the next month. The total expected cash receipts during March are:
    a. $56,000.
    b. $53,000.
    c. $52,500.
    d. $50,000.

16. (S.O. 5) The Auermann Company's direct materials budget shows total cost of direct materials purchases for January $125,000, February $150,000 and March $175,000. Cash payments are 60% in the month of purchase and 40% in the following month. The budgeted cash payments for March are:
    a. $165,000.
    b. $160,000.
    c. $150,000.
    d. $130,000.

17. (S.O. 6) Which of the following statements about budgeted financial statements is **incorrect?**
    a. The budgeted balance sheet is developed entirely from the budgets for the current year.
    b. Once established, the budgeted income statement provides the basis for evaluating company performance.
    c. Cost of goods sold is determined by multiplying the budgeted unit sales by the budgeted total unit production cost.
    d. The budgeted income statement is developed from the budgets for the current year.

18. (S.O. 6) A purchases budget is used instead of a production budget by:
    a. merchandising companies.
    b. service enterprises.
    c. not-for-profit organizations.
    d. manufacturing companies.

19. (S.O. 6) Entities that budget on the basis of cash flows (expenditures and receipts) rather than on a revenue and expense basis are:
    a. merchandising companies.
    b. service enterprises.
    c. not-for-profit organizations.
    d. manufacturing companies.

20. (S.O. 6) Which of the following statements is **incorrect?**
    a. A continuous twelve-month budget results from dropping the month just ended and adding a future month.
    b. The production budget is derived from the direct materials and direct labor budget.
    c. The cash budget shows anticipated cash flows.
    d. In the budget process for not-for-profit organizations, the emphasis is on cash flow rather than on revenue and expenses.

The
Navigator

MATCHING

Match each term with its definition by writing the appropriate letter in the space provided.

Terms	Definitions

Terms

_____ 1. Budget committee.

_____ 2. Budget.

_____ 3. Cash budget.

_____ 4. Production budget.

_____ 5. Merchandise purchases budget.

_____ 6. Master budget.

_____ 7. Manufacturing overhead budget.

_____ 8. Direct materials budget.

_____ 9. Sales budget.

_____ 10. Direct labor budget.

_____ 11. Long-range planning.

_____ 12. Sales forecast.

Definitions

a. The projection of potential sales for the industry and the company's expected share of such sales.

b. An estimate of the quantity and cost of direct materials to be purchased.

c. The selection of strategies to achieve long-term goals and the development of policies and plans to implement the strategies.

d. A formal written summary of management's plan for a specified future time period expressed in financial terms.

e. A group responsible for coordinating the preparation of the budget.

f. An estimate of expected manufacturing overhead costs for the budget period.

g. A projection of the units that must be produced to meet anticipated sales.

h. A set of interrelated budgets that constitutes a plan of action for a specific time period.

i. The estimated cost of goods to be purchased in a merchandising company to meet expected sales.

j. A projection of anticipated cash flows.

k. An estimate of expected sales for the budget period.

l. A projection of the quantity and cost of direct labor to be incurred to meet production requirements.

The
Navigator

EXERCISES

EX. 23-1   (S.O. 3) Vendela has the following sales budget for the year ending December 31, 2010:

| | Quarter | | | | |
	1	2	3	4	Year
Expected unit sales	4,000	3,500	5,000	5,500	18,000

On the basis of past experiences, Vendela Company believes it can meet future sales requirements by maintaining an ending inventory equal to 10% of the next quarter's budgeted sales volume. On January 1, 2010, Vendela has beginning finished goods of 400 units. Vendela expects sales for the first quarter of 2011 to be 6,000 units.

Instructions
Prepare a production budget for Vendela Company for the year ending December 31, 2010.

VENDELA COMPANY
Production Budget
For the Year Ending December 31, 2010

EX. 23-2   (S.O. 3) Brinkley Company's production budget for 2010 by quarters is as follows: (1) 6,000, (2) 7,000, (3), 8,000, and (4) 9,000. For the first quarter of 2011, the budget is 8,000 units. The manufacture of each unit requires three pounds of direct materials and an expected cost per unit of $2. The ending inventory of direct materials is expected to be 20% of the next quarter's production needs. At December 31, 2009, Brinkley had 3,600 pounds of direct materials.

Instructions
Prepare a direct materials budget for Brinkley Company for the year ending December 31, 2010.

BRINKLEY COMPANY
Direct Materials Budget
For the Year Ending December 31, 2010

EX. 23-3   (S.O. 3 and 4) The Ireland Company has accumulated the following budget data for the year 2010.

1. Sales 30,000 units; unit selling price $100.
2. Cost of one unit of finished goods; direct materials $15, direct labor $30, and manufacturing overhead 60% of direct labor cost.
3. Selling and administrative expenses: variable 5% of sales, fixed $320,000.

Instructions
Prepare a budgeted income statement for the year assuming an income tax rate of 30% on income before income taxes.

IRELAND COMPANY
Budgeted Income Statement
For the Year Ended December 31, 2010

The
Navigator

SOLUTIONS TO REVIEW QUESTIONS AND EXERCISES

TRUE-FALSE

1. (F) The budget itself, and the administration of the budget, are entirely management responsibilities.
2. (T)
3. (F) A budget is an aid to management; it is not a substitute for management.
4. (F) Management acceptance of budgets occurs more frequently when the flow of input data is from the lowest level of responsibility to the highest level of responsibility.
5. (T)
6. (F) The budget committee is usually made up of people inside the organization such as the president, treasurer, chief accountant (controller), and management personnel from each of the major areas of the company.
7. (T)
8. (F) Budgeting is concerned with meeting annual profit objectives. Long-range planning involves the selection of strategies to achieve long-term goals and the development of policies and plans to implement the strategies.
9. (T)
10. (F) The production budget is derived from the sales budget.
11. (F) The production budget shows only unit production data.
12. (T)
13. (F) The direct labor budget contains both quantity and cost data.
14. (T)
15. (T)
16. (T)
17. (T)
18. (F) In service enterprises, the critical factor in budgeting is coordinating professional staff needs with anticipated services.
19. (T)
20. (T)

MULTIPLE CHOICE

1. (a) The accounting department is responsible for (1) providing historical data on revenues, costs and expenses, (2) translating management's plans into financial terms, and (3) preparing periodic budget reports.

2. (c) A budget does not always motivate personnel. If a manager views a budget as being unfair and unrealistic, he or she may become discouraged and uncommitted to the budget goals.

3. (d) In order for budgets to be effective it is recognized that there must be (1) a sound organizational structure, (2) research and analysis, and (3) management acceptance of the budget program.

4. (c) For management acceptance, the flow of input data for budgeting is from the lowest level of responsibility to the highest.

5. (d) The responsibility for coordinating the preparation of the budget is assigned to the budget committee.

6. (c) Long-range plans contain considerably less detail than a budget because the data are intended more for a review of progress toward long-range goals than for an evaluation of specific results to be achieved. Answers (a), (b), and (d) are correct statements.

7. (d) The sales budget is the starting point in preparing the master budget. Each of the other budgets is dependent on the sales budget.

8. (c) The production requirements are:

Expected sales	60,000
Add: Desired ending finished goods	15,000
Total required units	75,000
Less: Beginning finished goods	12,000
Units to be produced	63,000

9. (c) The desired ending finished goods is computed as follows:

Beginning finished goods	3,000
Units to be produced	14,000
Total units available	17,000
Less: Units expected to be sold	12,000
Desired ending finished goods	5,000

10. (d) The amount of direct materials to be purchased is as follows:

Units to be produced	44,000
Direct materials per unit	3
Total pounds needed for production	132,000
Add: Desired ending direct materials units	110,000
Total materials required	242,000
Less: Beginning direct materials	100,000
Direct materials purchases	142,000

11. (b) The cost of direct materials purchases is:

Total direct materials needed for production	13,500
Add: Desired ending direct materials	700
Total materials required	14,200
Less: Beginning direct materials	800
Direct materials purchases	13,400
Cost per unit	X $3
Total cost of direct materials purchases	$40,200

12. (c) The total direct labor cost is computed as follows:

Total units to be produced	8,350
Direct labor time (hours)	3
Total required direct labor hours	25,050
Direct labor cost	X $9
Total direct labor cost	$225,450

13.　(c)　The level of production is:

Expected units sales in March... 13,000
Add: Desired ending finished goods, March 31 (17,000
　X 10%).. 1,700
Total required units.. 14,700
Less: Beginning finished goods, March 1, (13,000 X 10%)... 1,300
Units to be produced 13,400

14.　(c)　The cash to be borrowed is:

Beginning cash balance .... $ 21,000
Add: Cash receipts 145,000
Total available cash... 166,000
Less: Cash disbursements 170,000
Excess (deficiency) of available cash over disbursements .... (4,000)
Financing 24,000
Ending cash balance .... $ 20,000

15.　(b)　The percentage of cash collected during the month of sale is 70% [40% + (60% X 50%)]. Therefore, 30% of the February sales will be collected in March, $18,000 ($60,000 X 30%) and 70% of the March sales will be collected in March, $35,000 ($50,000 X 70%).

16.　(a)　In March, $60,000 will be paid on February purchases ($150,000 X 40%) and $105,000 will be paid on March purchases ($175,000 X 60%).

17.　(a)　The budgeted balance sheet is developed from the budgeted balance sheet from the preceding year and the budgets for the current year.

18.　(a)　The major differences in the master budget of a merchandising company are that (1) a purchases budget is used instead of a production budget and (2) the manufacturing budgets are not applicable.

19.　(c)　The budget process for not-for-profit organizations is based on cash flows (expenditures and receipts) rather than on a revenue and expense basis.

20.　(b)　The production budget is derived from the budgeted sales units plus the desired ending finished goods units less the beginning finished goods units.

MATCHING

1.　e
2.　d
3.　j
4.　g
5.　i
6.　h

7.　f
8.　b
9.　k
10.　l
11.　c
12.　a

EXERCISES

EX. 23-1

VENDELA COMPANY
Production Budget
For the Year Ending December 31, 2010

	Quarter				
	1	2	3	4	Year
Expected unit sales	4,000	3,500	5,000	5,500	18,000
Add: Desired ending finished goods units	350	500	550	600	600
Total required units	4,350	4,000	5,550	6,100	18,600
Less: Beginning finished goods units	400	350	500	550	400
Required production units	3,950	3,650	5,050	5,550	18,200

EX. 23-2

BRINKLEY COMPANY
Direct Materials Budget
For the Year Ending December 31, 2010

	Quarter				
	1	2	3	4	Year
Units to be produced	6,000	7,000	8,000	9,000	30,000
Direct materials per unit	X 3	X 3	X 3	X 3	X 3
Total pounds needed for production	18,000	21,000	24,000	27,000	90,000
Add: Desired ending direct materials units	4,200	4,800	5,400	4,800	4,800
Total materials required	22,200	25,800	29,400	31,800	94,800
Less: Beginning direct materials units	3,600	4,200	4,800	5,400	3,600
Direct materials purchases	18,600	21,600	24,600	26,400	91,200
Cost per pound	X $2	X $2	X $2	X $2	X $2
Total cost of direct materials purchases	$37,200	43,200	49,200	52,800	$182,400

EX. 23-3

IRELAND COMPANY
Budgeted Income Statement
For the Year Ended December 31, 2010

Sales (30,000 X $100)	$3,000,000
Cost of goods sold (30,000 X $63)	1,890,000
Gross profit	1,110,000
Selling and administrative expenses [$320,000 + ($3,000,000 X 5%)]	470,000
Income before income taxes	640,000
Income tax expense (30% X $640,000)	192,000
Net income	$ 448,000

Chapter 24

BUDGETARY CONTROL AND RESPONSIBILITY ACCOUNTING

The Navigator ✓

■ Scan Study Objectives ☐
■ Read Preview ☐
■ Read Chapter Review ☐
■ Work Demonstration Problem ☐
■ Answer True-False Statements ☐
■ Answer Multiple-Choice Questions ☐
■ Match Terms and Definitions ☐
■ Solve Exercises ☐

CHAPTER STUDY OBJECTIVES

After studying this chapter, you should be able to:
1. Describe the concept of budgetary control.
2. Evaluate the usefulness of static budget reports.
3. Explain the development of flexible budgets and the usefulness of flexible budget reports.
4. Describe the concept of responsibility accounting.
5. Indicate the features of responsibility reports for cost centers.
6. Identify the content of responsibility reports for profit centers.
7. Explain the basis and formula used in evaluating performance in investment centers.

The Navigator

PREVIEW OF CHAPTER 24

In contrast to Chapter 23, we now consider how budgets are used by management to control operations. This chapter focuses on two aspects of management control: (1) budgetary control and (2) responsibility accounting. The content and organization of this chapter are as follows:

Budgetary Control and Responsibility Accounting

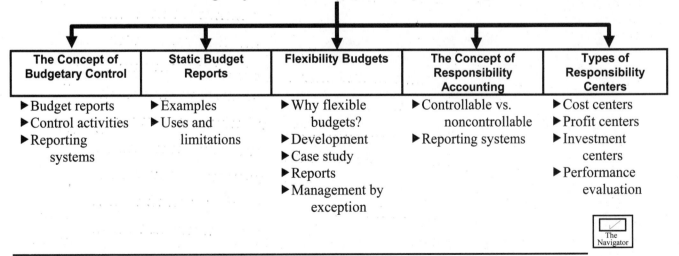

The Concept of Budgetary Control	Static Budget Reports	Flexibility Budgets	The Concept of Responsibility Accounting	Types of Responsibility Centers
▶ Budget reports ▶ Control activities ▶ Reporting systems	▶ Examples ▶ Uses and limitations	▶ Why flexible budgets? ▶ Development ▶ Case study ▶ Reports ▶ Management by exception	▶ Controllable vs. noncontrollable ▶ Reporting systems	▶ Cost centers ▶ Profit centers ▶ Investment centers ▶ Performance evaluation

The Navigator

CHAPTER REVIEW

Budgetary Control

1. (S.O. 1) The use of budgets in controlling operations is known as **budgetary control.** Such control takes place by means of budget reports that compare actual results with planned objectives. The budget reports provide management with feedback on operations.

2. **Budgetary control** involves:
   a. Developing budgets.
   b. Analyzing the differences between actual and budgeted results.
   c. Taking corrective action.
   d. Modifying future plans, if necessary.

3. Budgetary control works best when a company has a formalized reporting system. The system should
   a. Identify the name of the budget report such as the sales budget or the manufacturing overhead budget.
   b. State the frequency of the report such as weekly, or monthly.
   c. Specify the purpose of the report.
   d. Indicate the primary recipient(s) of the report.

Static Budget Reports

4. (S.O. 2) A **static budget** does not modify or adjust data regardless of changes in activity during the year. As a result, actual results are always compared with the budget data at the activity level used in developing the master budget.

5. A static budget is appropriate in evaluating a manager's effectiveness in controlling costs when (a) the actual level of activity closely approximates the master budget activity level, and/or (b) the behavior of the costs in response to changes in activity is fixed.

Flexible Budgets

6. (S.O. 3) A **flexible budget** projects budget data for various levels of activity. The flexible budget recognizes that the budgetary process is more useful if it is adaptable to changed operating conditions. This type of budget permits a comparison of actual and planned results at the level of activity actually achieved.

7. To develop the flexible budget, the following steps are taken:
   a. Identify the activity index and the relevant range of activity.
   b. Identify the variable costs, and determine the budgeted variable cost per unit of activity for each cost.
   c. Identify the fixed costs, and determine the budgeted amount for each cost.
   d. Prepare the budget for selected increments of activity within the relevant range.

8. For **manufacturing overhead costs,** the activity index is usually the same as the index used in developing the predetermined overhead rate; that is, direct labor hours or machine hours. For selling and administrative expenses, the activity index usually is sales or net sales.

9. The following **formula** may be used to determine total budgeted costs at any level of activity:

    Total budgeted costs = Fixed costs + (Total variable cost per unit X activity level)

10. Total budgeted costs at each level of activity can be shown **graphically.**
    a. In a graph, the activity index is shown on the horizontal axis and costs are shown on the vertical axis.
    b. The total budgeted costs for each level of activity are then identified from the total budgeted cost line.

11. **Flexible budget reports** are another type of internal report produced by managerial accounting. The flexible budget report consists of two sections: (a) production data such as direct labor hours and (b) cost data for variable and fixed costs. It also shows differences between budget and actual results.

12. **Management by exception** means that top management's review of a budget report is focused either entirely or primarily to differences between actual results and planned objectives. The guidelines for identifying an exception are based on materiality and controllability.

Responsibility Accounting

13. (S.O. 4) **Responsibility accounting** involves accumulating and reporting costs (and revenues, where relevant) on the basis of the manager who has the authority to make the day-to-day decisions about the items. A manager's performance is evaluated on matters directly under that manager's control.

14. Responsibility accounting can be used at every level of management in which the following **conditions** exist:
    a. Costs and revenues can be directly associated with the specific level of management responsibility.
    b. The costs and revenues are controllable at the level of responsibility with which they are associated.
    c. Budget data can be developed for evaluating the manager's effectiveness in controlling the costs and revenues.

15. Responsibility accounting is especially valuable in a decentralized company. **Decentralization** means that the control of operations is delegated to many managers throughout the organization. A **segment** is an identified area of responsibility in decentralized operations.

16. Responsibility accounting is an essential part of any effective system of budgetary control. It differs from budgeting in two respects:
    a. A distinction is made between controllable and noncontrollable items.
    b. Performance reports either emphasize or include only items controllable by the individual manager.

17. A cost is considered **controllable** at a given level of managerial responsibility if that manager has the power to incur it within a given period of time. Costs incurred indirectly and allocated to a responsibility level are considered to be **noncontrollable** at that level.

18. A **responsibility reporting system** involves the preparation of a report for each level of responsibility shown in the company's organization chart. A responsibility reporting system permits management by exception at each level of responsibility within the organization.

19. **Responsibility centers** may be classified into one of three types. A **cost center** incurs costs (and expenses) but does not directly generate revenues. A **profit center** incurs costs (and expenses) but also generates revenues. An **investment center** incurs costs (and expenses), generates revenues, and has control over investment funds available for use.

Cost Centers

20. (S.O. 5) A **responsibility report for cost centers** compares actual controllable costs with flexible budget data. Only controllable costs are included in the report, and no distinction is made between variable and fixed costs.

21. **Direct fixed costs** or **traceable costs** are costs that relate specifically to a responsibility center and are incurred for the sole benefit of the center. **Indirect fixed costs** or **common costs** pertain to a company's overall operating activities and are incurred for the benefit of more than one profit center.

Profit Centers

22. (S.O. 6) A responsibility report for a profit center shows budgeted and actual controllable revenues and costs. The report is prepared using the cost-volume-profit income statement format.

23. In the responsibility report for a profit center:
     a. Controllable fixed costs are deducted from contribution margin.
     b. The excess of contribution margin over controllable fixed costs is identified as controllable margin.
     c. Noncontrollable fixed costs are not reported.

24. Controllable margin is considered to be the best measure of the manager's performance in **controlling revenues and costs.**

Investment Centers

25. (S.O. 7) The primary basis for evaluating the performance of a manger of an investment center is **return on investment** (ROI). The **formula** for computing return on investment is: Investment Center Controllable Margin (in dollars) ÷ Average Investment Center Operating Assets = Return on Investment.
     a. **Operating assets** consist of current assets and plant assets used in operations by the center. Nonoperating assets such as idle plant assets and land held for future use are excluded.
     b. Average operating assets are usually based on the beginning and ending **cost or book values** of the assets.

26. A manager can improve ROI by (a) increasing controllable margin or (b) reducing average operating assets.

27. The return on investment approach includes **two judgmental factors:**
    a. Valuation of operating assets—cost, book value, appraised value, or market value.
    b   Margin (income) measure—controllable margin, income from operations, or net income.

28. Performance evaluation is a management function that compares actual results with budget goals. Performance evaluation includes both **behavioral and reporting principles.**

DEMONSTRATION PROBLEM (S.O. 7)

Comparative data for the following investment centers of Thorson Company are shown below.

	DeKalb	**Madison**	**Ann Arbor**	**Urbana**
Controllable margin	$ 48,000	(b)	120,000	$100,000
Average operating assets	400,000	500,000	800,000	(d)
Return on investment	(a)	14%	(c)	12%

Instructions
Compute the missing amounts using the ROI formula.

SOLUTION TO DEMONSTRATION PROBLEM

(a)   12% = ($48,000 ÷ $400,000).
(b) $70,000 = (14% X $500,000).
(c)   15% = ($120,000 ÷ $800,000).
(d) $833,333 = ($100,000 ÷ 12%).

REVIEW QUESTIONS AND EXERCISES

TRUE—FALSE

Indicate whether each of the following is true (T) or false (F) in the space provided.

_____   1. (S.O. 1) Budget reports provide the feedback needed by management to see whether actual operations are on course.

_____   2. (S.O. 2) A budget prepared for a single level of activity is called a static budget.

_____   3. (S.O. 2) A static budget is an effective means to evaluate a manager's ability to control costs, regardless of the actual activity level.

_____   4. (S.O. 3) A flexible budget recognizes that the budgetary process has greater usefulness if it is adaptable to changed operating conditions.

_____   5. (S.O. 3) One of the steps in developing a flexible budget is the combining of variable and fixed costs into one lump-sum cost.

_____   6. (S.O. 3) The flexible budget report evaluates a manager's performance in two areas: (1) production and (2) costs.

_____   7. (S.O. 3) Management by exception means that top management will investigate every difference.

_____   8. (S.O. 4) Under responsibility accounting, the evaluation of a manager's performance is based on the matters directly under the manager's control.

_____   9. (S.O. 4) Responsibility accounting is especially valuable in a centralized company.

_____   10. (S.O. 4) All costs are controllable by the top management of a company.

_____   11. (S.O. 4) The terms controllable costs and noncontrollable costs are synonymous with variable costs and fixed costs, respectively.

_____   12. (S.O. 4) The responsibility reporting system begins with the lowest level of responsibility and moves upward to each higher level.

_____   13. (S.O. 4) A responsibility reporting system permits management by exception at each level of responsibility within the organization.

_____   14. (S.O. 4) A profit center incurs costs (and expenses) but also generates revenues.

_____   15. (S.O. 5) A responsibility report for cost centers makes a clear distinction between variable and fixed costs.

_____ 16. (S.O. 5) Most direct fixed costs are **not** controllable by the profit center manager.

_____ 17. (S.O. 7) The formula for computing return on investment in responsibility accounting is controllable margin in dollars divided by average current assets.

_____ 18. (S.O. 7) The manager of an investment center can improve ROI by reducing average operating assets.

_____ 19. (S.O. 7) An advantage of the return on investment ratio is that no judgmental factors are involved.

_____ 20. (S.O. 7) Performance evaluation is a management function that compares actual results with budget goals.

The
Navigator

MULTIPLE CHOICE

Circle the letter that best answers each of the following statements.

1. (S.O. 1) Which of the following would **not** be considered an aspect of budgetary control?
    a. It assists in the determination of differences between actual and planned results.
    b. It provides feedback value needed by management to see whether actual operations are on course.
    c. It assists management in controlling operations.
    d. It provides a guarantee for favorable results.

2. (S.O. 1) Budgetary control involves all **but** one of the following:
    a. Modify future plans, if necessary.
    b. Analyze differences between actual and planned results.
    c. Take disciplinary action.
    d. Develop the budget.

3. (S.O. 1) Which of the following is **not** part of a formalized reporting system?
    a. Identify the name of the budget reports.
    b. State the corrective action that should be taken.
    c. Specify the purpose of the report.
    d. Indicate the primary recipient(s) of the report.

4. (S.O. 2) In a static budget,
    a. data are modified and adjusted according to changes in activity during the year.
    b. the actual results are always compared with budget data at the original budgeted activity level.
    c. it is important to select an activity index and a relevant range of activity.
    d. only budgeted fixed costs are compared with actual fixed costs.

5. (S.O. 2) A static budget is usually appropriate in evaluating a manager's effectiveness in controlling:
    a. fixed manufacturing costs and fixed selling and administrative expenses.
    b. variable manufacturing costs and variable selling and administrative expenses.
    c. fixed manufacturing costs and variable selling and administrative expenses.
    d. variable manufacturing costs and fixed selling and administrative expenses.

6. (S.O. 3) In the Johnson Company, indirect labor is budgeted for $24,000 and factory supervision is budgeted for $8,000 at normal capacity of 80,000 direct labor hours. If 90,000 direct labor hours are worked, flexible budget total for these costs is:
   a. $32,000.
   b. $36,000.
   c. $35,000.
   d. $33,000.

7. (S.O. 3) Vidmar Company uses flexible budgets. At normal capacity of 8,000 units, budgeted manufacturing overhead is: $64,000 variable and $180,000 fixed. If Vidmar had actual overhead costs of $250,000 for 9,000 units produced, what is the difference between actual and budgeted costs?
   a. $2,000 unfavorable.
   b. $2,000 favorable.
   c. $6,000 unfavorable.
   d. $8,000 favorable.

8. (S.O. 3) A flexible budget provides a basis for evaluating a manager's performance for:

	Production Control	Cost Control
a	No	No
b.	Yes	No
c.	No	Yes
d.	Yes	Yes

9. (S.O. 3) When production levels decline within a relevant range and a flexible budget is used, what effects would be anticipated with respect to each of the following?

	Total Fixed Costs	Total Variable Costs
a.	Decrease	Decrease
b.	Decrease	No change
c.	No change	No change
d.	No change	Decrease

10. (S.O. 3) A flexible budget is appropriate for:

	Direct Labor Costs	Manufacturing Overhead Costs
a.	No	No
b.	Yes	Yes
c.	Yes	No
d.	No	Yes

11. (S.O. 3) The criteria used in identifying an exception under management by exception are:
   a. materiality and frequency.
   b. controllability and frequency.
   c. materiality and controllability.
   d. none of the above.

12.   (S.O. 4) Responsibility accounting **cannot** be used effectively when:
    a.   costs are allocated to the responsibility level.
    b.   budget data can be developed for evaluating the manager's effectiveness in controlling costs.
    c.   costs are controllable at the level of responsibility with which they are associated.
    d.   costs can be directly associated with the specific level of responsibility.

13.   (S.O. 4) Controllable costs for responsibility accounting purposes are those costs that are directly influenced by:
    a.   a given manager within a given period of time.
    b.   a change in activity.
    c.   production volume.
    d.   sales volume.

14.   (S.O. 4) A responsibility reporting system:
    a.   begins with the highest level of responsibility and moves downward to the lowest level.
    b.   involves the preparation of a report for each level of responsibility shown in the company's organization chart.
    c.   does not permit comparative evaluations of responsibility centers.
    d.   does not permit management by exception at each level of responsibility.

15.   (S.O. 5) Responsibility reports for cost centers will include:

	Controllable Costs	**Noncontrollable Costs**
a.	No	No
b.	No	Yes
c.	Yes	No
d.	Yes	Yes

16.   (S.O. 5) Which of the following is **not** a direct fixed cost of a profit center?
    a.   Timekeeping for center's employees.
    b.   Depreciation on center's equipment.
    c.   Profit center manager's salary.
    d.   General office administrative costs.

17.   (S.O. 7) In the return on investment (ROI) formula:
    a.   sales are divided by average investment center operating assets.
    b.   controllable margin is divided by sales.
    c.   controllable margin is divided by average investment center operating assets.
    d.   sales are divided by net income.

18.   (S.O. 7) Which of the following will cause an increase in ROI?
    a.   An increase in variable costs.
    b.   An increase in average operating assets.
    c.   An increase in sales.
    d.   An increase in controllable fixed costs.

19.   (S.O. 7) Which of the following is **incorrect** about average operating assets?
    a.   Both current assets and plant assets are included.
    b.   Nonoperating assets are excluded.
    c.   The assets are valued at fair market values.
    d.   The average may be based on beginning and ending recorded balances.

20. (S.O. 7) If controllable margin is $300,000 and the average investment center operating assets are $1,000,000, the return on investment is:
    a. .33%.
    b. 3.33%.
    c. 10%.
    d. 30%.

MATCHING

Match each term with its definition by writing the appropriate letter in the space provided.

Terms		Definitions
_____	1. Budgetary control.	a. A projection of budget data for various levels of activity.
_____	2. Flexible budget.	b. The use of budgets to control operations.
_____	3. Static budget.	c. Costs incurred indirectly and allocated to a responsibility center that are not controllable at that level.
_____	4. Responsibility accounting.	d. Control of operations is delegated by top management to many managers throughout the organization.
_____	5. Noncontrollable costs.	
_____	6. Controllable costs.	e. Costs that a manager has the authority to incur within a given period of time.
_____	7. Responsibility reporting system.	f. The preparation of reports for each level of responsibility shown in the company's organization chart.
_____	8. Cost center.	g. A part of management accounting that involves accumulating and reporting revenues and cost on the basis of the individual manager who has the authority to make the day-to-day decisions about the items.
_____	9. Management by exception.	
_____	10. Profit center.	
_____	11. Investment center.	h. A responsibility center that incurs costs, generates revenues, and has control over the investment funds available for use.
_____	12. Decentralization.	i. A projection of budget data at one level of activity.
		j. The review of budget reports by top management directed entirely or primarily to differences between actual results and planned objectives.
		k. A responsibility center that incurs costs and also generates revenues.
		l. A responsibility center that incurs costs but does not directly generate revenues.

EXERCISES

EX. 24-1   (S.O. 3)   Hartung Company is in the midst of preparing its flexible budget for manufacturing overhead. At a production level of 10,000 units, unit costs are: Indirect materials $4, Indirect labor $3, Supplies $5, Depreciation $6, and Property taxes $2. Depreciation and property taxes are fixed costs.

Instructions
Complete the following four-column flexible budget for the manufacturing costs for the Hartung Company.

HARTUNG COMPANY
Flexible Manufacturing Overhead Budget

Activity level: Units	8,000	10,000	12,000	14,000
Variable costs:				
Indirect materials				
Indirect labor				
Supplies				
Total variable				
Fixed costs:				
Depreciation				
Property taxes				
Total fixed				
Total costs				

EX. 24-2 (S.O. 3) Gaylord Company has the following flexible budget for manufacturing overhead:

Activity level:			
Direct labor hours	20,000	25,000	30,000
Variable costs:			
Indirect materials	$10,000	$ 12,500	$ 15,000
Indirect labor	40,000	50,000	60,000
Supplies	30,000	37,500	45,000
Total	80,000	100,000	120,000
Fixed costs:			
Depreciation	30,000	30,000	30,000
Supervision	45,000	45,000	45,000
Total	75,000	75,000	75,000
Total costs $155,000	$175,000	$195,000	

In January, 22,000 direct labor hours were expected and 24,000 were worked.

Instructions
Given the following actual costs, complete the following budget report:

GAYLORD COMPANY
Manufacturing Overhead Budget Report
For the Month Ended January 31

	Budget at	Actual Costs at	Difference Favorable F Unfavorable U
Direct labor hours (DLH):			
Expected			
Actual	_____	_____	
Variable costs			
Indirect materials	$	$ 13,000	$
Indirect labor		47,500	
Supplies		35,200	
Total variable		95,700	
Fixed costs			
Depreciation		25,000	
Supervision		46,000	
Total fixed		71,000	_____
Total costs	_____	$166,700	_____

The Navigator

SOLUTIONS TO REVIEW QUESTIONS AND EXERCISES

TRUE-FALSE

1. (T)
2. (T)
3. (F)   A static budget is an effective means to evaluate a manager's ability to control costs provided (1) the actual level of activity closely approximates the master budget activity level, or (2) the behavior of the costs in response to changes in activity is fixed.

4. (T)
5. (F)   To develop the flexible budget, the following steps are taken:
    1.   Identify the activity index and the relevant range of activity.
    2.   Identify the variable costs and determine the budgeted variable cost per unit of activity for each cost.
    3.   Identify the fixed costs and determine the budgeted amount for each cost.
    4.   Prepare the budget for selected increments of activity within the relevant range.

6. (T)
7. (F)   Management by exception does not mean that top management will investigate every difference. Exceptions are identified by materiality and controllability of the item.

8. (T)
9. (F)   Responsibility accounting is especially valuable in a decentralized company.
10. (T)
11. (F)   A controllable cost can be variable or fixed, and a noncontrollable cost can also be variable or fixed.

12. (T)
13. (T)
14. (T)
15. (F)   There is usually no distinction between variable and fixed costs in a responsibility report for cost centers.
16. (F)   Most direct fixed costs are controllable by the profit center manager.
17. (F)   The basic formula for computing return on investment is controllable margin (in dollars) divided by average operating assets.

18. (T)
19. (F)   A number of judgmental factors are involved such as the proper valuation of operating assets and selection of the income measure to be used.

20. (T)

MULTIPLE CHOICE

1. (d)   Budgetary control assists management in controlling operations by providing feedback to see whether actual operations are on course, but budgetary control does not guarantee favorable results

2. (c)   Budgetary control involves taking corrective action but not necessarily disciplinary action.

3. (b)   A formalized reporting system does not require stating the corrective action. The missing part of the reporting system is specifying the frequency of the reports.

4. (b)   In a static budget, the actual results are always compared with the budget data at the original budgeted activity level. Answers (a) and (c) are aspects of a flexible budget, and answer (d) is false because a static budget includes variable as well as fixed costs.

5. (a)   A static budget is based on one level of activity. Thus, it is not usually appropriate in evaluating a manager's performance in controlling variable costs that should change at different levels of activity.

6. (c)   Indirect labor is a variable cost that is budgeted at $.30 per direct labor hour ($24,000 ÷ 80,000). Factory supervision is a fixed cost that remains the same at each activity level. The total cost, therefore, is $35,000 [(90,000 X $.30) + $8,000].

7. (b)   The per unit variable factory overhead is $8.00 ($64,000 ÷ 8,000). Therefore, for 9,000 units produced, variable factory overhead was expected to be $72,000 ($8.00 X 9,000). The addition of $180,000 fixed factory overhead gives a total budget overhead of $252,000; thus, there is a $2,000 favorable difference ($252,000 - $250,000).

8. (d)   A flexible budget provides a basis for evaluating a manger's performance for production control and cost control.

9. (d)   As production levels decrease, total fixed costs will remain the same, and total variable costs will decrease directly and proportionately.

10. (b)   Many different types of flexible budgets may be prepared. The direct labor and manufacturing overhead budgets are usually based on hours performed.

11. (c)   The usual criteria are materiality and controllability.

12. (a)   Costs allocated to the responsibility level are considered to be noncontrollable costs which are outside the scope of responsibility accounting.

13. (a)   Controllable costs are defined as the costs a manager has the power to incur within a given period of time.

14. (b)   Choice (a) is incorrect because the reporting begins at the lowest level and moves upward to the highest level. Comparative evaluations are possible (c), and management by exception is possible (d).

15. (c)   Only controllable costs are included in the responsibility report.

16. (d)   General office administrative costs are considered common fixed costs. Answers (a), (b), and (c) are all considered direct fixed costs.

17. (c) The return on investment (ROI) formula is:

$$\frac{\text{Controllable Margin (in dollars)}}{\text{Average Operating Assets}} = \text{Return on Investment}$$

18. (c) The return on investment is equal to controllable margin divided by average operating assets; therefore, an increase in sales will increase the controllable margin which will also increase the return on investment. The other choices will cause a decrease in controllable margin or an increase in average operating assets.

19. (c) The recorded book values of these assets are used in determining average operating assets.

20. (d) The return on investment is controllable margin divided by the average investment center operating assets, 30% ($300,000 ÷ $1,000,000).

MATCHING

1. b	5. c	9. j
2. a	6. e	10. k
3. i	7. f	11. h
4. g	8. l	12. d

EXERCISES

EX. 24-1

HARTUNG COMPANY
Flexible Manufacturing Overhead Budget

Activity level: Units	8,000	10,000	12,000	14,000
Variable costs:				
Indirect materials	$ 32,000	$ 40,000	$ 48,000	$ 56,000
Indirect labor	24,000	30,000	36,000	42,000
Supplies	40,000	50,000	60,000	70,000
Total variable	96,000	120,000	144,000	168,000
Fixed costs:				
Depreciation	60,000	60,000	60,000	60,000
Property taxes	20,000	20,000	20,000	20,000
Total fixed	80,000	80,000	80,000	80,000
Total costs	$176,000	$200,000	$224,000	$248,000

EX. 24-2

GAYLORD COMPANY
Manufacturing Overhead Budget Report
For the Month Ended January 31

	Budget at	Actual Costs at	Difference Favorable F Unfavorable U
Direct labor hours (DLH):			
Expected 22,000	24,000 DLH	24,000 DLH	
Actual 24,000			
Variable costs			
Indirect materials	$ 12,000	$ 13,000	$ 1,000 U
Indirect labor	48,000	47,500	(500) F
Supplies	36,000	35,200	(800) F
Total variable	96,000	95,700	(300) F
Fixed costs			
Depreciation	30,000	25,000	(5,000) F
Supervision	45,000	46,000	1,000 U
Total fixed	75,000	71,000	(4,000) F
Total costs	$171,000	$166,700	$(4,300) F

Chapter 25

STANDARD COSTS AND BALANCED SCORECARD

The Navigator ✓
- Scan Study Objectives ☐
- Read Preview ☐
- Read Chapter Review ☐
- Work Demonstration Problem ☐
- Answer True-False Statements ☐
- Answer Multiple-Choice Questions ☐
- Match Terms and Definitions ☐
- Solve Exercises ☐

CHAPTER STUDY OBJECTIVES

After studying this chapter, you should be able to:
1. Distinguish between a standard and a budget.
2. Identify the advantages of standard costs.
3. Describe how companies set standards.
4. State the formulas for determining direct materials and direct labor variances.
5. State the formula for determining the total manufacturing overhead variance.
6. Discuss the reporting of variances.
7. Prepare an income statement for management under a standard costing system.
8. Describe the balanced scorecard approach to performance evaluation.
*9. Identify the features of a standard cost accounting system.

*Note: All **asterisked** (*) items relate to material contained in the Appendix to the chapter.

PREVIEW OF CHAPTER 25

In this chapter we continue the study of controlling costs by considering additional measures that permit the evaluation of performance. The content and organization of the chapter are as follows:

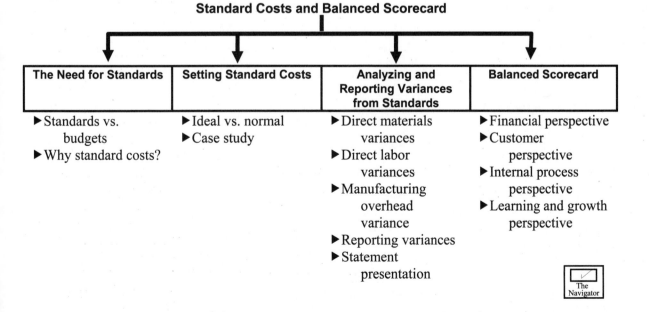

Standard Costs and Balanced Scorecard

The Need for Standards	Setting Standard Costs	Analyzing and Reporting Variances from Standards	Balanced Scorecard
▶ Standards vs. budgets ▶ Why standard costs?	▶ Ideal vs. normal ▶ Case study	▶ Direct materials variances ▶ Direct labor variances ▶ Manufacturing overhead variance ▶ Reporting variances ▶ Statement presentation	▶ Financial perspective ▶ Customer perspective ▶ Internal process perspective ▶ Learning and growth perspective

CHAPTER REVIEW

Standards and Budgets

1. (S.O. 1) In concept, **standards** and budgets are essentially the same. Both are pre-determined costs and both contribute significantly to management planning and control.
   a. A standard is a **unit** amount, whereas a budget is a **total** amount.
   b. Standard costs may be incorporated into a cost accounting system.

Why Standard Costs?

2. (S.O. 2) Standard costs offer the following advantages to an organization:
   a. They facilitate **management planning.**
   b. They promote **greater economy** by making employees more "cost conscious."
   c. They are useful in **setting selling prices.**
   d. They contribute to **management control** by providing a basis for the evaluation of cost control.
   e. They are useful in highlighting variances in **management by exception.**
   f. They **simplify the costing of inventories** and reduce clerical costs.

Setting Standard Costs

3. (S.O. 3) Setting standards requires input from all persons who have responsibility for costs and quantities. Standards may be set at one of two levels. **Ideal standards** represent optimum levels of performance under perfect operating conditions. **Normal standards** represent efficient levels of performance that are attainable under expected operating conditions.

4. To establish the standard cost of producing a product, it is necessary to establish standards for each manufacturing cost element—direct materials, direct labor, and manufacturing overhead. The standard for each element is derived from a consideration of the standard price to be paid and the standard quantity to be used.

Direct Materials

5. The **direct materials price standard** is the cost per unit of direct materials that should be incurred.
   a. This standard is based on the purchasing department's best estimate of the cost of raw materials.
   b. This standard should include an amount for related costs such as receiving, storing, and handling.

6. The **direct materials quantity standard** is the quantity of direct materials that should be used per unit of finished goods.
   a. This standard is expressed as a physical measure, such as pounds, barrels, or board feet.
   b. This standard should include allowances of unavoidable waste and normal storage.

7. The **standard direct materials cost per unit** is the standard direct materials price times the standard direct materials quantity.

Direct Labor

8. The **direct labor price standard** is the rate per hour that should be incurred for direct labor.
    a. This standard is based on current wage rates adjusted for anticipated changes, such as cost of living adjustments included in many union contracts.
    b. This standard generally includes employer payroll taxes and fringe benefits.

9. The **direct labor quantity standard** is the time that should be required to make one unit of the product.
    a. This standard is especially critical in labor-intensive companies.
    b. In setting this standard, allowances should be made for rest periods, cleanup, machine setup and machine downtime.

10. The **standard direct labor cost per unit** is the standard direct labor rate times the standard direct labor hours.

Manufacturing Overhead

11. The **manufacturing overhead standard** is based on a **standard predetermined overhead rate.**
    a. This overhead rate is determined by dividing budgeted overhead costs by an expected standard activity index.
    b. The **standard manufacturing overhead rate per unit** is the predetermined overhead rate times the activity index quantity standard.

Variances

12. A **variance** is the difference between total actual costs and total standard costs. An unfavorable variance suggests that too much was paid for materials, labor, and manufacturing overhead or that there were inefficiencies in using materials, labor, and manufacturing overhead. Favorable variances indicate efficiencies in incurring costs and in using materials, labor, and manufacturing overhead.

13. **Analyzing variances** begins with a determination of the cost elements that comprise the variance. For each manufacturing cost element, a total dollar variance is computed. Then this variance is analyzed into a price variance and a quantity variance.

Direct Materials Variances

14. (S.O. 4) The formulas for the direct materials variances are:

Actual Quantity X Actual Price (AQ) X (AP)	−	Standard Quantity X Standard Price (SQ) X (SP)	=	Total Materials Variance (TMV)
Actual Quantity X Actual Price (AQ) X (AP)	−	Actual Quantity X Standard Price (AQ) X (SP)	=	Materials Price Variance (MPV)
Actual Quantity X Standard Price (AQ) X (SP)	−	Standard Quantity X Standard Price (SQ) X (SP)	=	Materials Quantity Variance (MQV)

15. A **variance matrix** can be used in analyzing variances. In such cases, the formulas for each cost element are computed first and then the variances.

16. Materials price variances are usually the responsibility of the purchasing department, whereas materials quantity variances are usually attributable to the production department.

Direct Labor Variances

17. The formulas for the direct labor variances are:

Actual Hours X Actual Rate (AH) X (AR)	−	Standard Hours X Standard Rate (SH) X (SR)	=	Total Labor Variance (TLV)
Actual Hours X Actual Rate (AH) X (AR)	−	Actual Hours X Standard Rate (AH) X (SR)	=	Labor Price Variance (LPV)
Actual Hours X Standard Rate (AH) X (SR)	−	Standard Hours X Standard Rate (SH) X (SR)	=	Labor Quantity Variance (LQV)

18. Labor price variances usually result from paying workers higher wages than expected and/or misallocation of workers. Labor quantity variances relate to the efficiency of the workers and are the responsibility of the production department.

Manufacturing Overhead Variance

19. (S.O. 5) The computation of the **manufacturing overhead variances** is conceptually the same as the computation of the materials and labor variances. For manufacturing overhead, however, both variable and fixed overhead must be considered. The formulas are:

Actual Overhead	−	Overhead Applied*	=	Total Overhead Variance
Actual Overhead	−	Overhead Budgeted*	=	Overhead Controllable Variance
Fixed Overhead Rate X		(Normal Capacity Hours − Standard Hours Allowed)	=	Overhead Volume Variance

20. The overhead controllable variance shows whether overhead costs were effectively controlled.
    a. Budgeted costs are determined from the **flexible manufacturing overhead budget** for standard hours allowed.
    b. Most controllable variances are associated with **variable costs** which are controllable costs.

21. The overhead volume variance indicates whether plant facilities were efficiently used during the period.
    a. This variance relates solely to **fixed costs.**
    b. It measures the amount that fixed overhead costs are under- or overapplied.

22. In computing the overhead variances,
    a. Standard hours allowed are used in each of the variances.
    b. Budgeted costs are derived from the flexible budget.
    c. The controllable variance generally pertains to variable costs.
    d. The volume variance pertains solely to fixed costs.

23. The controllable overhead variance includes variable manufacturing overhead and therefore is the responsibility of the production department. The overhead volume variance may be the responsibility of either the production or sales departments.

Reporting of Variances

24. (S.O. 6) All variances should be reported to appropriate levels of management as soon as possible. **Variance reports** facilitate the principle of "management by exception." Rather than analyze every variance, top management will normally look for significant variances.

Statement Presentation of Variances

25. (S.O. 7) In income statements prepared for management under a standard cost accounting system, cost of goods sold is stated at standard cost and the variances are separately disclosed. In financial statements prepared for stockholders and other external users, standard costs may be used.

Balanced Scorecard

26. (S.O. 8)   Many companies use both financial and nonfinancial measures to evaluate performance. This approach is known as the **balanced scorecard.** The four most commonly employed perspectives are as follows:
    a. The **financial perspective** employs financial measures of performance.
    b. The **customer perspective** evaluates how well the company is performing from the viewpoint of those people who buy and use its product.
    c. The **internal process perspective** evaluates the internal operating processes critical to success.
    d. The **earning and growth perspective** evaluates how well the company develops and retains its employees.

The different perspectives are linked together so a company can better understand how to achieve its goals and what measures to use to evaluate performance.

Standard Cost Accounting System

*27. (S.O. 9) A **standard cost accounting system** is a double-entry system of accounting in which standard costs are used in making entries and variances are formally recognized in the accounts. A standard cost system may be used with either job order or process costing.

*28. As an example, the purchase of raw materials inventory for $5,000 when the standard cost is $6,000 would be recorded as follows:

Raw Materials Inventory..	6,000	
Materials Price Variance..		1,000
Accounts Payable..		5,000

    a.   A debit balance in a variance account indicates an unfavorable variance.
    b.   A credit balance in a variance account indicates a favorable variance.

*29. In income statements prepared for management, cost of goods sold is stated at standard cost and the variances are separately disclosed.

*30. Standard costs may be used in costing inventories in financial statements prepared for **stockholders** when there are no significant differences between actual and standard costs. However, if the difference is material, the inventories and cost of goods sold must be reported at actual costs.

The
Navigator

DEMONSTRATION PROBLEM (S.O. 4, 5, 6, 7)

Morgan Inc. is a small company that manufactures baseball caps. For the past several years, the company has used a standard cost accounting system. Cole prepares monthly income statements for management with variances reported within the statement. In April 2010, 67,500 caps were produced. There were no finished caps on hand at either April 1 or April 30. The selling price per cap was $10.00. The following standard and actual cost data applied to the month of April when normal capacity was 14,000 direct labor hours.

Cost Element	Standard (per unit)	Actual
Direct materials	1.5 yards at $3.00 per yard	$318,600 for 108,000 yards ($2.95 yard)
Direct labor	.2 hour at $11.00 per hour	$158,760 for 14,175 hours ($11.20 per hour)
Overhead	.2 hour at $ 5.00 per hour	$49,000 fixed overhead
		$20,000 variable overhead

Overhead is applied on the basis of direct labor hours. At normal capacity, budgeted fixed overhead costs were $49,000 and budgeted variable costs were $21,000.

Instructions

(a)   Compute the total, price, and quantity variances for (1) materials, (2) labor, and (3) the total, controllable, and volume variances for manufacturing overhead (assuming no beginning or ending material balances).

(b)   Journalize the entries to record the variances and the completion and sale of the caps.

SOLUTION TO DEMONSTRATION PROBLEM

(a)
Direct Material Variances

Total	= $318,600 ($2.95 X 108,000) - $303,750 (1.5 X $3.00 X 67,500)	=	$14,850 U
Price	= $318,600 ($2.95 X 108,000) - $324,000 ($3.00 X 108,000)	=	$5,400 F
Quantity	= $324,000 ($3.00 X 108,000) - $303,750 (1.5 X $3.00 X 67,500)	=	$20,250 U

Direct Labor Variances

Total	= $158,760 ($11.20 X 14.175) - $148,500 (.2 X $11.00 X 67,500)	=	$10,260 U
Price	= $158,760 ($11.20 X 14.175) - $155,925 ($11.00 X 14,175)	=	$2,835 U
Quantity	= $155,925 ($11.00 X 14,175) - $148,500 (.2 X $11.00 X 67,500)	=	$7,425 U

Overhead Variances

Total	= $69,000	-	$67,500	=	$1,500 U
	($49,000 + $20,000)		($5 X 67,500 X .2)		
Controllable	= $69,000	-	$69,250	=	$250 F
			[$49,000 + ($1.50* X 67,500 X .2)]		
Volume	= $3.50 X (14,000 – 13,500)			=	$1,750 U**

*$21,000 ÷ 14,000 = $1.50
**Alternatively: $69,250 - $67,500 = $1,750 U

(b)

1. Raw Materials Inventory 324,000
       Materials Price Variance   5,400
       Accounts Payable   318,600
         (To record purchase of materials)

2. Factory Labor 155,925
   Labor Price Variance   2,835
       Wages Payable   158,760
         (To record direct labor costs)

3. Manufacturing Overhead 69,000
       Accounts Payable/Cash/Acc. Depreciation   69,000
         (To record overhead incurred)

4. Work in Process Inventory 303,750
   Materials Quantity Variance 20,250
       Raw Materials Inventory 324,000
         (To record issuance of raw materials)

5. Work in Process Inventory 148,500
   Labor Quantity Variance   7,425
       Factory Labor 155,925

6. Work in Process Inventory 67,500
       Manufacturing Overhead   67,500
         (To assign overhead to jobs)

7. Finished Goods Inventory 519,750
       Work in Process Inventory 519,750
         (To record transfer of completed work to finished goods)

8. Accounts Receivable 675,000
   Cost of Goods Sold 519,750
       Sales 675,000
       Finished Goods Inventory 519,750
         (To record sale of finished goods and the cost of
          goods sold)

9. Overhead Volume Variance 1,750
       Overhead Controllable Variance   250
       Manufacturing Overhead   1,500
         (To recognize overhead variances)

REVIEW QUESTIONS AND EXERCISES

TRUE—FALSE

Indicate whether each of the following is true (T) or false (F) in the space provided.

_____ 1. (S.O. 1)   In concept, standards and budgets are essentially the same.

_____ 2. (S.O. 2)   Standards may be useful in setting selling prices for finished goods.

_____ 3. (S.O. 3)   Ideal standards represent an efficient level of performance under normal operating conditions.

_____ 4. (S.O. 3)   The materials price standard is based on the purchasing department's best estimate of the cost of raw materials.

_____ 5. (S.O. 3)   The direct labor quantity standard is based on current wage rates adjusted for anticipated changes such as cost of living adjustments included in many union contracts.

_____ 6. (S.O. 3)   The standard predetermined overhead rate is based on an expected standard activity index.

_____ 7. (S.O. 3)   An unfavorable variance suggests efficiencies in incurring costs and in using materials and labor.

_____ 8. (S.O. 4)   The materials price variance is the difference between actual quantity of materials purchased times the standard cost and the standard quantity of materials times the standard cost.

_____ 9. (S.O. 4)   The materials quantity variance is the difference between the standard cost times the actual quantity of materials used and the standard cost times the standard quantity used.

_____ 10. (S.O. 4)   The materials price variance is normally caused by the production department.

_____ 11. (S.O. 4)   Material quantity variances can be caused by inexperienced workers, faulty machinery, or carelessness.

_____ 12. (S.O. 4)   The labor quantity variance is the difference between the actual rate times the standard hours and the standard rate times the standard hours.

_____ 13. (S.O. 4)   The use of an inexperienced worker instead of an experienced employee can result in a favorable labor price variance but probably an unfavorable quantity variance.

_____ 14. (S.O. 5)   The overhead controllable variance is the difference between the actual overhead costs incurred and the budgeted costs for the standard hours allowed.

_____ 15. (S.O. 5)   An increase in the cost of indirect manufacturing costs such as fuel and maintenance may cause an overhead volume variance.

_____ 16. (S.O. 6) All variances should be reported to appropriate levels of management as soon as possible.

_____ 17. (S.O. 6) In using variance reports, top management normally looks carefully at every variance.

_____ *18. (S.O. 9) A standard cost system may be used with either job order or process costing.

_____ *19. (S.O. 9) Under a standard cost accounting system, a favorable labor price variance will result in a credit to Labor Price Variance.

_____ *20. (S.O. 9) The use of standard costs in inventory costing is prohibited in financial statements.

MULTIPLE CHOICE

Circle the letter that best answers each of the following statements.

1. (S.O. 3) A standard that represents the optimum level of performance under perfect operating conditions is called a(n):
    a. normal standard.
    b. controllable standard.
    c. ideal standard.
    d. materials price standard.

2. (S.O. 4) The standard unit cost is used in the calculation of which of the following variances?

	Materials Price Variance	Materials Quantity Variance
a.	No	No
b.	No	Yes
c.	Yes	No
d.	Yes	Yes

3. (S.O. 4) In the Norton Company, each unit of finished goods requires one pound of direct materials at $2 per pound. In producing 50,000 units, 45,000 pounds of materials are used at $2.10 per pound. The materials price variance is:
    a. $4,500 unfavorable.
    b. $5,000 favorable.
    c. $5,000 unfavorable.
    d. $10,000 favorable.

4. (S.O. 4) Using the data in question 3 above, the materials quantity variance is:
    a. $10,500 favorable.
    b. $10,000 favorable.
    c. $10,500 unfavorable.
    d. $4,500 unfavorable.

5. (S.O. 4) In the Delaney Company, the standard material cost for the silk used in making a dress is $27.00 based on three square feet of silk at a cost of $9.00 per square foot. The production of 1,000 dresses resulted in the use of 3,400 square feet of silk at a cost of $9.20 per square foot. The materials quantity variance is:
    a. $600 unfavorable.
    b. $680 unfavorable.
    c. $3,600 unfavorable.
    d. $3,680 unfavorable.

6. (S.O. 4) The difference between the actual labor rate multiplied by the actual labor hours worked and the standard labor rate multiplied by the standard labor hours is the:
    a. total labor variance.
    b. labor price variance.
    c. labor quantity variance.
    d. labor efficiency variance.

7. (S.O. 4) The labor price variance is the difference between the:
    a. standard and actual rate multiplied by actual hours.
    b. standard and actual rate multiplied by standard hours.
    c. standard and actual hours multiplied by actual rate.
    d. standard and actual hours multiplied by the difference between standard and actual rate.

8. (S.O. 4) In the Wetzel Company 20,000 direct labor hours were worked when standard hours were 21,000 and the actual pay rate was $6.30 when the standard rate was $6.50. The labor quantity variance is:
    a. $6,300 favorable.
    b. $6,300 unfavorable.
    c. $6,500 favorable.
    d. $6,500 unfavorable.

9. (S.O. 4) Using the data in question 8, the labor price variance is:
    a. $4,000 unfavorable.
    b. $4,000 favorable.
    c. $4,200 unfavorable.
    d. $4,200 favorable.

10. (S.O. 4) An unfavorable labor quantity variance means that:
    a. the actual rate was higher than the standard rate.
    b. the total labor variance must also be unfavorable.
    c. actual hours exceeded standard hours.
    d. actual hours were less than standard hours.

11. (S.O. 4) Information on Engstrom's direct labor costs for the month of August is as follows:

Actual rate	$7.50
Standard hours	11,000
Actual hours	10,000
Direct labor price variance—unfavorable	$5,000

    What was the standard rate for August?
    a. $6.95.
    b. $7.00.
    c. $8.00.
    d. $8.05.

12. (S.O. 4) An unfavorable material price variance generally is the responsibility of the following department:
    a. Quality control.
    b. Purchasing.
    c. Engineering.
    d. Production.

13. (S.O. 4) Which department is usually responsible for a labor price variance attributable to misallocation of workers?
    a. Quality control.
    b. Purchasing.
    c. Engineering.
    d. Production.

14. (S.O. 5) The total overhead variance is:
    a. the difference between actual overhead costs and overhead applied.
    b. based on actual hours worked for the units produced.
    c. the difference between overhead budgeted and overhead applied.
    d. the difference between actual overhead costs and overhead budgeted.

15. (S.O. 5) The overhead controllable variance is the difference between the:
    a. budgeted overhead based on standard hours allowed and the overhead applied to production.
    b. budgeted overhead based on standard hours allowed and budgeted overhead based on actual hours worked.
    c. actual overhead and the overhead applied to production.
    d. actual overhead and budgeted overhead based on standard hours allowed.

16. (S.O. 5) Budgeted overhead for the Henderson Company at normal capacity of 30,000 direct labor hours is $6 per hour variable and $4 per hour fixed. In May, $310,000 of overhead was incurred in working 31,500 hours when 32,000 standard hours were allowed. The overhead controllable variance is:
    a. $5,000 favorable.
    b. $2,000 favorable.
    c. $10,000 favorable.
    d. $10,000 unfavorable.

17. (S.O. 5) Using the data in question 16, the overhead volume variance is:
  a. $8,000 favorable.
  b. $11,000 favorable.
  c. $5,000 favorable.
  d. $10,000 favorable.

18. (S.O. 5) The overhead volume variance is the difference between the:
  a. overhead budget based on standard hours allowed and overhead budget based on actual hours worked.
  b. normal capacity hours and standard hours allowed times the fixed overhead rate.
  c. actual overhead and the overhead budget based on standard hours allowed.
  d. actual overhead and the overhead applied.

19. (S.O. 6) In reporting variances,
  a. promptness is relatively unimportant.
  b. management normally investigates all variances.
  c. the reports should facilitate management by exception.
  d. the reports are not departmentalized.

*20. (S.O. 9) A standard cost system may be used in:

	Job Order Costing	**Process** Costing
a.	No	No
b.	Yes	No
c.	No	Yes
d.	Yes	Yes

The
Navigator

MATCHING

Match each term with its definition by writing the appropriate letter in the space provided.

Terms	Definitions

Terms

_____ 1. Variances.

_____ 2. Materials price variance.

_____ 3. Standard hours allowed.

_____ 4. Standard cost accounting system.

_____ 5. Ideal standards.

_____ 6. Standard predetermined overhead rate.

_____ 7. Materials quantity variance.

_____ 8. Overhead controllable variance.

_____ 9. Labor price variance.

_____ 10. Normal standards.

_____ 11. Overhead volume variance.

_____ 12. Total materials variance.

_____ 13. Total overhead variance.

_____ 14. Total labor variance.

_____ 15. Labor quantity variance.

_____ 16. Standard costs.

Definitions

a. A double entry system of accounting in which standard costs are used in making entries and variances are recognized in the accounts.

b. Predetermined unit costs which are used as measures of performance.

c. The difference between the actual quantity of materials times the actual price and the actual quantity times the standard price.

d. The difference between the actual overhead incurred and overhead budgeted for the standard hours allowed.

e. Standards based on an efficient level of performance that are attainable under expected operating conditions.

f. The difference between actual hours times the standard rate and standard hours times the standard rate.

g. The difference between actual hours times the actual rate and standard hours times the standard rate for labor.

h. The difference between the actual quantity of materials times the standard price and the standard quantity times the standard price.

i. The difference between normal capacity hours and standard hours allowed times the fixed overhead rate.

j. Standards based on the optimum level of performance under perfect operating conditions.

k. The difference between actual overhead incurred and overhead costs applied to work done.

l. The differences between total actual costs and total standard costs.

m. The difference between the actual hours times the actual wage rate and the actual hours times the standard rate.

n. The hours that should have been worked for the units produced.

o. The difference between the actual quantity times the actual price and the standard quantity times the standard price of materials.

p. An overhead rate determined by dividing budgeted overhead costs by an expected standard activity index.

The Navigator

EXERCISES

EX. 25-1   (S.O. 4, 5) Lindsey Company manufactures coats with fur-lined hoods. The following information pertains to the standard costs of manufacturing the hood of one coat:

Direct Material	1 yard at $30 per yard
Direct Labor	2 hours at $10 per hour
Variable Overhead	1/2 hour at $2 per hour
Fixed Overhead	1/2 hour at $3 per hour

Other data:

1. Coats produced during June—10,000.
2. 11,000 yards were purchased and used at $29 per yard.
3. Actual direct labor costs were $209,000 for 19,000 hours worked.
4. Normal capacity was 5,500 direct labor hours.
5. Actual variable overhead costs were $9,500.
6. Actual fixed overhead costs were $16,100.

Instructions
Compute the following variances for Lindsey Company:

	Computation	**Amount**
a. Total Materials		_____
b. Materials Price		_____
c. Materials Quantity		_____
d. Total Labor		_____
e. Labor Price		_____
f. Labor Quantity		_____
g. Total Overhead		_____
h. Overhead Controllable		_____
i. Overhead Volume		_____

*EX. 25-2 (S.O. 8)   A. Carlson uses a standard cost accounting system.   The following transactions occurred during the year:

Feb.   20   Purchased raw materials on account, $8,800 when the standard cost was $9,300.

Mar.   5   Incurred direct labor costs, $15,200 when the standard labor cost was $14,900.

May   10   Incurred manufacturing overhead costs, $11,000 (credit Accounts Payable).

June   18   Issued raw materials for production, $8,200 when the standard cost was $9,000.

Aug.   3   Assigned factory labor to production, $14,900 when the standard cost was $14,500.

Sept.   10   Applied manufacturing overhead to production, $10,150.

Oct.   2   Transferred completed work to finished goods, $29,700.

Nov.   22   Sold the finished goods for $42,000.

Dec.   31   Recognized unfavorable overhead variances: controllable $550 and volume $300.

Instructions
Prepare the entries for A. Carlson in the following general journal.

General Journal			J1
Date	**Account Title**	**Debit**	**Credit**

	General Journal		J
Date	**Account Title**	**Debit**	**Credit**

The
Navigator

SOLUTIONS TO REVIEW QUESTIONS AND EXERCISES

TRUE-FALSE

1. (T)
2. (T)
3. (F)   Ideal standards represent the optimum level of performance under perfect operating conditions.   Normal standards represent an efficient level of performance under normal operating conditions.
4. (T)
5. (F)   It is the direct labor price standard that is based on current wage rates adjusted for anticipated changes such as cost of living adjustments.
6. (T)
7. (F)   An unfavorable variance has a negative connotation. It suggests that too much was paid for materials and labor or that there were inefficiencies in using materials and labor.
8. (F)   The materials price variance is the difference between the actual quantity of materials purchased times the actual cost and the actual quantity times the standard cost.
9. (T)
10. (F)   The materials price variance is normally the responsibility of the purchasing department.
11. (T)
12. (F)   The labor quantity variance is the difference between the actual hours times the standard rate and the standard hours times the standard rate.
13. (T)
14. (T)
15. (F)   An increase in the cost of indirect manufacturing costs such as fuel and maintenance may cause an overhead controllable variance.
16. (T)
17. (F)   In using variance reports, top management normally looks for significant variances. The variance reports facilitate the principle of "management by exception."
18. (T)
19. (T)
20. (F)   The use of standard costs in inventory costing is in accordance with generally accepted accounting principles when there are no significant differences between actual and standard costs.

MULTIPLE CHOICE

1. (c)   A standard that represents the optimum level of performance under perfect operating conditions is the ideal standard. A normal standard (a) represents an efficient level of performance under normal operating conditions.

2. (d)   The materials price variance is equal to the difference between the actual quantity times the actual unit cost and the actual quantity times the standard unit cost. The materials quantity variance is equal to the difference between the actual quantity times the standard unit cost and the standard quantity times the standard unit cost.

3. (a)   The materials price variance is: (45,000 X $2.10) - (45,000 X $2.00) = $4,500 U.

4.   (b)   The materials quantity variance is: (45,000 X $2.00) - (50,000 X $2.00) = $10,000 F.

5.   (c)   The materials quantity variance is: (3,400 X $9.00) - (3,000 X $9.00) = $3,600 U.

6.   (a)   The total labor variance is equal to the difference between the actual labor rate multiplied by the actual labor hours worked and the standard labor rate multiplied by the standard labor hours.

7.   (a)   The labor price variance is equal to the difference between the actual hours times the actual rate and actual hours times the standard rate.

8.   (c)   The labor quantity variance is: (20,000 X $6.50) - (21,000 X $6.50) = $6,500 F.

9.   (b)   The labor price variance is: (20,000 X $6.30) - (20,000 X $6.50) = $4,000 F.

10. (c)   The labor quantity variance is equal to the difference between the actual hours times the standard rate and the standard hours times the standard rate. Therefore, an unfavorable variance results when actual hours exceeds standard hours.

11. (b)   The labor price variance is: (10,000 X $7.50) - ($10,000 X $X) = $5,000 U.

12. (b)   Generally, the purchasing department is responsible for an unfavorable materials price variance. In some cases however, inflation may be the cause, and the production department may be responsible if a rush order caused the higher price.

13. (d)   Misallocation of workers occurs when an inexperienced worker is used instead of an experienced worker and vice versa. The production department is generally responsible for a labor price variance attributable to this cause.

14. (a)   The total overhead variance is the difference between actual overhead incurred and overhead applied.

15. (d)   The overhead controllable variance is the difference between the actual overhead costs incurred and the budgeted costs for the standard hours allowed.

16. (b)   The overhead controllable variance is: $310,000 - [(32,000 X $6.00) + (30,000 X $4.00] = $2,000 F.

17. (a)   The overhead volume variance is: $4.00 X (30,000 – 32,000) = $8,000 F.

18. (b)   The overhead volume variance is the difference between the overhead budgeted based on standard hours allowed and the overhead applied.

19. (c)   Variances should be reported as soon as possible (a). Management normally investigates significant variances (b). The reports are usually departmentalized (d).

20. (d)   A standard cost accounting system may be used in either a job order or process costing system.

MATCHING

1.	l	5.	j	9.	m	13.	k
2.	c	6.	p	10.	e	14.	g
3.	n	7.	h	11.	i	15.	f
4.	a	8.	d	12.	o	16.	b

EXERCISES

EX. 25-1

	Variances	**Computations**
a.	Total materials	(11,000 X $29) - (10,000 X $30) = $19,000 U
b.	Materials price	(11,000 X $29) - (11,000 X $30) = $11,000 F
c.	Materials quantity	(11,000 X $30) - (10,000 X $30) = $30,000 U
d.	Total labor	(19,000 X $11) - (20,000 X $10) = $ 9,000 U
e.	Labor price	(19,000 X $11) - (19,000 X $10) = $19,000 U
f.	Labor quantity	(19,000 X $10) - (20,000 X $10) = $10,000 F
g.	Total overhead	($9,500 + $16,100) - [5,000 X ($2 + $3)] = $600 U
h.	Overhead controllable	($9,500 + $16,100) - [(5,000 X $2) + $16,500] = $ 900 F
i.	Overhead volume	$3 X (5,500 – 5,000) = $1,500 U

EX. 25-2

	General Journal			**J1**
Date	**Account Title**	**Debit**	**Credit**	
Feb. 20	Raw Materials Inventory	9,300		
	Materials Price Variance		500	
	Accounts Payable		8,800	
Mar. 5	Factory Labor	14,900		
	Labor Price Variance	300		
	Wages Payable		15,200	
May 10	Manufacturing Overhead	11,000		
	Accounts Payable		11,000	

	General Journal		J2
Date	**Account Title**	**Debit**	**Credit**
June 18	Work in Process Inventory	9,000	
	Materials Quantity Variance		800
	Raw Materials Inventory		8,200
Aug. 3	Work in Process Inventory	14,500	
	Labor Quantity Variance	400	
	Factory Labor		14,900
Sept. 10	Work in Process Inventory	10,150	
	Manufacturing Overhead		10,150
Oct. 2	Finished Goods Inventory	29,700	
	Work in Process Inventory		29,700
Nov. 22	Accounts Receivable	42,000	
	Cost of Goods Sold	29,700	
	Sales		42,000
	Finished Goods Inventory		29,700
Dec. 31	Overhead Controllable Variance	550	
	Overhead Volume Variance	300	
	Manufacturing Overhead		850

Chapter 26

INCREMENTAL ANALYSIS AND CAPITAL BUDGETING

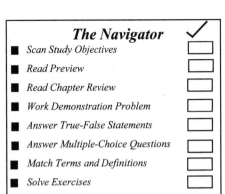

The Navigator ✓

- Scan Study Objectives ☐
- Read Preview ☐
- Read Chapter Review ☐
- Work Demonstration Problem ☐
- Answer True-False Statements ☐
- Answer Multiple-Choice Questions ☐
- Match Terms and Definitions ☐
- Solve Exercises ☐

CHAPTER STUDY OBJECTIVES

After studying this chapter, you should be able to:

1. Identify the steps in management's decision-making process.
2. Describe the concept of incremental analysis.
3. Identify the relevant costs in accepting an order at a special price.
4. Identify the relevant costs in a make-or-buy decision.
5. Give the decision rule in deciding whether to sell or process materials further.
6. Identify the factors to consider in retaining or replacing equipment.
7. Explain the relevant factors in whether to eliminate an unprofitable segment.
8. Determine which products to make and sell when resources are limited.
9. Contrast annual rate of return and cash payback in capital budgeting.
10. Distinguish between the net present value and internal rate of return methods.

PREVIEW OF CHAPTER 26

An important purpose of management accounting is to provide management with relevant information for decision making. This chapter begins with an explanation of management's decision-making process. It then considers the topics of incremental analysis and capital budgeting. The organization and content of this chapter are as follows:

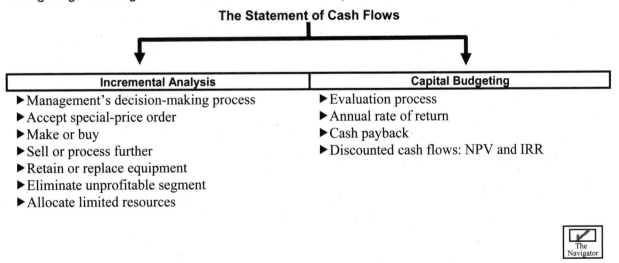

The Statement of Cash Flows

Incremental Analysis	Capital Budgeting
▶ Management's decision-making process	▶ Evaluation process
▶ Accept special-price order	▶ Annual rate of return
▶ Make or buy	▶ Cash payback
▶ Sell or process further	▶ Discounted cash flows: NPV and IRR
▶ Retain or replace equipment	
▶ Eliminate unprofitable segment	
▶ Allocate limited resources	

CHAPTER REVIEW

Incremental Analysis

1. (S.O. 1) **Management's decision-making process** frequently involves the following steps:
    a. Identify the problem and assign responsibility.
    b. Determine and evaluate possible courses of action.
    c. Make a decision.
    d. Review results of decision.

2. (S.O. 2) Business decisions involve a choice among alternative courses of action. In making such decisions, management ordinarily considers both financial and nonfinancial information. The process used to identify the financial data that change under alternative courses of action is called **incremental analysis.**
    a. Incremental analysis includes the probable effects of the decision on **future earnings.**
    b. Data for incremental analysis involves estimates and uncertainty.
    c. Gathering data may involve market analysts, engineers, and accountants.

3. In incremental analysis, **both costs and revenues** may change. However, in some cases (1) variable costs may not change under the alternative courses of action, and (2) fixed costs may change.

Accept an Order at a Special Price

4. (S.O. 3) An **order at a special price** should be accepted when the incremental revenue from the order exceeds the incremental costs.
    a. It is assumed that sales in other markets will not be affected by the special order.
    b. If the units can be produced within existing plant capacity, generally only variable costs will be affected.

Make or Buy

5. (S.O. 4) In a **make or buy** decision, management must determine the costs which are different under the two alternatives. If there is an opportunity to use the productive capacity for another purpose, opportunity cost should be considered. **Opportunity cost** is the potential benefit that may be obtained by following an alternative course of action. This cost is an additional cost of making the component.

Sell or Process Further

6. (S.O. 5) The basic decision rule in a **sell or process further** decision is: Process further as long as the incremental revenue from such processing exceeds the incremental processing costs. Incremental revenue is the increase in sales which results from processing the product further.

Retain or Replace Equipment

7. (S.O. 6) In a decision to **retain or replace equipment,** management compares the costs which are affected by the two alternatives. Generally, these are variable manufacturing costs and the cost of the new equipment.
    a. The **book value** of the old machine is a sunk cost which does not affect the decision. A **sunk cost** is a cost that cannot be changed by any present or future decision.

b.   However, any **trade-in allowance** or **cash disposal value** of the existing asset must be considered.

Eliminate an Unprofitable Segment

8.   (S.O. 7) In deciding whether to **eliminate an unprofitable segment,** management should choose the alternative which results in the highest net income. Often fixed costs allocated to the unprofitable segment must be absorbed by the other segments. It is possible, therefore, for net income to **decrease** when an unprofitable segment is eliminated.

Allocate Limited Resources

9.   (S.O. 8) When a company has limited resources (floor space, raw materials, or machine hours), management must decide which products to make and sell. In an **allocation of limited resources** decision, it is necessary to find the **contribution margin per unit of limited resource.**
   a.   This is obtained by dividing the contribution margin per unit of each product by the number of units of the limited resource required for each product. For example, if the unit contribution margin for a product is $6 and three machine hours are required, the contribution margin per unit of limited resource is $2 ($6 ÷ 3).
   b.   Production should be geared to the product with the highest contribution margin per unit of limited resource.

Capital Budgeting

10.   (S.O. 9) The process of making capital expenditure decisions is known as **capital budgeting.** The three most commonly used capital budgeting techniques are (a) annual rate of return, (b) cash payback, and (c) discounted cash flow.

Annual Rate of Return

11.   The **annual rate of return** technique is based on accounting data. It indicates the **profitability of a capital expenditure.** The formula is:

Expected Annual Net Income ÷ Average Investment = Annual Rate of Return

Average investment is based on the following:

$$\frac{\text{Original investment} + \text{Value at end of useful life}}{2} = \text{Average investment}$$

12.   A project is considered acceptable if its rate of return is greater than management's minimum rate of return (also called the **hurdle rate** or **cutoff rate).**
   a.   The hurdle rate is based on the company's **cost of capital,** which is the rate of return management expects to pay on all borrowed and equity funds.
   b.   When choosing among several acceptable projects, the higher the annual rate of return, the more attractive the investment.
   c.   This technique is simple and familiar, but it does not consider the time value of money.

Cash Payback

13. The **cash payback technique** identifies the time period required to recover the cost of the capital investment from the annual cash inflow produced by the investment. The formula for computing the cash payback period is:

Cost of Capital Investment ÷ Annual Cash Inflow = Cash Payback Period

Annual or net cash inflow is approximated by adding depreciation expense to net income.

14. The evaluation of the payback period is often related to the expected useful life of the asset.
a. With this technique, the shorter the payback period, the more attractive the investment.
b. This technique is useful as an initial screening tool.
c. This technique ignores both the expected profitability of the investment and the time value of money.

Discounted Cash Flow

15. (S.O. 10) The **discounted cash flow technique** is generally recognized as the best conceptual approach to making capital budgeting decisions. This technique considers both the estimated total cash inflows and the time value of money. Two methods are used with the discounted cash flow technique: net present value and internal rate of return.

Net Present Value Method

16. Under the **net present value method,** cash inflows are discounted to their present value and then compared with the capital outlay required by the investment. The difference between these two amounts is the **net present value (NPV).**
a. The interest rate used in discounting the future cash inflows is the required minimum rate of return.
b. A proposal is acceptable when NPV is zero or positive.
c. The higher the positive NPV, the more attractive the investment.

17. When there are **equal annual cash inflows,** the table showing the present value of an annuity of 1 can be used in determining present value. When there are **unequal annual cash inflows,** the table showing the present value of a single future amount must be used in determining present value.

Internal Rate of Return Method

18. The **internal rate of return method** results in finding the **interest yield** of the potential investment. This is the interest rate that will cause the present value of the proposed capital expenditure to equal the present value of the expected annual cash inflows. Determining the true interest rate involves two steps:
a. An **internal rate of return factor** is computed by dividing the capital investment by the annual cash inflows.
b. The factor is then used with the annuity of 1 table to find the approximate internal rate of return.

19. The **decision rule** is: Accept the project when the internal rate of return is equal to or greater than the required rate of return, and reject the project when the internal rate of return is less than the required rate.

20. In **practice,** the internal rate of return and cash payback methods are most widely used.

DEMONSTRATION PROBLEM (S.O. 7)

Lynn Devers, a recent graduate of Smith's accounting program, evaluated the operating performance of Knutson Company's six divisions. Lynn made the following presentation to Knutson's Board of Directors and suggested the Adams Division be eliminated. "If the Adams Division is eliminated," she said, "Our net income would increase by $23,200."

	The Other Five Divisions	Adams Division	Total
Sales	$2,422,600	$249,400	$2,672,000
Cost of goods sold	1,712,500	199,300	1,911,800
Gross profit	710,100	50,100	760,200
Operating expenses	456,000	73,300	529,300
Net income	$ 254,100	$(23,200)	$ 230,900

The cost of goods sold for Adams Division is 30% fixed, and its operating expenses are 60% fixed. None of Adams Division's fixed costs will be eliminated if the division is discontinued.

Instructions
Is Lynn right about eliminating the Adams Division? Prepare a schedule to support your answer.

SOLUTION TO DEMONSTRATION PROBLEM

No, net income would decrease $80,570 ($230,900 - $150,330).

	The Other Five Divisions	Adams Division	Total
Sales	$2,422,600	$ -0-	$2,422,600
Cost of goods sold	1,712,500	59,790*	1,772,290
Gross profit	710,100	(59,790)	650,310
Operating expenses	456,000	43,980**	499,980
Net income	$ 254,100	$(103,770)	$ 150,330

*$199,300 X 30% = $59,790 fixed.
**$73,300 X 60% = $43,980 fixed.

REVIEW QUESTIONS AND EXERCISES

TRUE—FALSE

Indicate whether each of the following is true (T) or false (F) in the space provided.

_____ 1. (S.O. 1) Accounting contributes to management's decision making process through internal reports that review the actual impact of the decision.

_____ 2. (S.O. 2) The process used to identify the financial data that change under alternative courses of action is called allocation of limited resources.

_____ 3. (S.O. 2) Variable costs may **not** change under alternative courses of action, while fixed costs may change.

_____ 4. (S.O. 3) When deciding whether to accept an order at a special price, management should make its decision on the basis of the total cost per unit and the expected revenue.

_____ 5. (S.O. 3) If a company is operating at full capacity, the incremental costs of a special order will likely include fixed manufacturing costs.

_____ 6. (S.O. 4) An example of a capital budgeting decision is make or buy.

_____ 7. (S.O. 4) Opportunity cost is the potential benefit that may be obtained by following an alternative course of action.

_____ 8. (S.O. 5) The basic decision rule in a sell or process further decision is: sell without further processing as long as the incremental revenue from processing exceeds the incremental processing costs.

_____ 9. (S.O. 6) An important factor to be considered in a retain or replace equipment decision is the book value of the old equipment.

_____ 10. (S.O. 7) In deciding on the future status of an unprofitable segment, management should recognize that net income could decrease by eliminating the unprofitable segment.

_____ 11. (S.O. 8) When deciding how to allocate limited resources, the contribution margin per unit of limited resource must be determined.

_____ 12. (S.O. 9) The process of making capital expenditure decisions in business is known as capital budgeting.

_____ 13. (S.O. 9) The annual rate of return is computed by dividing expected annual net income by average investment.

_____ 14. (S.O. 9) The cost of capital is the cost of funding a specific project.

_____ 15. (S.O. 9)   The cash payback technique identifies the time period required to recover the cost of the capital investment from the annual cash inflow produced by the investment.

_____ 16. (S.O. 10) The most informative and best conceptual approach to capital budgeting is the discounted cash flow technique.

_____ 17. (S.O. 10) The discounted cash flow technique considers estimated total cash inflows from the investment but **not** the time value of money.

_____ 18. (S.O. 10) Under the net present value method, a proposal is acceptable only when there is a positive net present value.

_____ 19. (S.O. 10) The lower the positive net present value, the more attractive the investment.

_____ 20. (S.O. 10) Under the internal rate of return method, the project is rejected when the internal rate of return is less than the required rate.

The
Navigator

MULTIPLE CHOICE

Circle the letter that best answers each of the following statements.

1. (S.O. 2) A number of different types of decisions may be made by management that involve incremental analysis. Which of the following types of decisions do **not** involve incremental analysis?
    a. Retain or replace equipment.
    b. Make or buy.
    c. Allocation of limited resources.
    d. All of the above are considered to involve incremental analysis.

2. (S.O. 3) It costs Crabbe Company $26 per unit ($18 variable and $8 fixed) to produce their product, which normally sells for $38 per unit. A foreign wholesaler offers to purchase 2,000 units at $21 each. Crabbe would incur special shipping costs of $2 per unit if the order were accepted. Crabbe has sufficient unused capacity to produce the 2,000 units. If the special order is accepted, what will be the effect on net income?
    a. $2,000 decrease.
    b. $2,000 increase.
    c. $6,000 increase.
    d. $36,000 increase.

3. (S.O. 4) Which of the following would generally **not** affect a make or buy decision?
    a. Selling expenses.
    b. Direct labor.
    c. Variable manufacturing costs.
    d. Opportunity cost.

4. (S.O. 4) Opportunity cost is:
    a. the total difference in costs for two alternatives.
    b. the potential benefit that may be obtained by following an alternative course of action.
    c. a cost that cannot be changed by any present or future decision.
    d. the annual cash inflow from a capital investment.

5. (S.O. 5) Which of the following would generally **not** affect a sell or process further decision?
    a. Sales.
    b. Direct materials.
    c. Direct labor.
    d. Fixed manufacturing overhead.

6. (S.O. 6) A cost that **cannot** be changed by any present or future decision is a (an)
    a. incremental cost.
    b. opportunity cost.
    c. sunk cost.
    d. variable cost.

7.   (S.O. 7) If an unprofitable segment is eliminated:
     a.   it is impossible for net income to decrease.
     b.   fixed expenses allocated to the eliminated segment will be eliminated.
     c.   variable expenses of the eliminated segment will be eliminated.
     d.   it is impossible for net income to increase.

8.   (S.O. 8) In the Rossetto Company, contribution margin per unit is $6 for Product X and $10
     for Product Y. Product X requires 4 machine hours and Product Y requires 8 machine
     hours. What is the contribution margin per unit of limited resource for each product?

	X	Y
a.	$1.50	$1.25
b.	$2.50	$1.50
c.	$1.25	$ .75
d.	$2.50	$ .75

9.   (S.O. 9) Which of the following is **incorrect?**
     a.   Capital budgeting is the process of making capital expenditure decisions.
     b.   Capital budgeting decisions are the opposite of incremental analysis.
     c.   Accounting data are indispensable in capital budgeting decisions.
     d.   Capital budgeting involves the allocation of limited resources.

10. (S.O. 9) The formula for the annual rate of return technique is:
     a.   Annual Cash Flow ÷ Cost of Capital Investment.
     b.   Annual Cash Flow ÷ Average Investment.
     c.   Expected Annual Net Income ÷ Cost of Capital Investment.
     d.   Expected Annual Net Income ÷ Average Investment.

11. (S.O. 9) In the annual rate of return technique, the minimum rate of return is **not**:
     a.   based on the cost of capital.
     b.   also called the annual rate of return.
     c.   also called the hurdle rate.
     d.   also called cutoff rate.

12. (S.O. 9) Ehrlich Company had an investment which cost $260,000 and had a salvage value
     at the end of its useful life of zero. If Ehrlich's expected annual net income is $20,000, the
     annual rate of return is:
     a.   7.7%.
     b.   13%.
     c.   15.4%.
     d.   20%.

13. (S.O. 9) Which of the following is **not** correct about the annual rate of return technique?
     a.   The calculation is simple.
     b.   The accounting terms used are familiar to management.
     c.   The time value of money is considered.
     d.   The timing of the cash inflows is not considered.

14. (S.O. 9) The cash payback formula is:
    a.   Cost of Capital Investment ÷ Net Income.
    b.   Cost of Capital Investment ÷ Annual Cash Inflow.
    c.   Average Investment ÷ Net Income.
    d.   Average Investment ÷ Annual Cash Inflow.

15. (S.O. 9) Sue Bonno Company has identified that the cost of a new computer will be $40,000, but with the use of the new computer, net income will increase by $5,000 a year. If depreciation expense is $3,000 a year, the cash payback period is:
    a.   20 years.
    b.   10 years.
    c.   8 years.
    d.   5 years.

16. (S.O. 9) To determine annual cash inflow, depreciation is:
    a.   subtracted from net income because it is an expense.
    b.   subtracted from net income because it is an outflow of cash.
    c.   added back to net income because it is an inflow of cash.
    d.   added back to net income because it is not an outflow of cash.

17. (S.O. 10) Which of the following is **not** part of the discounted cash flow technique?
    a.   Annual rate of return.
    b.   Net present value method.
    c.   Internal rate of return method.
    d.   All of the above are part of the discounted cash flow technique.

18. (S.O. 10) Which of the following is **not** considered in the net present value method?
    a.   Present value of annual cash inflows.
    b.   Present value of depreciation expense.
    c.   Present value of liquidation proceeds.
    d.   Capital investment.

19. (S.O. 10) A **negative** net present value means that the:
    a.   project's rate of return exceeds the required rate of return.
    b.   project's rate of return is less than the required rate of return.
    c.   project's rate of return equals the required rate of return.
    d.   project is acceptable.

20. (S.O. 10) Which of the following statements about the internal rate of return method is **false?**
    a.   It is widely used in practice.
    b.   It results in finding the interest yield of the potential investment.
    c.   The first step in the method is computing the net present value.
    d.   The internal rate of return factor is computed by dividing the capital investment by the annual cash inflows.

The
Navigator

MATCHING

Match each term with its definition by writing the appropriate letter in the space provided.

Terms

_____ 1. Incremental analysis.

_____ 2. Discounted cash flow technique.

_____ 3. Opportunity cost.

_____ 4. Sunk cost.

_____ 5. Capital budgeting.

_____ 6. Annual rate of return technique.

_____ 7. Cost of capital.

_____ 8. Cash payback technique.

_____ 9. Net present value method.

_____ 10. Internal rate of return method.

Definitions

a. A technique of determining the profitability of a capital expenditure by dividing expected annual net income by the average investment.

b. A method used in capital budgeting in which cash inflows are discounted to their present value and then compared to the capital outlay required by the investment.

c. The process of identifying the financial data that change under alternative courses of action.

d. The process of making capital expenditure decisions in business.

e. The rate of return that management expects to pay on all borrowed and equity funds.

f. A method used in capital budgeting that results in finding the interest yield of the potential investment.

g. The potential benefit that may be obtained by following an alternative course of action.

h. A cost that cannot be changed by any present or future decision.

i. A capital budgeting technique which identifies the time period required to recover the cost of the capital investment from the annual cash inflows produced by the investment.

j. A capital budgeting technique that considers both the estimated total cash inflows from the investment and the time value of money.

The Navigator

EXERCISES

EX. 26-1   (S.O. 4) Calvin Company manufactures its own subassembly units known by the code name "ekrob." Calvin incurs the following annual costs in producing 40,000 ekrobs:

Direct materials	$ 60,000
Direct labor	90,000
Variable overhead	50,000
Fixed overhead	80,000
Total	$280,000

Calvin can purchase the ekrobs from Hobbes Corporation for $6.00 per unit. If they purchase the ekrobs, only $30,000 of the fixed overhead will be eliminated. However, the vacant factory space can be used to increase production of another product, which would generate annual income of $22,000.

Instructions
Prepare an incremental analysis to determine whether Calvin should make or buy ekrobs.

	Make	**Buy**	**Net Income Incr. (Decr.)**

EX. 26-2   (S.O. 9 and 10)   Jenny Durdil Company is considering an investment of $200,000 in new equipment which will be depreciated on a straight-line basis (8-year life, no salvage value). The expected annual revenues and costs of the new product that will be produced from the equipment are:

Sales...		$292,000
Less costs and expenses:		
Manufacturing costs..	$200,000	
Equipment depreciation	25,000	
Selling and administrative	43,900	268,900
Income before income taxes..		23,100
Income tax expense (30%)...		6,930
Net income...		$ 16,170

Instructions
(a) Compute the annual rate of return.
(b) Compute the cash payback period.
(c) Compute the net present value assuming a 12% required rate of return.
(d) Determine the internal rate of return.

(a)

(b)

(c)

(d)

_____

_____

_____

_____

_____

The
Navigator

SOLUTIONS TO REVIEW QUESTIONS AND EXERCISES

TRUE-FALSE

1. (T)
2. (F) The process used to identify the financial data that change under alternative courses of action is called incremental analysis.
3. (T)
4. (F) When deciding whether to accept an order at a special price, management should make its decision on the basis of the incremental cost per unit and the expected revenue.
5. (T)
6. (F) Make or buy is an example of an incremental analysis decision.
7. (T)
8. (F) The basic decision rule is: process further as long as the incremental revenue from such processing exceeds the incremental processing costs.
9. (F) In a retain or replace equipment decision, the book value of the old machine is a sunk cost which does not affect the decision.
10. (T)
11. (T)
12. (T)
13. (T)
14. (F) The cost of capital is the rate of return that management expects to pay on all borrowed and equity funds. It does not relate to the cost of funding a specific project.
15. (T)
16. (T)
17. (F) The discounted cash flow technique considers both estimated total cash inflows and the time value of money.
18. (F) A proposal is acceptable when net present value is zero or positive.
19. (F) The higher the positive net present value, the more attractive the investment.
20. (T)

MULTIPLE CHOICE

1. (d)   Common types of management decisions that involve incremental analysis are (1) acceptance of an order at a special price, (2) make or buy, (3) sell or process further, (4) retain or replace equipment, (5) elimination of an unprofitable segment, and (6) allocation of limited resources.

2. (b)   The incremental analysis is:

	Reject Order	Accept Order	Net Income Increase (Decrease)
Revenues	$ -0-	$42,000	$ 42,000
Costs: Manufacturing	-0-	(36,000)	(36,000)
Shipping	-0-	(4,000)	(4,000)
Net income	$ -0-	$ 2,000	$ 2,000

3. (a)   Selling expenses should not change under the two alternatives (make or buy). Choices (b), (c) and (d) all represent incremental costs which could change depending upon which alternative is chosen.

4. (b)   Opportunity cost is the potential benefit that may be obtained by following an alternative course of action. Choice (a) is the incremental cost, (c) is a sunk cost, and (d) is simply called annual cash inflow.

5. (d)   Generally, total fixed manufacturing overhead will be the same whether the product is sold or processed further. Choices (a), (b) and (c) would usually change under the two alternatives.

6. (c)   A sunk cost is a cost that cannot be changed by any present or future decision.

7. (c)   If an unprofitable segment is eliminated, the segment's variable costs will be completely eliminated. Net income may increase or decrease, depending on the situation (a). The fixed expenses which are allocated to the eliminated segment will have to be absorbed by the other segments (b).

8. (a)   The contribution margin per unit of limited resource for each product is:

	X	Y
Contribution margin per unit (a)	$6.00	$10.00
Machine hours required (b)	4.00	8.00
Contribution margin per unit of limited resource (a) ÷ (b)	$1.50	$1.25

9. (b)   Incremental analysis involves decision making for alternative courses of action. Capital budgeting is similar in that it involves choosing among various capital projects.

10. (d)   The formula for the annual rate of return is expected annual net income divided by average investment.

11. (b)   The minimum rate of return, also called the hurdle rate (c) or cutoff rate (d), is based on the cost of capital (a). It is not the same as the annual rate of return.

12. (c) The annual rate of return is expected annual net income, $20,000, divided by average investment of $130,000 [($260,000 + 0)/2].

13. (c) A major limitation is that this technique does not consider the time value of money. The other statements are correct.

14. (b) The formula for computing cash payback is cost of capital investment divided by annual cash inflow.

15. (d) The cash payback period is calculated by dividing the cost of the capital investment by the annual cash inflow (net income + depreciation expense), [$40,000 ÷ ($5,000 + $3,000)].

16. (d) To determine annual cash inflow, depreciation expense is added back to net income because it is an expense which is not an outflow of cash.

17. (a) The discounted cash flow technique includes the net present value method and the internal rate of return method. The annual rate of return does not consider the time value of money and therefore is not part of the discounted cash flow technique.

18. (b) Net present value is computed as the present value of future cash inflows (annual cash inflows and liquidation proceeds) less the capital investment. Depreciation expense is not considered because it is not a cash flow.

19. (b) A negative net present value means the project's rate of return is less than the required rate of return and is therefore unacceptable.

20. (c) The first step is determining the internal rate of return factor by dividing the capital investment by annual cash inflows making choice (c) incorrect. The other answer choices are correct.

MATCHING

1.	c	6.	a
2.	j	7.	e
3.	g	8.	i
4.	h	9.	b
5.	d	10.	f

EXERCISES

EX. 26-1

	Make	Buy	Net Income Incr. (Decr.)
Direct materials	$ 60,000	$ -0-	$ 60,000
Direct labor	90,000	-0-	90,000
Variable overhead	50,000	-0-	50,000
Fixed overhead	30,000	-0-	30,000
Purchase price (40,000 X $6)		240,000	(240,000)
Opportunity cost	22,000		22,000
Total annual cost	$252,000	$240,000	$ 12,000

The analysis indicates that if the ekrobs are purchased from Hobbes, Calvin will increase net income by $12,000.

EX. 26-2

(a) $16,170 ÷ [($200,000 + $0)/2] = 16.17%.

(b) $200,000 ÷ ($16,170 + $25,000) = 4.86 years.

(c)
Present value of annual cash inflows ($41,170 X 4.96764)	$204,518
Capital investment	200,000
Positive net present value	$ 4,518

(d) $200,000 ÷ $41,170 = 4.8579 internal rate of return factor. The approximate internal rate of return is slightly greater than 12%.

Appendix C

Present Value Concepts

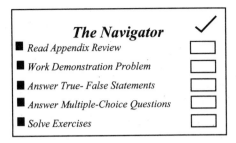

The Navigator

■ *Read Appendix Review* ☐

■ *Work Demonstration Problem* ☐

■ *Answer True- False Statements* ☐

■ *Answer Multiple-Choice Questions* ☐

■ *Solve Exercises* ☐

APPENDIX REVIEW

1. A present value computation is based on the concept of the **time value of money.** The present value is based on three variables:
    a. the dollar amount to be received (future amount).
    b. the length of time until the amount is received (number of periods), and
    c. the interest rate (the discount rate).

2. The present value may be determined through tables that show the present value of 1 for N periods. Different percentages represent the periodic interest rates or discount rates, and the 5-digit numbers in the respective columns are the present value of 1 factors.

3. A higher discount rate produces a smaller present value. In addition, the further removed from the present the future amount is, the smaller the present value.

4. A series of periodic receipts or payments are called **annuities.** In computing the present value of an annuity, it is necessary to know the:
    a. discount rate.
    b. number of discount periods, and
    c. amount of the periodic receipts or payments.

5. Like the computation of present value of a single amount, tables may be used to compute the present value of an annuity. The tables show the present value of 1 to be received periodically for a given number of periods.

6. Discounting may be done on an annual basis or over shorter periods of time such as monthly, quarterly, or semiannually. When the time frame is less than one year, it is necessary to convert the annual interest rate to the applicable time frame.

7. The present value (or market price) of a long-term note or bond is a function of three variables:
    a. the payment amounts.
    b. the length of time until the amounts are paid, and
    c. the discount rate.

8. To compute the present value of a bond, both the interest payments and the principal amount must be discounted.

The
Navigator

DEMONSTRATION PROBLEM

Gardner Co. is about to issue $1,000,000 of 10-year bonds paying a 10% interest rate, with interest payable semiannually. The discount rate for such securities is 8%. How much can Gardner expect to receive for the sale of these bonds?

SOLUTION TO DEMONSTRATION PROBLEM

Present value of principal to be received at maturity
$1,000,000 X PV of 1 due in 20 periods at 4%
$1,000,000 X .45639 (Table 1) $ 456,390

Present value of interest to be received periodically over the term of the bonds
$50,000 X PV of 1 due periodically for 20 periods at 4%
$50,000 X 13.5903 (Table 2)   679,515
Present value of bonds $1,135,905

REVIEW QUESTIONS AND EXERCISES

TRUE—FALSE

Indicate whether each of the following is true (T) or false (F) in the space provided.

_____   1.   Present value is based on three variables: (1) the dollar amount to be received (future amount), (2) the probability of receiving that amount in the future, and (3) the interest rate (the discount rate).

_____   2.   The process of determining the present value is referred to as discounting the future amount.

_____   3.   In computing the present value of an annuity, it is necessary to know the (1) discount rate, (2) the number of discount periods, and (3) the present value.

_____   4.   Discounting may also be done over shorter periods of time such as monthly, quarterly, or semiannually.

_____   5.   The present value (or market price) of a bond is a function of three variables: (1) the payment amounts, (2) the length of time until the amounts are paid, and (3) the discount rate.

MULTIPLE CHOICE

1. Using Table 1, the present value factor for 2 periods at a discount rate of 8% is:
   a.   .89000.
   b.   .92593.
   c.   .91743.
   d.   .85734.

2. A higher discount rate produces:
   a.   a smaller present value.
   b.   a higher present value.
   c.   the same present value.
   d.   a greater length of time.

3. The present value of $5,000 due in 10 years using a discount rate of 12% is:
   a. $1,609.85.
   b. $1,927.70.
   c. $2,837.15.
   d. $3,219,70.

4. Which of the following is **not** necessary to know when computing the present value of an annuity?
   a.   The discount rate.
   b.   The amount of the periodic receipts or payments.
   c.   The number of discount periods.
   d.   The probability of receiving the amount due.

5. Alan Hirsch earns 15% on an investment that pays back $12,000 at the end of each of the next five years. Using Table 2, what is the amount Hirsch invested to earn the 15% rate of return?
   a. $201,129.60.
   b. $60,000.00.
   c. $40,225.92.
   d. $34,259.76.

EXERCISES

EX. C-1 a. If Tim Foran invests $20,900 now and wants to receive $100,000 at the end of 15 years, what annual rate of interest will Tim Foran earn on his investment?

b. Bova Corporation receives a $20,000, 8-year note bearing interest of 10% (paid annually) from a customer at a time when the discount rate is 8%. What is the present value of the note received by Bova?

SOLUTIONS TO REVIEW QUESTIONS AND EXERCISES

TRUE-FALSE

1. (F)   Present value is based on three variables: (1) the dollar amount to be received (future amount), (2) the length of time until the amount is received (number of periods), and (3) the interest rate (the discount rate).

2. (T)

3. (F)   In computing the present value of an annuity, it is necessary to know (1) the discount rate, (2) the number of discount periods, and (3) the amount of the periodic receipts or payments.

4. (T)

5. (T)

MULTIPLE CHOICE

1. (d)   Using Table 1 going down the 8% column and across the 2 periods row, the number .85734 represents the present value of 1.

2. (a)   A higher discount rate produces a smaller present value. A lower discount rate produces a higher present value.

3. (a)   Using Table 1 going down the 12% column and across the 10 periods row, the number .32197 represents the present value of 1. Multiplying the amount from the table by $5,000 results in an answer of $1,609.85 ($5,000 X .32197).

4. (d)   In computing the present value of an annuity, it is necessary to know (1) the discount rate, (2) the number of discount periods, and (3) the amount of the periodic receipts or payments.

5. (c)   The present value of interest to be received periodically over the term of the note is equal to $12,000 multiplied by the present value of 1 due in five periods at 15% ($12,000 X 3.35216 = $40,225.92).

EXERCISES

EX. C-1

a. $20,900 ÷ $100,000 = .20900.
    Using Table 1 and going across period row 15, .20900 is under the 11% column indicating an annual rate of interest of 11% must be earned.

b. Present value of principal to be received at maturity:
    $20,000 X PV of 1 due in 8 periods at 8%
    $20,000 X .54027 (Table 1) $10,805

    Present value of interest to be received periodically over the term of the note:
    $2,000 X PV of 1 due periodically for 8 periods at 8%
    $2,000 X 5.74664 (Table 2)   <u> 11,493</u>
        Present value of note   <u>$22,298</u>

NOTES

NOTES

NOTES

NOTES

NOTES

NOTES

NOTES

NOTES

NOTES

NOTES

NOTES

NOTES

NOTES

NOTES

NOTES

NOTES

NOTES

NOTES